THE
PARIS
COOKBOOK

For Julia Child & Joël Robuchon, the two people who have influenced me most in the world. With immense gratitude for their example, their inspiration, their support and encouragement.

First published in Great Britain 2001 by
Kyle Cathie Limited
122 Arlington Road
London NW1 7HP
general.enquiries@kyle-cathie.com

ISBN 1 85626 379 7

Text © 2001 Patricia Wells
Photography © 2001 Tim Winter

Senior Editor: Helen Woodhall
Editorial Assistant: Andrie Morris and Esme West
Designers:Mark Buckingham and Mick Hodson
Production: Lorraine Baird and Sha Huxtable
Index: Helen Snaith

Patricia Wells is hereby identified as the author of this work in accordance with Section 77 of the Copyright, Designs and Patents Act 1988.

A Cataloguing In Publication record for this title is available from the British Library.

Printed and bound by Eurolitho, Italy

THE
PARIS
COOKBOOK

Patricia Wells

KYLE CATHIE LIMITED

Contents

Introduction

———◦———

When I moved to Paris in the first week of January 1980, there was no way to know that it would be 'for good'. My husband and I had both left jobs as journalists at *The New York Times* – Walter as an assistant national editor and I as a food writer – to live in Paris for two years. That week, Walter began his job as the new deputy editor of *The International Herald Tribune*, and I began life as a freelance writer.

I was thirty-three years old and had an immense passion for food, and for learning all that there was to know about it. Paris seemed like the perfect spot for my little sabbatical – the ideal city to use as my testing and tasting ground for what I call my PhD in food.

In those early years, my greatest luxury was time. Walter worked long days, and I was alone – all day, and into the evening. So I walked and wandered this all-embracing city, pressing my nose against pastry show windows and boulangeries, making regular pilgrimages to the famed Androuët cheese shop (then in the 9th arrondissement, near the place de Clichy), sampling food from every bistro on my ever-growing lists of places to try, studying the menus posted outside every eating place in town, and weaving my way through the surprising list of restaurants run by young, up-and-coming chefs, with names like Guy Savoy, Joël Robuchon and Alain Dutournier.

I remember my first visit to the Rue Poncelet outdoor food market in our new Right Bank neighbourhood. It was a cold and dark afternoon in January, and I literally stumbled upon the market as I was exploring the blocks that fanned off from our home on Rue Daru. I almost cried with joy as I saw it, marvelling at the array of gorgeous, impeccably displayed fruits and vegetables, fish, meats and poultry. I was shocked to see rabbits on display, hanging by their still-attached furry feet, and an entire wild boar – head, feet and all – carefully draped over a table outside the butcher's shop. I was awed by all of the sounds I heard, as vendors hawked and cajoled, teased and shouted. I could not believe my good fortune.

A combination of innocence and naïvety, energy and enthusiasm, and an intense curiosity for all things culinary and French propelled me through life in those days. Everything, it seemed, was new. And everything was worth commenting upon and reporting. Soon I began my regular restaurant reviews for *The International Herald Tribune*, and sent regular dispatches to *The New York Times, Travel & Leisure and Food & Wine*.

Two years grew into three and, before we knew it, returning 'home' to New York was no longer a topic of conversation. I had begun a new career, begun writing books and, quite literally, never looked back.

Paris was now our home and, on Walter's free evenings when we were not dining out, I was learning how to use the huge array of fresh ingredients that were all so new to me. There was so much material for great meals: rabbit and game, the immense variety of fish and shellfish, the brilliant selection of meats, the tender young vegetables, juicy fresh fruits, not to mention the tempting selection of cheeses.

Years before, as a novice cook, a favourite pastime and challenge was to reproduce dishes that I had sampled in restaurants. Now, in Paris, I not only had this embarrassingly rich larder, but thousands of cookbooks, a codified cuisine, and a nation full of Frenchmen and women willing to share each and every recipe.

As part of my restaurant-review research, I regularly spent mornings in restaurant kitchens, to see what really went on behind the scenes, and to gather knowledge as well as cooking tips and recipes.

This, my latest book, really began that first month of January 1980. For twenty years, Paris and its markets, its people, and its restaurants, have been my classroom. Wherever I go, it seems that people talk to me about food – in the dentist's chair, at the hairdresser's, in taxis and, of course, in markets and restaurants. I am constantly jotting down tips and *'trucs'*, recipes and menu ideas on the back of receipts or strips of paper. I never stop learning, and doubt that food will ever be a topic that does not interest me immensely.

In Paris as a city, in France as a country, the world of food has changed tremendously since those early days. Then, there were perhaps two or three varieties of potatoes in the markets; today, there are a dozen or more. Paris markets now offer delicious tomatoes all year round, excellent varieties of strawberries throughout the year, and, it seems that with each season, the selection of fresh and wild mushrooms, the variety of fish and shellfish, the choice of new and aged cheese, the shape, colour and style of breads, grows by the day.

Yet, happily, France remains a nation of tradition. And so this cookbook includes many of the most classic and renowned of French dishes: a classic Tarte Tatin from chef Benoît Guichart at Jamin; the late night favourite, French Onion Soup, from the Left Bank Brasserie Balzar; an outrageously rich and irresistible version of Potatoes Anna from chef David van Laer; and, a classic Hanger Steak from one of my preferred wine bars, Le Mauzac. For dessert, La Maison du

Chocolat agreed to share their scrumptious chocolate mousse, while a Left Bank pastry shop, La Bonbonnerie de Buci, provided inspiration for a puckery lemon tart.

Cafés and bistros suggest an entire collection of traditional salads, and here I share Allard's Lamb's Lettuce and Beets, Café Bonaparte's Chicken Salad, Le Nemrod's Salade Auvergnate, and Chez Maître Paul's Salad of Frisée, Ham, Comté and Walnuts. The modern world loves greens, too, so I have included such contemporary creations as Cap Vernet Garden Salad, as well as Le Bistrot Mazarin's Spinach, Bacon, Avocado and Tomato Salad. Not to mention *the* salad of the 1980s: Joël Robuchon's Herb Salad (Salade Pastorale), a veritable festival of greens and varied fresh herbs.

Paris remains the cutting edge of modern cuisine, so it is only fitting that this cookbook offers popular contemporary fare, such as Spring Noirmoutier Potatoes with Fleur de Sel, Slow-Roasted Salmon with Sorrel Sauce, chef William Ledeuil's Fresh Cod Brandade and his remarkable Cream of Corn Soup from the bistro Les Bookinistes, along with Tante Louise's innovative Caramelised Cauliflower Soup with Foie Gras.

My daily trips to markets around Paris inspired many of the recipes between these pages, such as the Boulevard Raspail Cream of Mushroom Soup from the Sunday morning organic market; a Wednesday morning discovery – a delicious wintertime Guinea Hen with Sauerkraut and Sausages – from the Place Monge market; and, one of my favourite recipes in the entire book, The Apple Lady's Apple Cake from the Left Bank market, in the shadow of the Eiffel Tower, a row of stands that stretch out along the Avenue de Breteuil every Thursday and Saturday morning.

Grand Parisian restaurants continue to offer daily inspiration and learning, in the form of Taillevent's Cream of Watercress Soup with Caviar, Frédéric Anton's Four-Hour Pork Roast, Guy Savoy's amazing Lentil Ragoût with Black Truffles, and a vegetable dish inspired by L'Ambroisie's chef-owner, Bernard Pacaud, in the form of a perky and simply sublime dish of White Beans with Mustard and Sage.

Fish restaurants offer their share of stimuli, with Le Duc's very simple and satisfying Hot Curried Oysters; the unforgettable Sole Meunière, with tips from Le Dôme's chef Frank Graux; the outgoing Gerard Allemandou's easy and ethereal Sea Scallops with Warm Vinaigrette, from his trendy bistro La Cagouille; and the Dôme's bistro favourite: Clams with Fresh Thyme.

Paris restaurants offer an almost endless choice of specialities from all of the regions of France, and here I have included a sampling of dishes from throughout the country: from the

Auvergne, a rich salad of flinty lentils from regional restaurant Ambassade d'Auvergne; from the Basque region, a spicy-crusted leg of lamb from Jean-Guy Lousteau's bistro Au Bascou; and, of course, from Alsace, the fortifying, invigorating regional speciality of sausages, meats and sauerkraut, a choucroute from the lively Alsatian bar Alsaco.

The French – and Parisians in particular – never seem to get enough of a sweet thing, and so the dessert chapter is overflowing with some of my favourite dishes, many of them inspired by the fruits of the market. From Rue Poncelet's Cherries in Sweet Red Wine, to a Fresh Fig and Almond Gratin, and on to a popular and easy-to-prepare Ultra-Thin Apple Tart, fresh fruits have their moment in the sun.

This, then is *my* Paris. You may not be able to spend a day or a week, a month or a year, in this remarkable city, but in opening my kitchen to you, I hope that you can stroll through the markets with me, walk from one end of town to the next, share specialities from my favourite cafes, bistros, wine bars, markets, cheese shops and restaurants, and let Paris live in your kitchen, in your home and in your soul every day of the year.

Patricia Wells
Paris
December 2000

Starters and Appetisers

Starters and Appetisers
Les Entrées et les Amuse-Gueules

Asparagus Velouté
Velouté d'Asperges

Molard's Ham and Goat's Cheese Wraps
Bouchette Charcutier

Taillevent Goat's Cheese and Dried Tomato Appetiser
Amuse-gueule Taillevent

Artichokes and Goat's Cheese Chez Michel
Chez Michel Fondante de Chèvre et Artichaut

Toasty Salted Almonds
Amandes Salées Poelées

Domaine Saint Luc's Cake aux Olives
Cake aux Olives Domaine Saint Luc

Rue Saint Dominique 'Caviar'
'Caviar' Rue Saint Dominique

Arpège Eggs with Maple Syrup
Chaufroid d'Oeuf au Sirop d'Erable

Ledoyen's Quick Sautéed Foie Gras with Garlic and Lemon Purée
Foie Gras, Purée d'Ail et Citron

Laurent's Foie Gras with Spicy Black Beans
Foie Gras aux Haricots Noirs Pimentés

Hors d'Oeuvres Variés:
Beetroot/Les Betteraves, Carrots/Les Carottes and Celeriac
Rémoulade/Rémoulade de Celériac

Joël Robuchon's Parmesan Crisps
Tuiles au Parmesan Joël Robuchon

Chunky Green Olive Pistou-Tapenade
Pistou-Tapenade aux Olives Vertes

Black Olive Tapenade
Tapenade Noir

Marinated Red Peppers
Poivrons Rouges Marinés

Marinated Paris Mushrooms
Champignons de Paris Marinés

Scrambled Eggs with Truffles
Oeufs Brouillés aux Truffes

Asparagus Velouté
Velouté d'Asperges

———○———

Parisian restaurants are famous for getting the most out of every kitchen ingredient. I confess that in the past I have been a bit wasteful with asparagus. I love the sweet green tips and tender portion of this magical vegetable, but when it comes to those often tough and woody stems, I am less charmed. By studying what restaurant chefs do to come up with creative new amuse-bouches, or surprise starters, I established a favoured way to deal with the tougher portion of the asparagus: Whenever I cook asparagus I cut off the woody ends and freeze them until I have enough to make this soup. Then I thaw and slice the asparagus and sweat it with a bit of leek. The mixture is puréed into a smooth, rich, brilliant green velouté, which I serve in tiny portions as a first course. Be sure to include a good part of the green portion of the leek, which will keep the soup a brilliant green colour. Hot or cold, this surprise starter always attracts raves.

———○———

SERVES 4

2 tablespoons extra-virgin olive oil
Fine sea salt to taste
1 leek, white portion and most of the green portion, rinsed and cut into thin rings
About 500g (1lb) stem portion of trimmed green asparagus, finely chopped
About 375ml (13 fl oz) Homemade Chicken Stock (page 274)

1. In a large stock pan, combine the oil, a pinch of salt and the leeks. Cover and sweat – cook, covered, over low heat without colouring, until soft and translucent – about 5 minutes. Add the asparagus, cover and sweat for about 5 minutes more. Add the chicken stock, cover and simmer over low heat for 15 minutes more.

2. Transfer the mixture to the bowl of a food processor. Process to a purée. Pass the soup through the fine blade of a food mill to remove any remaining fibres and to create a perfectly smooth, velvety, soup. Taste for seasoning. Transfer to small espresso cups and serve hot or cold.

Molard's Ham and Goat's Cheese Wraps
Bouchette Charcutier

———○———

*Something wonderful happens to young, fresh goat's cheese when it is warmed and melted –
here wrapped in a fragrant bundle of smoky bacon. The marriage of the cured meat and the
cheese is one that manages to make two plus two taste like 25, as the sweet lactic flavour of the
cheese merges with the smoky richness of the bacon. My favourite version of this now common
Parisian appetiser – seen at many cheese shops and outdoor markets – comes from the reputable
cheese shop Molard, situated along the lively Rue des Martyrs market street in the city's 9th
arrondissement*

———○———

SERVES 4

*About 1 tablespoon finely chopped
fresh herbs, such as chives, chervil,
tarragon, thyme, or a mixture
4 small goat's cheese rounds, each
about 30g (2oz)
8 extra-thin slices smoked bacon,
pancetta, or smoked ham, each about
3 x 20cm (1½ x 8 in)*

I always associate goat's
cheese with the flinty flavour of
a white Sancerre, for that's
where – in the Loire valley –
I tasted my first goat's cheese
many years ago. Whatever you
choose, make sure it is chilled,
dry and white.

1. Sprinkle the herbs on each side of the goat's cheese rounds,
pressing down lightly so they adhere to the cheese.

2. Wrap two slices of bacon, criss-cross fashion, around each
round of goat's cheese. The goat's cheese can be prepared to
this stage up to 8 hours in advance. Cover and keep the cheese
in a cool spot.

3. Heat a large, dry non-stick frying-pan over moderate heat.
Add the wrapped cheese and cook until the meat is browned,
about 2 minutes per side. Serve as a cheese course, with a
tossed green salad alongside.

La Maison du Fromage, 'Molard'

48, rue de Martyrs

Paris 9

Telephone: 01 45 26 84 88

Métro: Nôtre Dame de Lorette

Taillevent Goat's Cheese and Dried Tomato Appetiser
Amuse-gueule Taillevent

In October 1999, Michel Del Burgo took over the kitchens of the famed Taillevent. This simple appetiser – what is called an amuse-gueule *or 'palate teaser' – was the first creation I sampled from his hands. When I dipped my demitasse spoon into this ethereal, pungent mixture, I knew that Del Burgo was on the path to success. This has become a favourite for entertaining, as it is quick, easy, and can be prepared in advance. It is delicious both hot and at room temperature.*

SERVES 8

EQUIPMENT:
8 porcelain egg cups or miniature ramekins

150g (5oz) fresh goat's cheese
2 tablespoons finely-chopped fresh chives
About 1 teaspoon extra-virgin olive oil
About 2 tablespoons Sun-Dried Tomato Paste (page 279)

1. In the bowl of a food processor, combine the goat's cheese, chives and 1 teaspoon of oil. Process to blend. Add additional oil if the mixture is too firm. Spoon the mixture into 8 porcelain egg cups. Spoon a thin layer of Sun-dried Tomato Paste over the cheese.

2. The egg cups can be prepared up to 2 hours in advance, stored covered, at room temperature. Alternatively, the appetiser can be served warm. Place beneath a preheated grill and grill until the tomato paste sizzles, about one minute.

Champagne, always champagne.

Taillevent

15, rue Lammenais

Paris 8

Telephone: 01 44 95 15 01 Fax: 01 42 25 95 18

Métro: Charles-de-Gaulle-Etoile or George V

Artichokes and Goat's Cheese chez Michel
Chez Michel Fondante de Chèvre et Artichaut

———◇———

I sampled this appealing first course the first time I visited the reincarnated Chez Michel in the 1980s. The dish combines all the foods I love: artichokes, goat's cheese, salad greens and basil, all pulled together with my homemade vinaigrette. It can be prepared in a matter of minutes if you have best-quality frozen artichokes on hand.

———◇———

SERVES 4

*90g (3oz) soft goat's cheese
2 tablespoons extra-virgin olive oil
8 frozen artichoke bottoms, thawed
20 basil leaves, cut into a chiffonnade
(very fine ribbons)
200g (7oz) mesclun, mixed salad
greens (about 2 litres, loosely packed)
to include a mix of red and
green-tipped oak leaf lettuce, rocket
or rocket, romaine, chervil, red radicchio or trevise, curly white as well as
green endive, escarole and
bitter dandelion greens
Classic Vinaigrette (page 260) to taste*

PREHEAT THE GRILL

1. In the bowl of a food processor, combine the goat's cheese and oil, and process until smooth. Spread the cheese mixture into the craters of the artichokes bottoms, smoothing out with a spatula. Arrange the artichoke bottoms side by side on a baking sheet. Place the baking sheet on oven rack about 7.5cm (3in) from the heat. Grill until the cheese is golden brown and bubbly, 2 to 3 minutes.

2. Meanwhile, toss the mesclun with the basil chiffonnade. Toss the salad with vinaigrette. Arrange on 4 large salad plates. Place two grilled artichoke bottoms alongside.

With this, I first sampled the well-made white Burgundy, the Mâcon-Villages Mâcon-Clessé from wine-maker Jean Thévenet's Domaine de Bongrand. It is a remarkably big and fragrant white, and one that pairs well with the combination of goat's cheese and artichokes.

Chez Michel

10, rue Belzunce, Paris 10

Telephone: 01 44 53 06 20 Fax: 01 44 53 61 31

Métro: Poissonnière or Gare du Nord

Toasty Salted Almonds
Amandes Salées Poelées

———○———

I love almonds, and am always looking for ways to introduce a new almond appetiser to my repertoire. This is a 'back of the box' recipe from a package of French Vanihe brand almonds. The whole almonds are toasted in a frying-pan, as you spray them with a fine shower of brine. The salt spray creates a delicate white film on the almonds. That salty tang on the tongue wakes up the palate and puts your appetite into gear.

———○———

SERVES 12 AS A NIBBLE

EQUIPMENT:
A perfume atomiser or small garden mister

1 teaspoon fine sea salt
4 tablespoons water
250g (8oz) whole, unblanched almonds

1. Fill a perfume atomiser or a small garden mister with the salt and water. Shake to dissolve the salt.

2. Place the almonds in a dry frying-pan over moderate heat. Cook, stirring or shaking the pan frequently to prevent burning, spraying from time to time, until the almonds are toasted and covered with a delicate white film and begin to release their fragrance, about 4 minutes.

3. Transfer the nuts to a baking sheet to cool. Serve at room temperature. The almonds can be stored, covered, in a cool dry place for up to 2 weeks.

Any aperitif wine is ideal here: Champagne, a fino dry sherry, a Riesling or a Chenin Blanc.

Domaine Saint Luc's Cake aux Olives
Cake aux Olives Domaine Saint Luc

———◦———

Eliane Cornillon is one of the best home cooks I know. When in Provence, we often share a meal at their lively ferme auberge (a working farm that takes in guests and serves a family meal each evening), sipping away at Ludovic Cornillon's fine wines. In Paris, we are lucky enough to find his wines at many restaurants and wine shops. This moist and fragrant light olive cake always receives raves, and I thank Eliane for sharing it with me. While black olives are traditional in a French olive cake, you can use pitted green olives, or a combination.

———◦———

SERVES 8

EQUIPMENT:
One 1.5-litre (2½-pint) rectangular loaf pan, preferably non-stick

Butter for preparing the loaf pan
4 tablespoons flour
2 teaspoons baking powder
½ teaspoon salt
4 large eggs, lightly beaten
250ml (9fl oz) whole milk
90g (3oz) freshly grated Parmigiano-Reggiano or Swiss Gruyère
90g (3oz) black Nyons olives, pitted and halved lengthways
1 tablespoon extra-virgin olive oil
About 250ml (9fl oz) Homemade Tomato Sauce (page 269)

Try a fragrant white wine, or one of the more powerful Côtes du Rhône, such as Ludovic Cornillon's Domaine St Luc Coteaux du Tricastan.

1. Butter the loaf pan and set aside.

2. In a large bowl, combine the flour, baking powder and salt, and stir to blend. Slowly add the eggs, whisking to incorporate. Whisk in the milk, cheese, olives and oil. Set aside for 2 hours to allow the flour to absorb the liquids, making for a lighter cake.

3. Preheat the oven to 220C/425F/gas mark 7.

4. Stir the batter to blend once again. Pour the batter into the prepared loaf pan. Place in the centre of the oven and bake until firm and golden, about 30 minutes. Serve at room temperature. As an appetiser, slice and cut into cubes. As a first course, slice and serve with a fresh tomato sauce.

Cave Viard

9, rue de Quatre Vents

Paris 6

Telephone: 01 43 54 99 30 Fax: 01 44 07 27 73

Métro: Odéon

Rue Saint Dominique 'Caviar'
'Caviar' Rue Saint Dominique

———○———

On my first visit to Christian Constant's Left Bank restaurant, Le Violin d'Ingres, on the Rue Saint Dominique, the waiter arrived with crusty rolls accompanied by a generous pat of butter sprinkled with this vibrant salt, pepper and spice mixture that I've now dubbed Rue Saint Dominique Caviar. What a delightful way to change the way one looks at 'buttered bread'. This simple blend of coarsely ground black pepper, white pepper and allspice combined with the precious fleur de sel make for a palate-opening blend that is particularly delicious spread on tangy sourdough bread. I keep a batch of this in a separate pepper mill, and guests never fail to ask, 'What's in it?'

———○———

2 tablespoons black peppercorns (preferably Indian Tellicherry)
2 tablespoons white peppercorns
2 tablespoons whole allspice berries
Unsalted butter, at room temperature
Fleur de sel or fine sea salt to taste

1. Combine the peppercorns and allspice berries in a pepper mill. At serving time, place several pats of butter on a small plate. Coarsely grind the spice mix over the butter. Sprinkle with a touch of fleur de sel. Serve.

Le Violin d'Ingres

135, rue Saint-Dominique

Paris 7

Telephone: 01 45 55 15 05 Fax: 01 45 55 48 42

Métro: Ecole Militaire

Arpège Eggs with Maple Syrup
Chaufroid d'Oeuf au Sirop d'Erable

———◦———

*Ninety percent of the time, my first impressions remain unchanged for life. The first time I
sampled Alain Passard's food at Arpège in the very early 1980s, I was not terribly impressed.
Save for his brilliant chocolate puff pastry that I had sampled at his previous restaurant in the
Paris suburbs, I just couldn't figure out what all the fuss was about. But palates I respected urged
me on, and I persisted. After about half a dozen visits to Arpège, in Paris's 7th arrondissement, I
became a convert, and today remain one of Passard's staunchest advocates. One dish that won
me over immediately was this adorable appetiser — a surprising mixture of egg, cream, maple
syrup, and sherry vinegar all served in the shell – that properly awakens your palate with a jolt
of surprise and a clap of acclamation. I knew that Passard's wife was Canadian, so it was no
surprise to find maple syrup on his menu. But it was his unusual use of this very
special sweetener that set it apart: With the richness of the egg, the sweetness of the maple
syrup, set off by slightly acidic cream, this is a true* amuse-bouche *or 'palate pleaser'. When
preparing this, be sure to count on a few extra eggs, for there is always a chance that one
shell will crack. This recipe is a little tricky at first, but once you get the knack, you will
make it over and over again.*

———◦———

SERVES 6

EQUIPMENT:
An egg cutter; 6 porcelain egg cups

60ml (3fl oz) double cream
About ¾ teaspoon sherry vinegar,
or to taste
Sea salt to taste
6 very fresh eggs, at room
temperature
2 teaspoons finely-chopped
fresh chives
Freshly ground black pepper to taste
About 2 teaspoons maple syrup

1. In the chilled bowl of a heavy-duty mixer, whisk the cream
until soft peaks form. Season to taste with sherry vinegar and
salt. Set aside.

2. Place an egg in your hand, tapered side up. Using an egg
cutter or very sharp knife, carefully slice off about the top third
of the egg shell. Carefully pour the egg white out of the shell
into a small bowl, holding back the yolk with the flat side of a
knife. (Reserve the white for another use.) With a damp paper
towel, wipe off the bottom of the shell. Place the egg in a
porcelain egg cup. (If you return the eggs to the egg carton,
they are likely to stick and will be impossible to remove from

the carton.) Repeat with the remaining eggs.

3. Select a large, shallow frying-pan, large enough to hold the eggs in their shells in a single layer. Add water to about 5cm (2in) in depth. Bring just to a simmer.

4. Carefully place the egg in the shell in the simmering water (the egg shell should just bob on top of the water), cooking just until the yolk begins to set around the edges, about 3 minutes. Carefully remove the egg shells from the water with your fingertips and return each to an egg cup.

WHAT'S AN EGG CUTTER?
An egg cutter is a small utensil, sometimes of metal and sometimes of metal and plastic, that can be used to cleanly cut the top third portion of an egg shell. The utensil can be found in most well-equipped kitchenware shops.

5. Sprinkle each cooked egg yolk with chopped chives. Season with salt and pepper. Carefully spoon the cream and vinegar mixture over the yolk up to the rim. Drizzle with maple syrup and serve immediately.

Although this dish can easily stand alone without an accompanying wine, it is perfect with a glass of champagne, or with whatever white wine you will be enjoying with your first course.

Arpège
84, rue de Varenne
Paris 7
Telephone: 01 45 51 47 33 Fax: 01 44 18 98 39
Métro: Varenne

Ledoyen's Quick Sautéed Foie Gras with Garlic and Lemon Purée
Foie Gras, Purée d'Ail et Citron

———————◦———————

When I spend time in restaurant kitchens I like to sleuth about, sticking my nose in pots and asking questions. How else is one to learn? When passing a morning with chef Christian Le Squer at Ledoyen one spring day, I enquired about the whole cloves of garlic simmering away on the stove. Le Squer explained that the garlic was cooked in milk until tender, them peeled and puréed with cubes of lemon. The purée serves as a lively, refreshing condiment for slices of seared fresh foie gras. I also love to use this puckery, pungent creation as a condiment for roasted meats and poultry.

———————◦———————

SERVES 4 TO 6

*FOR THE GARLIC AND
LEMON PURÉE:
4 plump, fresh heads garlic,
separated into cloves but skin intact
1 litre (1¾ pints) whole milk
1 lemon, preferably organic, rinsed,
sliced and cut into a small dice
Fine sea salt to taste*

*THE FOIE GRAS:
1 fresh duck foie gras
(500–750g/1–1½lb)
Fleur de sel or fine sea salt to taste
Coarsely ground white pepper
2 tablespoons finely-chopped
fresh chives*

1. To prepare the garlic and lemon purée: Place the garlic in a small saucepan. Cover with about 500ml (18fl oz) of the milk. Bring just to a simmer over moderate heat. Pour the garlic and milk into a fine-mesh sieve set over a bowl. Discard the milk. Return the garlic to the pan, cover with the remaining 500ml (18fl oz) of the milk and simmer, uncovered, over low heat until the garlic is soft and a small knife inserted into the clove of garlic meets no resistance, about 20 minutes. Let the garlic cool in the milk.

2. Gently press the garlic cloves between your fingers, releasing them from their skin. Transfer the garlic cloves to the bowl of a food processor. Purée. Add the diced lemon and pulse just to blend. Add salt to taste. The purée can be stored, covered and refrigerated, for up to 2 days.

3. To prepare the foie gras: Note that a duck liver consists of two lobes, one small and one large. With the tip of a small, sharp knife, carefully remove any traces of green from the surface of the foie gras. With your hands, separate the larger

lobe from the smaller lobe of the liver by pulling them apart gently. With the tip of a small, sharp knife, remove the thin, transparent skin surrounding each piece of duck liver. With the tip of the knife remove and discard the thin, red blood vessel that runs lengthways through the inside of each lobe. With a sharp knife, slice the foie gras on a bias into escalopes about 2cm- (¾in-) thick. Cover with plastic wrap and refrigerate until serving time.

4. Heat a large, non-stick frying-pan with no added fat until very hot. Add the foie gras and sear for 30 seconds on each side, turning carefully with tongs. Transfer the cooked foie gras to a platter covered with paper towels to drain. Sprinkle with fleur de sel, coarsely ground white pepper and chives. Transfer to warmed salad plates.

5. Spoon a small spoonful of Garlic and Lemon Purée alongside the foie gras. Serve.

Certainly the most traditional wine with foie gras is Sauternes, but don't limit it to the sweet, famed Bordeaux. Try a Riesling or a Gewürztraminer, a wine with its own lemony tang.

Ledoyen

Carré des Champs-Elysées

Paris 8

Telephone: 01 47 42 35 98 Fax: 01 47 42 55 01

Métro: Champs Elysées-Clemenceau

Laurent's Foie Gras with Spicy Black Beans
Foie Gras aux Haricots Noirs Pimentés

———○———

I first sampled this elegant dish of spicy black beans and foie gras at the grand Parisian restaurant, Laurent, where chef Philippe Braun manages to surprise us with dishes that totally stray from the French tradition. Here, the spice serves as a perfect foil for the richness of the foie gras. Note the double smokiness of flavours and aromas, both from the smoked bacon and the smoky hot red pepper. When chef Braun is not into surprising us, his repertoire might include the most sublime and simple of French fare, such as a thick and meaty veal chop teamed up with green asparagus from Provence and Spring morel mushrooms. There are few restaurants as romantic as Laurent, whether you are indoors listening to the soothing music coming from the baby grand piano, or, in good weather, seated at one of the precious tables set at the edge of the gardens of the Champs Elysées.

———○———

SERVES 4

EQUIPMENT:
A food mill, fitted with the medium blade; a hand-held immersion blender

FOR THE FOIE GRAS:
1 fresh duck foie gras (500–750g/1–1½lb)
1 teaspoon fleur de sel or fine sea salt
1 teaspoon coarsely ground black pepper
2 tablespoons finely-chopped fresh chives
6 tablespoons double cream
150g (5oz) unsalted butter

FOR THE BLACK BEANS:
1.5 litres (2½ pints) Homemade Chicken Stock (page 274), plus additional as necessary
500g (1lb) black beans

1. To prepare the foie gras: Prepare the duck liver by removing all traces of green from the surface, separating the larger lobe from the smaller lobe by pulling them apart, removing the transparent skin around each piece of the liver, and discarding the thin red blood vessel that runs through each lobe (see page 21–22). With a sharp knife, slice the foie gras on a bias into a total of four escalopes, each about 120g (4oz). Cover with plastic wrap and refrigerate until serving time.

2. Preheat the oven to 180°C/350°F/gas mark 4

3. To prepare the beans: Bring 1.5 litres (2½ pints) of water to boil in large saucepan. When the water is boiling, add the black beans and cook just until the water returns to a boil, about 1 to 2 minutes. Remove the pan from the heat and drain the beans, discarding the water. Return the beans to the pan. Cover with the stock. Add the bacon, garlic, onion, tomato, red pepper, hot

50g (2oz) smoked bacon, in a single slice
3 plump, fresh garlic cloves, peeled, halved and degermed
1 onion, peeled and halved
1 tomato, cored, peeled, seeded and chopped
1 sweet red pepper, trimmed and cut into fine cubes
1 small smoked hot pepper, such as chipoltes adobados, or to taste
2 teaspoons coarse salt

1 BOUQUET GARNI:
several branches of fresh or dried thyme, several branches of celery and several branches of parsley, tied securely with cotton twine

pepper, salt and bouquet garni. Cover and place in the centre of the oven. Bake until the beans are tender, 2½ to 3 hours. Cooking time will depend upon the freshness of the beans. Younger beans cook more quickly than older beans.

4. Once the beans are cooked, remove about 2 ladles of the whole beans and several tablespoons of the cooking liquid, and transfer to a small saucepan. Cover and keep warm.

5. Remove and discard the bacon, onion, hot pepper and bouquet garni. Leave the red bell pepper and the garlic with the beans. Transfer the beans and remaining cooking liquid to the bowl of a food processor and purée. The purée should be fairly liquidy, not a thick paste. If necessary, thin out with additional chicken stock.

6. Place a food mill fitted with a medium screen on top of a large saucepan. Pass the purée through the mill into the saucepan. Stir in the cream and 90g (3oz) of the butter. Taste for seasoning. Process the mixture in a food processor or with a hand-held immersion blender until emulsified into a smooth-textured mixture. Keep warm.

7. Add the remaining 60g (2oz) of the butter to the whole beans in the small saucepan. Keep warm.

8. Heat a large, non-stick frying-pan with no added fat until very hot. Add the foie gras and sear for 30 seconds on each side, turning carefully with tongs. Transfer the cooked foie gras to a platter covered with paper towels to drain. Sprinkle with the pepper, chives and fleur de sel.

9. Pour a ladleful of the puréed bean mixture into each of four warmed, shallow soup bowls. Place the whole beans on top. Place the foie gras on top of the whole beans and serve immediately.

Laurent's sommelier Patrick Lair suggests two very different wines to accompany this racy dish: Either a Tokay Pinot Gris from Trimbach, vintage 1995, or Pierre Gaillard's Côte Rôtie 'Rose Pourpre' 1996.

Laurent

41, avenue Gabriel

Paris 8

Telephone: 01 42 25 00 39 Fax: 01 45 62 45 21

Métro: Champs Elysées-Clemenceau

Hors d'Oeuvres Variés: Beetroot
Les Betteraves

———○———

In France, beetroot is generally sold cooked, a practice begun during the Second World War, when beetroot-growers began to cook their crops in giant cauldrons in the field in order to save precious fuel for farmers and French housewives by cooking in bulk. This turned out to be a great sales technique: fuel was expensive, and housewives were certainly more likely to buy cooked beets over the raw version. Pickled beetroot makes a colourful addition to any vegetable platter.

———○———

SERVES 4

500g (1lb) cooked beetroot, peeled and diced
250ml (9fl oz) champagne vinegar (or cider vinegar or white vinegar)
250ml (9fl oz) water
100g (3oz) sugar
1 teaspoon fine sea salt
Freshly ground black pepper to taste

1. Place the beets in a medium-size bowl. Set aside.

2. In a small saucepan, combine the vinegar, water, sugar and salt; bring to a boil over high heat. Cook for 2 minutes, stirring to dissolve the sugar. Pour the vinegar mixture over the beetroot and let cool, uncovered, to room temperature. Cover and refrigerate for at least 12 hours, stirring once or twice during that time.

The salad can be stored for up to one week, securely covered and refrigerated. Serve as part of a vegetable platter, as a first-course salad on its own, or as an accompaniment to cooked beef.

COOKING BEETROOT

I like steamed beetroot the best. Here's an easy method:

Bring 1 litre (1¾ pints) of water to a simmer in the bottom of a steamer. Place the beetroot on the steaming rack. Place the rack over simmering water, cover and steam until the beetroot can be penetrated with a paring knife, about 20 minutes for baby beetroots, up to 1 hour for larger ones. You may have to add water from time to time to keep the steamer from running dry. Drain and let cool just long enough so you can handle them. Most of the peel will just slip off, but stubborn patches can be peeled off with a paring knife. Cut off the root end and dice.

Carrots

Les Carottes

———○———

Carrots and cumin are a marriage made in heaven. Here, the cool sweetness of the carrots mingles with the fragrant warmth of the cumin seed, creating an appealing, mouth-watering salad. To benefit from cumin's fragrance and flavour, grind the grain in a spice mill at the very last moment.

———○———

SERVES 4

6 carrots, peeled and julienned
2 shallots, finely chopped
2 tablespoons sugar
½ teaspoon salt
½ teaspoon freshly ground cumin
Freshly ground black pepper to taste
3 tablespoons freshly squeezed lemon juice
Several tablespoons finely-chopped parsley leaves

1. In a large bowl, combine the carrots and shallots. In a small bowl, combine the sugar, salt and cumin. Add to the carrots and toss to blend.

2. Add the lemon juice and toss again.

3. Set aside, uncovered, to marinate for 1 hour. Sprinkle with parsley and serve at room temperature. The salad should be served the day it is made or the flavours will fade.

Celeriac Rémoulade
Rémoulade au Céleriac

———◇———

The French manage to find many clever uses for celeriac, or celery root, generally a much under-utilised vegetable. My favourite method is to grate it finely and then to toss it with a mustard-puckery homemade mayonnaise.

———◇———

SERVES 6 TO 8

*500g (1lb) small to medium celeriac
About 250ml (9oz) Mustard
Mayonnaise (page 264)*

1. Peel the celeriac and cut it into quarters. Grate it using the grating blade of a food processor or the finest blade of a hand grater.

2. Place in a bowl, add the mayonnaise and toss to coat evenly. Taste for seasoning.

The salad may be prepared several hours in advance. Cover securely and refrigerate. Serve chilled or at room temperature.

Joël Robuchon's Parmesan Crisps
Tuiles au Parmesan Joël Robuchon

———◦———

As consultant, Joël Robuchon has created a marvellously modern table at the elegant Restaurant de l'Astor in the Right Bank Hotel Astor. When the restaurant first opened in 1997, this Parmesan chip was a popular appetiser on the menu. The addition of verdant fresh herbs makes for lively colour as well as flavour.

———◦———

MAKES 25 TO 30 CRISPS

About 125g (4oz) freshly grated Parmigiano-Reggiano cheese
Assorted fresh herbs: choose from chervil, tarragon, parsley, dill, fennel fronds, thyme, stemmed

PREHEAT THE OVEN TO 200C/400F/GAS MARK 6.

1. With a cheese grater, grate the cheese into a small bowl.

2. Using a 5cm- (2in-) round metal biscuit cutter as a guide, sprinkle 1 tablespoon of grated cheese onto a cold, non-stick baking sheet. Take care to spread the cheese as thinly as possible so that the chips bake evenly. Move the cutter and repeat, leaving enough space between rounds to allow the cheese to spread as it cooks. Sprinkle each 'crisp' with one or two sprigs of each herb.

3. Place the baking sheet in the centre of the oven and bake just until firm, 2 to 3 minutes. Watch carefully to prevent the crisps from browning, which would cause them to taste bitter. Remove from the oven. Immediately transfer each crisp to a cool surface to cool. Serve immediately.

Champagne, always champagne. Make mine Veuve-Clicquot

Astor

11, rue Astor

Paris 8

Telephone: 01 53 05 05 20 Fax: 01 53 05 05 30

Métro: Saint-Augustin

Chunky Green Olive Pistou-Tapenade
Pistou-Tapenade aux Olives Vertes

———○———

*Laced with garlic and pungent with basil, this chunky green olive pistou-tapenade
was inspired by the delectable green olives of my good friend and olive merchant Jean-Louis
Martin from Provence. I prepare this as soon as the first Autumn crop of olives – olives
cassés de les Baux – arrive in the olive markets in late September. The olives have the
forward flavours of the wild fennel with which they are cured, and are as
fragrant as the Provençal hills.*

———○———

MAKES 325ML (12FL OZ)

EQUIPMENT:
A food processor

200g (7oz) green olives, pitted
Small handful basil leaves
4 plump, fresh garlic cloves, peeled,
halved and degermed
2 tablespoons extra-virgin olive oil

1. In the bowl of a food processor, combine the olives, basil and garlic and process to a chunky purée. Add enough olive oil to form a chunky tapenade.

2. Transfer to a small bowl and smooth out the top with a spatula. Serve on toast.

An excellent Parisian source for good quality olives is:

Oliviers & Co.

28, rue de Buci

Paris 6

Telephone: 01 44 07 15 43

Métro: Saint-Germain des Prés or Odéon

Black Olive Tapenade
Tapenade Noir

———◇———

This classic spread combines all of the favourite flavours of Provence: the tang of the home-cured black olives in brine, the saltiness of the tiny anchovy, the briny flavour of the caper, the vibrant sharpness of garlic, the heady scent of thyme, and the unifying quality of a haunting olive oil.

———◇———

MAKES 325ML (12 FL OZ)

10 anchovy fillets
4 tablespoons milk
300g (about 10oz) best-quality French brine-cured black olives, pitted
1 tablespoon capers, drained
1 teaspoon French Dijon mustard
1 plump, fresh clove garlic, peeled, degermed and finely chopped
¼ teaspoon fresh thyme, leaves only
6 tablespoons extra-virgin olive oil
Freshly ground black pepper to taste

1. In a small, shallow bowl, combine the anchovies and milk. Set aside for 15 minutes to rid the anchovies of their salt and to soften and plump them. Drain and set aside.

2. In the bowl of a food processor combine the drained anchovies, olives, capers, mustard, garlic and thyme. Process to form a thick paste.

3. With the food processor running, add the oil in a steady stream until it is thoroughly incorporated into the mixture. Season with black pepper. Taste for seasoning.

Marinated Red Peppers
Poivrons Rouges Marinés

———————○———————

Paris market stalls are filled with giant red peppers all year long, with winter varieties coming from Spain and Israel between November and July, and from the southwest of France and Provence between June and November. I love anything pickled, and these are among my favourites. They are delicious appetisers and have a multitude of uses. Eat and enjoy!

———————○———————

MAKES 1 LITRE (1¾ PINTS)

500ml (18fl oz) extra-virgin olive oil (or substitute peanut oil)
250ml (9fl oz) best-quality white wine vinegar
1 tablespoon sea salt
2 tablespoons sugar
4 red peppers, rinsed, trimmed and cut lengthways into thin strips

1. In a shallow, non-reactive pan combine the oil, vinegar, salt and sugar. Bring to a boil over high heat.

2. Add the pepper strips, stirring constantly over high heat for exactly 2 minutes. Remove from the heat and allow the peppers to cool in the liquid.

3. Transfer to a sterilised jar and cover securely. Refrigerate. Once the jar is opened, be sure the peppers remain immersed in liquid to prevent them from spoiling. Serve as part of an antipasto platter with sausages and ham, or use in sandwiches or as pizza topping.

Marinated Paris Mushrooms
Champignons de Paris Marinés

———◦———

Plain old 'button' mushrooms, or what the French call 'champignons de Paris', tend to be ignored in this world of exotic wild and domesticated mushrooms. During Napoleon's reign the mushrooms were cultivated in the quarried outrock of Paris's 15th arrondissement, thus the name Paris mushroom. Today, they are more likely to be found growing north of Paris or in the Loire Valley. This is a quick and easy way of preserving their goodness.

———◦———

*MAKES ABOUT 500ML
(18 FL OZ)*

*500ml (18fl oz) best-quality white wine vinegar
250ml (9fl oz) dry white wine
2 tablespoons sea salt
6 bay leaves
Several sprigs fresh rosemary
500g (1lb) mushrooms, cleaned, trimmed and thinly sliced
About 250ml (9fl oz) extra-virgin olive oil (or substitute peanut oil)*

1. In a shallow, non-reactive saucepan, combine the vinegar, wine, salt, 4 bay leaves and the rosemary. Bring to a simmer over moderate heat and simmer for 10 minutes to burn the alcohol from the wine and to infuse the liquid with herbs. Add the mushrooms and simmer for 10 minutes more. Transfer the mushrooms to a fine-mesh sieve to drain. Set aside to cool.

2. Transfer the mushrooms to a sterilised 500 ml (18fl oz) jar. Add the 2 remaining bay leaves. Cover with the oil and a secure lid. Refrigerate, waiting about 1 week before sampling the mushrooms. Once the jars are opened, be sure the mushrooms remain immersed in oil to prevent them from spoiling. Serve as part of an antipasto platter with sausages, olives and ham, or use in sandwiches or as a pizza topping.

Scrambled Eggs with Truffles
Oeufs Brouillés aux Truffes

———o———

This is not only my favourite way to prepare eggs, but one of the finest ways to experience a fresh truffle. Straining the eggs makes for an ethereally fine mixture. Although cooking the eggs over a pan of water is more time-consuming than cooking them directly in a frying-pan, it is well worth the effort. The results are so incredible, you will say: 'I can't believe I made these.' Take the time to store the truffle with the eggs for at least 4 hours and up to 2 days. The eggs will become imbued with the truffle's magic aroma. Before preparing the scrambled eggs, be sure to preheat your dinner plates or prepare clean egg shells for serving the eggs.

———o———

SERVES 2

6 ultra-fresh farm eggs
2 fresh truffles (each about 60g/2oz/
120g/4oz total weight), scrubbed
60g (2oz) unsalted butter,
cut into small pieces
Fine sea salt
Freshly ground white pepper
2 tablespoons crème fraîche
2 slices toasted Brioche
(page 65)
1 tablespoon Black Truffle Butter
(page 270)

1. At least 4 hours (and up to 2 days) before preparing the eggs, carefully arrange the truffles and eggs in a sterilised jar. Seal and refrigerate.

2. Remove the jar of eggs and truffles from the refrigerator about 2 hours before preparing the eggs. Slice half of the truffles into paper-thin slices with a truffle slicer or an extra-sharp knife. Finely chop the remaining truffles.

3. Break the eggs into a bowl and beat lightly with a fork. Set a coarse sieve over a bowl and strain the eggs through it. Stir in the finely chopped truffles and season with salt.

4. Transfer the eggs to the top of a pan or heat-proof bowl set over, but not touching, boiling water. Add 45g (1½oz) butter. Stir constantly with a wooden spoon until the eggs form a creamy, homogeneous mass. They should cook slowly and evenly. Remove from the heat and carefully stir in the remaining butter and the crème fraîche. Fluffy, just-cooked

eggs should take about 10 minutes. Taste for seasoning.

5. With a large spoon, transfer the mixture to two very hot dinner plates. Top with slices of truffle. Alternatively, spoon the scrambled eggs into clean egg shells set in egg cups and top with slices of truffle. Serve with toasted brioche spread with truffle butter.

While eggs can spoil the flavour of good wines and clash with others, one will rarely miss with a glass of bubbling champagne.

Menu·Carte

Make it Bistro, at Home

———○———

Hors d'Oeuvres Variés: Beets, Carrots and
Celeriac Rémoulade

———○———

Le Mauzac's Hanger Steak

———○———

David van Laer's Potatoes Anna

———○———

Chocolate Financiers

———○———

L'Astor's Vanilla Custard Tarts

Salads

Salads

Les Salades

Cap Vernet Garden Salad
Salade à la Maraîchère du Cap Vernet

Le Bistro Mazarin's Spinach, Bacon, Avocado and Tomato Salad
Salade Meli-Melo Bistrot Mazarin

Ladurée's Asparagus, Rocket and Parmesan Salad
Salade d'Asperges, Roquette and Parmesan Ladurée

Café Bonaparte Chicken Salad
Bonaparte Salade Apollinaire

Le Nemrod's Salade Auvergnate
Frisée, Jambon, Cantal et Noix

Chez Benoît's Spring Salad
Salade de Printemps chez Benoît

Joël Robuchon's Herb Salad
Salade Pastorale aux Herbes

Chez Maître Paul's Salad
Salade Comtoise Chez Maître Paul

Charpentier's Mesclun Salad with Roquefort Vinaigrette
Salade de Mesclun, Sauce Roquefort aux Charpentiers

Salad of Curly Endive, Bacon and Roquefort
Salade Frisée, Lardons et Roquefort

Spring Madness: Lamb's Lettuce and Beetroot
Salade de Mâche et Betterave

Winter Mesclun
Mesclun d'Hiver

Cap Vernet Garden Salad
Salade à la Maraîchère du Cap Vernet

———◦———

As often as my schedule permits in the winter months, I dip into Guy Savoy's brasserie Cap Vernet for lunch and an instant oyster fix. This restaurant has some of Paris' best and freshest oysters. I always have at least half a dozen of Yvon Madec's iodine-infused boudeuses from the far-north Breton port of Prat-au-Coum. The oyster orgy is generally followed by this refreshing salad of mixed dressed greens, decorated, teepee-style, with thin strips of moist, nutty, Parmigiano-Reggiano cheese. Chef Stéphane Perraud prepares this with a mix of greens, to contrast colour, texture and flavour. Just before serving the salad, I like to anoint the cheese with a few drops of balsamic vinegar, almost as a blessing for the feast. A maraîchère, by the way, is a market gardener, and the name of the dish comes from the many market gardeners who grow the freshest of greens in the rich soil on the outskirts of Paris.

———◦———

SERVES 2 AS A MAIN COURSE;
4 AS A FIRST OR SALAD COURSE

About 150g (5oz) loosely packed mixed greens, such as curly endive, radicchio and oak leaf-lettuce, washed, dried and torn into bite-sized pieces
Several tablespoons Classic Vinaigrette (page 260)
Sea salt
Freshly ground white pepper to taste
One 60g (2oz) chunk of Parmigiano-Reggiano cheese
A few drops of balsamic vinegar

1. In a large salad bowl, combine the greens and toss to blend evenly. Add enough vinaigrette to evenly coat the ingredients, tossing to thoroughly coat the greens with the dressing. Season with salt and pepper.

2. Transfer the salad to large dinner plates.

3. Using a vegetable peeler, shave the cheese into long thick strips. Arrange the strips of cheese, teepee style, on top of the dressed greens. Drizzle with a few drops of balsamic vinegar. Serve.

Cap Vernet

82, avenue du Marceau

Paris 8

Telephone: 01 47 20 20 40 Fax: 01 47 20 95 36

Métro: Charles de Gaulle-Etoile

Le Bistrot Mazarin's Spinach, Bacon, Avocado and Tomato
Salade Meli-Melo Bistrot Mazarin

———◇———

When I was restoring my office/studio on the Left Bank Rue Jacob in the late 1990s, Bistrot Mazarin was one of my hangouts. I remember a particularly cold winter, when I visited my unheated worksite almost daily, to meet with masons and plumbers, painters and cabinet-makers. The tradesmen and I would often have lunch at the nearby Bistrot Mazarin, which had moved its outdoor gas heaters indoors to supplement the heat on icy days. In summer months, the terrace is always lively. This salad appeared as a daily special one day in May. I never get enough greens, and this one hit the spot as an evening's first course.

———◇———

SERVES 2 AS A MAIN COURSE;
4 AS A FIRST OR SALAD COURSE

250g (8oz) baby spinach leaves, washed, dried and stemmed
1 ripe avocado, peeled and cubed
4 tomatoes, cored, peeled and cut into eight wedges (only the walls of the tomato, not the inner pulp)
90g (about 3oz) smoked slab bacon, cubed
Sea salt
Freshly ground black pepper to taste
Several tablespoons Classic Vinaigrette (page 260)

1. Place the spinach, avocado and tomatoes in a large salad bowl. Set aside.

2. Place the bacon in a large frying-pan. Adding no additional fat, cook, stirring frequently, over medium-high heat just until the bacon begins to give off its fat and browns, 4 to 5 minutes.

3. With a slotted spoon, scatter the bacon over the salad. Toss to blend evenly. Add enough vinaigrette to coat the ingredients. Toss to blend evenly. Season with salt and pepper to taste.

Bistrot Mazarin

42, rue Mazarine

Paris 6

Telephone: 01 43 29 99 01

Métro: Mabillon

Ladurée's Asparagus, Rocket and Parmesan Salad
Salade d'Asperges, Roquette and Parmesan Ladurée

———○———

One day I was fortunate enough to spend the entire day at the Ladurée pastry shop with Pierre Hermé, then the famed shop's pastry chef. We sampled everything, from buttery croissants to the entire line of chocolates. We had to stop for lunch, of course, and this is the spring salad I sampled on that glorious day.

———○———

SERVES 4

EQUIPMENT:
One 4-litre (7-pint) pasta pan fitted with a colander

16 plump asparagus spears (about 680g/1½lb)
Fine sea salt
4 large, extra-fresh farm eggs
1 tablespoon distilled vinegar
1 tablespoon extra-virgin olive oil
About 250g (8oz) fresh rocket, rinsed, spun dry and stemmed
One 60g (2oz) chunk of Parmigiano-Reggiano cheese
Several tablespoons Classic Vinaigrette (page 260)
Freshly ground black pepper

1. Trim off and discard the thick white portion of the asparagus. With a vegetable peeler, peel (discarding the peels) the lower 5cm (2in) of the asparagus. Trim and reserve the peeled section for soup. Set aside the asparagus.

2. Prepare a large bowl of iced water.

3. Fill the pasta pan with water and bring to a boil over high heat. Add 4 tablespoons of salt and the asparagus spears and cook, uncovered, until crisp-tender, about 5 minutes. Cooking time will vary, according to the size and tenderness of the asparagus. Immediately remove the colander from the water, allow the water to drain from the asparagus, and plunge the colander with the asparagus into the iced water so the vegetables cool down as quickly as possible. The asparagus will cool in 1 to 2 minutes. If you leave them longer, they will become soggy and begin to lose flavour. Transfer the asparagus to a tea towel and wrap to dry. The asparagus can be cooked up to 4 hours in advance. Keep the spears wrapped in the towel. Unless the kitchen is very hot, store at room temperature; the asparagus will reheat more quickly at serving time.

4. Shortly before serving, warm four dinner plates.

5. Poach the eggs: In a shallow, 25cm-(10in-) frying-pan, bring 7cm (3in) of water to a boil over high heat. Add the distilled vinegar. (The vinegar will help the white of the egg cook faster so it does not spread out too much.) Turn off the heat and immediately break the 4 eggs directly into the pan, carefully opening the shells close to the water's surface, so the eggs slip into the water in one piece. Immediately cover the pan with a tight-fitting lid to retain the heat and cook the eggs. Do not disturb the pan. After 3 minutes, remove the lid. The eggs are ready when the whites are opaque and the yolks are covered with a thin, translucent layer of white. Rinse the eggs gently under cold running water to rid them of any taste of vinegar.

6. While the eggs cook, in a large, non-stick frying-pan large enough to hold the asparagus, heat the oil over high heat until hot but not smoking. Add the cooked asparagus, reduce heat to low, and gently reheat, 2 to 3 minutes.

7. Place the rocket in a large bowl. Drizzle with several tablespoons of Classic Vinaigrette and toss to coat evenly with the dressing. Arrange on the dinner plates. Arrange 4 asparagus spears on each of the dinner plates. Cover the asparagus with a poached egg. Cover the rocket with several pieces of shaved cheese. Season generously with freshly ground black pepper. Serve.

Ladurée

73, avenue Champs-Elysées

Paris 8

Telephone: 01 40 75 08 75

Métro: Georges V

Café Bonaparte Chicken Salad
Bonaparte Salade Apollinaire

———○———

About once a week I get a hankering for this simple, wholesome, filling salad, a satisfying combination of chicken, greens, hard-boiled eggs, tomatoes and cucumbers. So late in the morning, just when I begin to have that falling-down-with-hunger feeling, I give a call to a friend and just pop the question: 'Is this a Bonaparte salad day?' The answer is usually yes and, if we are lucky, we secure a table on the terrace in the shadow of the Saint-Germain church, with a front row seat on all the activity of the heart of Saint-Germain des Prés. Le Bonaparte is what some might consider a second-string café in the neighbourhood, lined up right behind the glittery Café Flore and Les Deux Magots, the two stars of the 6th arrondissement. Le Bonaparte's bright red and blue décor always cheers me up, service is generally friendly and swift, and the clientèle international. The salad, by the way, goes by the name of Salade Apollinaire, for the café faces the brief Rue Guillaume Apollinaire. One might also call it The Endless Plate of Salad, for no matter how much I eat, it seems as though the ingredients almost continue to grow on the plate. Of course, I always finish every last bite.

———○———

SERVES 2

AS A MAIN COURSE SALAD

About 250g (8oz) cooked, skinned and cubed chicken
Sea salt
Freshly ground black pepper to taste
3 small tomatoes, cored and cut lengthways into eighths
1 small cucumber, peeled and thinly sliced
1 small head lettuce, washed, dried and torn into bite-sized pieces
Classic Vinaigrette to taste (page 260)
2 large hard-cooked eggs, peeled and quartered lengthways

1. Place the chicken in a large salad bowl. Season well with salt and pepper. Add the tomatoes and cucumbers and season once again. Add the lettuce. Toss the mixture carefully with your hands. Season with the vinaigrette, tossing with your hands until all the ingredients are evenly distributed. Taste for seasoning. Divide the salad between two large salad plates. Arrange the egg quarters all around. Serve.

Le Bonaparte

42, rue Bonaparte

Paris 6

Telephone: 01 43 26 41 81

Métro: Saint-Germain des Prés

Le Nemrod's Salade Auvergnate
Frisée, Jambon, Cantal, et Noix

Café owners Richard and Michelle Bonal run a great neighbourhood café, Le Nemrod, in the heart of the Left Bank. Here, you will find an assortment of cold sandwiches on the sublime Poilâne bread, as well as this hearty salad that combines the best ingredients of the Auvergne region in south-central France: silken ham, earthy and lactic Cantal cheese and fresh walnuts. Toss this all with the freshest of curly endive and a great homemade vinaigrette. And don't forget a nice touch of freshly ground black pepper at the end, to tie it all together.

*SERVES 2 AS A MAIN COURSE;
4 AS A FIRST OR SALAD
COURSE*

*About 150g (5oz) curly endive,
washed and dried
About 30g (1 oz) matchstick-
sliced ham
About 120g (4oz) cubed French
Cantal cheese (or substitute
an aged cheddar)
About 90g (3oz) walnut halves
Several tablespoons Classic
Vinaigrette (page 260)
Sea salt
Freshly ground black pepper to taste*

1. In a large salad bowl, combine the curly endive, ham, cheese and walnuts. Toss to blend evenly. Add enough vinaigrette to evenly coat the ingredients. Toss to blend evenly. Season with salt and freshly ground black pepper.

Beaujolais, Beaujolais and more Beaujolais.

Le Nemrod

51, rue du Cherche-Midi

Paris 6

Telephone: 01 45 48 17 05

Métro: Sèvres-Babylone

Chez Benoît's Spring Salad
Salade de Printemps chez Benoît

———◦———

At least four times a year I make a ritual-like pilgrimage to this most classic and most beautiful of Paris bistros. Owner Michel Petit manages to keep the menu traditional without becoming stale, and each season adds a new dish that warms the soul. This dish has become a modern favourite in our family. Sometimes I set it on a bed of dressed and tossed baby mesclun leaves, for a true 'Salad as a Meal'.

———◦———

SERVES 2 AS A MAIN COURSE;

4 AS A SALAD COURSE

EQUIPMENT:
One 6-litre (10-pint) pasta pan fitted with a colander

500g (1lb) asparagus
250g (8oz) green beans, rinsed, trimmed at both ends and quartered
Fine sea salt to taste
250g (8oz) snow peas, rinsed, trimmed at both ends and quartered
Several tablespoons finely chopped fresh chives
Several tablespoons fresh chervil leaves (or substitute fresh tarragon leaves)

FOR THE WALNUT OIL DRESSING:
2 tablespoons freshly squeezed lemon juice
Fine sea salt to taste
5 tablespoons walnut oil (or substitute hazelnut oil or extra-virgin olive oil)

1. Trim the asparagus to about 10cm (4in), discarding the woody end. Reserve the ends for other uses. Cut the asparagus on the diagonal into three or four bite-sized pieces. Set aside.

2. Prepare several large bowls of iced water.

3. Fill the pasta pan with water and bring to a boil over high heat. Add 4 tablespoons of salt and the green beans, and cook in rapidly boiling water, uncovered, until crisp-tender, 3 to 4 minutes. Cooking time will vary, according to their size and tenderness. Immediately remove the colander from the water, allow the water to drain from the beans, and plunge the colander with the beans into the iced water so they cool down quickly. The beans will cool in 1 to 2 minutes. If you leave them longer, they will become soggy and begin to lose flavour. Transfer the beans to a strainer, drain and wrap in a thick towel to dry. The beans can be cooked up to 4 hours in advance. Keep them wrapped in the towel and refrigerate, if desired

4. Repeat with the snow peas: Bring the water back to a boil, add the snow peas and cook in rapidly boiling water, uncovered, until they are crisp-tender, 2 to 3 minutes. Cooking time will

vary, according to their size and tenderness. Immediately drain the peas and plunge them into the iced water so they cool down quickly. Transfer the peas to a strainer, drain and wrap in a thick towel to dry. The peas can also be cooked up to 4 hours in advance. Keep them wrapped in the towel and refrigerate.

5. Repeat with the asparagus: Add the asparagus and cook in rapidly boiling water, uncovered, until crisp-tender, about 3 minutes. Cooking time will vary according to their size. Immediately drain the asparagus tips and plunge them into iced water so they cool down quickly and retain their crispness and bright green colour. The asparagus will cool in 1 to 2 minutes. After that, they will soften and begin to lose crispness and flavour. Transfer to a colander, drain and wrap in a thick towel to dry. The asparagus can be cooked up to 2 hours in advance. Keep them wrapped in the towel at room temperature.

6. Prepare the walnut oil dressing: In a small bowl combine the lemon juice and salt. Whisk in the oil and taste for seasoning. Set aside. Do not dress the salad until the very last moment or the vegetables will turn soggy and discolour from the acid in the dressing.

7. To serve, combine all the vegetables in a large, shallow bowl. Sprinkle with chives and chervil. Drizzle with the vinaigrette. Toss very gently to blend. Taste for seasoning. Serve as a first course or as a main luncheon dish.

Benoît

20, rue Saint Martin

Paris 4

Telephone: 01 42 72 25 76 Fax: 01 42 72 45 68

Métro: Châtelet or Hôtel de Ville

Joël Robuchon's Herb Salad
Salade Pastorale aux Herbes

———○———

It took a chef with the talent of Joël Robuchon to bring the common tossed salad to a place of honour at the three-star table. From the early days of the 1980s when Robuchon tended the stoves at Jamin, this salad – served in tiny portions, with each leaf meticulously cut into tiny, bite-sized pieces – was served with every meal.

———○———

SERVES 6

FOR THE VINAIGRETTE:
Salt to taste
1 tablespoon red wine vinegar
1 tablespoon sherry vinegar
6 tablespoons extra-virgin olive oil
Freshly ground white pepper

FOR THE SALAD:
Large handfuls (about 30g/1oz) of:
curly endive
oak leaf lettuce
curly red-leaf lettuce
radicchio
romaine lettuce
lamb's lettuce or corn salad
rocket
Small handfuls (about 10g/⅓oz) of:
chervil leaves
basil leaves
flat-leaf parsley leaves
dill leaves
marjoram leaves
tarragon leaves

TO GARNISH:
6 small leaves fresh mint
6 small leaves celery
Several drops of red wine vinegar

1. To prepare the vinaigrette: In a small bowl, combine the salt and vinegars and whisk to blend. Slowly whisk in the oil. Season with pepper. Taste for seasoning.

2. Wash, stem and dry the salads and herbs. Tear into small, bite-sized pieces and transfer to a large salad bowl. Toss to blend. Slowly add the vinaigrette, tossing to coat the greens.

3. Place the salad in domes on each of six salad plates. Garnish with the mint and celery leaves. Drizzle with a few more drops of vinegar. Serve.

WHAT IS MESCLUN?

Mesclun, also known as mesclum, is a Provençal blend of up to ten different salad greens and herbs. A mix might include red- and green-tipped oak-leaf lettuce, rocket, romaine, chervil, red radicchio or trevise, curly white and green endive, escarole and bitter dandelion greens. Generally, fresh herbs – such as sage, dill and tarragon – are also added to the mix. Today mesclun is ubiquitous, but more often than not is a pale version of its true self, often just two or three greens and a few tangles of herbs. The best versions, like this one here, are made of a variety of fresh greens that are cut into small bite-sized pieces and tossed together at the last moment.

Chez Maître Paul's Salad
Salade Comtoise Chez Maître Paul

—○—

The first time I visited Chez Maître Paul – an old-time Left Bank bistro – was in 1983 while working on the first version of The Food Lover's Guide to Paris. *My friend and assistant Susan Loomis and I feasted on this marvellously simple and hearty salad, one that must be made with the very freshest of ingredients. Chez Maître Paul's current owner, François Debert, suggests using a French Comté cheese that has been aged at least 6 to 8 months. Likewise, a top-quality lightly smoked ham – he suggests the lightly smoked white ham from the village of Luxeuil in the Franche Comté – will add an essential smoky balance to the rich and fragrant cheese. Make an effort to find the freshest of walnuts, freshly cracked. And the mix of herbs – the famous French* fines herbes – *turns a rustic salad into a very elegant one.*

—○—

SERVES 2 AS A MAIN COURSE;
4 AS A FIRST OR SALAD COURSE

About 250g (8oz) escarole, washed, dried and broken into bite-sized pieces
About 60g (2oz) sliced smoked ham cut into matchsticks
About 125g (4oz) French Comté cheese or Swiss Gruyère cut into matchsticks
About 90g (3oz) freshly cracked walnut halves
Finely-chopped fines herbes, *a mixture of fresh chervil, tarragon, chives and parsley leaves*
Mustard Vinaigrette to taste (page 267)
Sea salt
Freshly ground black pepper to taste

1. In a large salad bowl, combine the curly endive, ham, cheese, walnuts and herbs. Toss to blend evenly. Add enough vinaigrette to evenly coat the ingredients. Toss to blend evenly. Season with salt and freshly ground black pepper.

On one of my latest visits, owner François Debert offered me an astonishing Pinot Noir Vieilles Vignes from the Franche-Comté, a simple but outstanding *vin de pays*. A young Burgundy as well as a Beaujolais make a worthy substitute.

Chez Maître Paul

12, rue Monsieur le Prince

Paris 6

Telephone: 01 43 54 74 59 Fax: 01 46 34 58 33

Métro: Odéon or RER Luxembourg

Charpentiers's Mesclun Salad with Roquefort 'Vinaigrette'
Salade de Mesclun, Sauce Roquefort aux Charpentiers

For some twenty years I have been a regular at the family-style bistro Aux Charpentiers, where one finds such simple daily specials as roast chicken or duck, roasted saddle of lamb and varied daily specials. One summer's evening we sat on the restaurant's sidewalk terrace and sampled this very simple first course. Select a good variety of greens for a modern allure. I created the sauce, motivated by chef-owner Paul Bardeche's own inspiration.

SERVES 4

150g (5oz) loosely packed mesclun, or a mixture of radicchio, curly endive, lamb's lettuce, dandelion greens, oak leaf lettuce, romaine, escarole, rocket and chervil, washed, dried and torn into bite-sized pieces

FOR THE ROQUEFORT 'VINAIGRETTE':
3 tablespoons freshly squeezed lemon juice
125ml (4fl oz) best-quality walnut oil
About 120g (4oz) Roquefort cheese, crumbled
Fine sea salt
Freshly ground black pepper

1. Place the greens in a large salad bowl. Set aside.

2. To prepare the Roquefort 'vinaigrette': In a small jar, combine the lemon juice, walnut oil and cheese. Cover securely and shake to blend. The cheese will remain in crumbled bits. Toss over salad, seasoning with plenty of freshly ground black pepper.

Aux Charpentiers

10, rue Mabillon

Paris 6

Telephone: 01 43 26 30 05 Fax: 01 46 33 07 98

Métro: Mabillon

Salad of Curly Endive, Bacon and Roquefort
Salade Frisée, Lardons et Roquefort

There is no limit to the varieties of salad one finds in Parisian cafés and bistros. This one, with the ever-present curly endive, full of colour and crunch, pairs two deliciously salty ingredients, creamy Roquefort cheese and crispy warm bacon.

SERVES 2 AS A MAIN COURSE;
4 AS A FIRST OR SALAD COURSE

150g (5oz) curly endive, washed, dried and torn into bite-sized pieces
125g (4oz) Roquefort cheese, crumbled
150g (5oz) smoked slab bacon, rind removed and cut into cubes
Several tablespoons Classic Vinaigrette, to taste (page 260)
Sea salt
Freshly ground black pepper to taste

1. In a large salad bowl, combine the curly endive and cheese. Set aside.

2. Place the bacon in a large frying-pan. Adding no additional fat, cook, stirring frequently over medium-high heat just until the bacon begins to give off its fat and browns, 4 to 5 minutes. With a slotted spoon, scatter the bacon over the salad. Toss to blend evenly.

3. Add enough vinaigrette to evenly coat the ingredients. Toss to blend evenly. Season with salt and pepper to taste.

Although wine is not always served with a salad, a chilled glass of Beaujolais is always in order.

Spring Madness: Lamb's Lettuce and Beetroot
Salade de Mâche et Betterave

———o———

One of the most welcome signs of spring in Paris is the arrival of the popular classic mix of tender green lamb's lettuce paired with the just slightly sweet cooked red beetroot IN Salade de Mâche et Betterave. In vegetable markets, the two are always found side by side, contrasting the crimson red and the brilliant green, shouting out: 'Buy me, take me home for dinner.' The salad is also classic Parisian bistro fare, and is usually on the spring menu at one of my favourite old-time bistros, Chez Allard.

———o———

SERVES 4

FOR THE VINAIGRETTE:
1 tablespoon best-quality sherry-wine vinegar
Fine sea salt to taste
4 tablespoons extra-virgin olive oil

FOR THE SALAD:
2 medium cooked beetroots (500g/1lb), peeled and cubed
About 150g (5oz) fresh lamb's lettuce, rinsed and dried
1 small shallot, peeled and cut into thin rounds

1. To prepare the vinaigrette: In a large salad bowl, combine the vinegar and salt. Whisk to blend. Add the oil, whisking to blend. Taste for seasoning.

2. Add the beetroot and toss to thoroughly coat it with the dressing. Set aside for at least 5 minutes and up to 30 minutes.

3. At serving time, add the lamb's lettuce and shallots. Toss gently to thoroughly coat the ingredients with the dressing. Serve on salad plates, being sure to evenly distribute the beetroot, which tends to fall to the bottom of the bowl.

Chez Allard

1, rue de l'Epéron

Paris 6

Telephone: 01 43 26 48 23

Métro: Odéon

Winter Mesclun
Mesclun d'Hiver

———○———

One weekday just before Christmas, I strolled into my neighbourhood greengrocer and he proudly announced: 'Even Pierre Gagnaire hasn't seen this yet!' Chef Gagnaire and I share the same produce merchant, who held up an alabaster ball of lettuce tinged with a deep ruby red. It was white radicchio, a winter version with colours the exact reverse of the common red version. I gathered it up, along with all of the following baby greens in his larder, and for lunch friends and I had a veritable feast.

———○———

SERVES 6

*Large handfuls (about 30g/1oz of:
lamb's lettuce leaves
baby spinach leaves, stemmed
rocket leaves, stemmed
dandelion greens, stemmed
sorrel leaves, stemmed (optional)
45g (1½oz) red radicchio leaves,
torn into bite-sized pieces
white radicchio leaves, torn into bite-
sized pieces (optional)
6 leaves Belgian endive, cut
into ribbons (chiffonnade)
Small handfuls (about 5g/¼oz) of:
mint leaves
dill leaves
tarragon leaves
chervil leaves (optional)
Several tablespoons Classic
Vinaigrette (page 260)*

1. Rinse and dry all the greens and herbs. Be sure that they are all carefully stemmed.

2. Place in a large bowl and toss with your hands to mix. Drizzle with Classic Vinaigrette and toss to coat evenly with the dressing. Taste for seasoning. Serve.

Le Jardin de Courcelles

96, rue de Courcelles

Paris 17

Telephone 01 47 63 70 55

Métro: Courcelles

Menu·Carte

Left Bank Madness

—◇—

Spring Madness: Lamb's Lettuce and Beetroot

—◇—

Chez Henri's Sautéed Potatoes

—◇—

Benoît's Fricassée of Chicken with Morels

—◇—

Carton's Ultra-Thin Apple Tart

—◇—

Breads

Breads
Les Pains

—◦—

Rue Jacob Walnut Bread
Pain aux Noix de Rue Jacob

—◦—

Eight-Grain Parisian Bread
Pain aux Huit Céréales

—◦—

Parmesan Bread
Pain Parmesan

Rye Crackers
Biscuits au Seigle

—◦—

Brioche
Brioche

—◦—

Chickpea-Flour Crêpes from Nice
Socca

Rue Jacob Walnut Bread
Pain aux Noix de Rue Jacob

———o———

Some of the finest walnut oil and most deliciously fresh walnuts in France can be found at the minuscule family-run boutique Huilerie Artisanale Leblanc on the Left Bank Rue Jacob. Using their products, I created this walnut bread, bursting with fragrant walnuts and perfumed with the nut's own rich oil. It is one of the most rewarding treats I know. I love to pair the bread with fresh, tangy goat's milk cheese. The milk in this dough makes for a light, almost cake-like bread. The triple rise at room temperature makes for a bread that has a richly developed flavour. Be sure to use the freshest nuts and oil you can find.

———o———

*MAKES 1 LOAF (ABOUT
12 SLICES)*

*EQUIPMENT:
One 1-litre (1¾-pint) rectangular loaf
tin, preferably non-stick*

*1 package (2½ teaspoons) active
dry yeast
1 teaspoon sugar
330ml (12fl oz) lukewarm milk
1 tablespoon walnut oil
2 teaspoons fine sea salt
About 500g (1lb 2oz) strong white
flour or strong wholewheat flour
125g (4oz) walnuts,
coarsely chopped
1 large egg beaten with 1 tablespoon
cold water, for egg wash*

1. In the bowl of a heavy-duty electric mixer fitted with a dough hook, combine the yeast, sugar and milk, and stir to blend. Let stand until foamy, about 5 minutes. Stir in the oil and salt.

2. Add the flour and nuts all at once, mixing at medium low speed until most of the flour has been absorbed and the dough forms a ball. Continue to knead at medium low speed until soft and satiny but still firm, 4 to 5 minutes, adding additional flour to keep the dough from sticking.

3. Transfer the dough to a bowl, cover tightly with plastic wrap, and let rise until doubled in bulk, about 1 hour. Punch down the dough and let rise again until doubled in bulk, about 1 hour.

4. Punch down again. Form the dough into a tight rectangle. Place the dough in the loaf tin. Cover with a clean cloth and let rise until doubled in bulk, about 1 hour.

5. Preheat the oven to 220ºC/425ºF/gas mark 7.

6. Brush the top of the dough with the egg glaze. With a razor blade, slash the top of the dough several times, so that it can expand regularly during baking. Place the loaf tin on the bottom shelf of the oven. Once the bread is lightly browned and nicely risen – about 15 minutes – reduce the heat to 190ºC/375ºF/gas mark 5. Rotate the loaf so that it browns evenly. Bake until the crust is firm and golden brown, and the bread sounds hollow when tapped on the bottom, about 30 minutes more, for a total baking time of 45 minutes.

7. Transfer the bread to a rack to cool. Do not slice the bread for at least 1 hour, for it will continue to bake as it cools.

WHAT I LEARNED

When baking any bread that contains milk (as opposed to water), bake at a lower temperature than you would dough prepared with water. The sugar in the milk will make the dough brown more quickly and the bread could easily burn at a higher temperature. Note that the bread and the crust will be softer and more golden than bread made with water.

WHY DOES WALNUT OIL TURNS RANCID SO QUICKLY?

In order to press the oil from walnuts, the nuts must first be heated. Unfortunately, in the heating process, the natural preservative that retards rancidity in the nut is broken down, making the oil fragile as well. Buy walnut oil from a reputable shop, store it in the refrigerator to preserve its fresh qualities, and use it within one year.

Huilerie Artisanale Leblanc et Fils

6, rue Jacob

Paris 6

Telephone: 01 46 34 61 55

Métro: Mabillon

Eight-Grain Parisian Bread
Pain aux Huit Céréales

———o———

In the past decade, Paris has undergone a major bread revival. On nearly every street corner one finds an incredible variety of breads, many of them studded with all manner of grains, from corn meal to sesame seeds, flax and poppy seeds and sometimes the popular French grain, épeautre, often called the poor man's wheat because it will grow on even the poorest of soils. Inspired by the wholesome breads of the city, I created this bread to reflect the modern style.

———o———

MAKES 1 LOAF
(ABOUT 12 SLICES)

EQUIPMENT:
One 1-litre (1¾-pint)
rectangular loaf tin,
preferably non-stick

1 teaspoon active dry yeast
1 teaspoon sugar
330ml (12fl oz) lukewarm water
2 teaspoon fine sea salt
About 500g (1lb 2oz) strong flour
2 teaspoons fine sea salt
2 tablespoons sesame seeds
3 tablespoons polenta (corn meal)
1 tablespoon pumpkin seeds
1 tablespoon oatmeal flakes
1 tablespoon épeautre or spelt (or substitute wheat berries)
1 tablespoon flax seeds
1 tablespoon sunflower seeds
1 large egg beaten with 1 tablespoon cold water, for egg wash

1. In the bowl of a heavy-duty electric mixer fitted with a dough hook, combine the yeast, sugar and 80ml (3fl oz) lukewarm water, and stir to blend. Let stand until foamy, about 5 minutes. Stir in the remaining water and the salt.

2. Add the flour all at once, mixing at medium speed until most of the flour has been absorbed and the dough forms a ball. Add the salt and all the seeds and grains and continue to knead until smooth and satiny, but still firm, 4 to 5 minutes, adding additional flour to keep the dough from sticking. Transfer to a clean, floured work surface and, by hand, continue to knead for 1 minute to help distribute the seeds and grains.

3. Return the dough to a clean bowl. Cover securely with plastic wrap. Place in the refrigerator. Let the dough rise until doubled or tripled in bulk, 8 to 12 hours. This slow, refrigerator rise will make for a more flavourful, well-developed bread.

4. Remove the dough from the refrigerator. Punch down the dough, cover securely with plastic wrap, and let rise until doubled in bulk, about 1 hour. Punch down the dough and let rise again until doubled in bulk, about 1 hour.

5. Punch down again. Form the dough into a tight rectangle. Place the dough in the non-stick loaf tin. Cover with a clean cloth and let rise until doubled in bulk, about 1 hour.

6. Preheat the oven to 220°C/425°F/gas mark 7.

7. Brush the top of the dough with the egg wash. With a razor blade, slash the top of the dough several times, so it can expand regularly during baking. Place the loaf tin on the bottom shelf of the oven. Bake until the crust is firm and golden brown, and the bread sounds hollow when tapped on the bottom, about 45 minutes, or until an instant-read thermometer plunged into the centre of the bread reads 100°C/200°F. Transfer the bread to a rack to cool. Do not slice the bread for at least 1 hour, for it will continue to bake as it cools

Parmesan Bread
Pain Parmesan

———○———

Inspired by a Gruyère bread I tasted at one of my favourite bakeries – Boulangerie Onfroy – I developed this rich, full-flavoured Parmesan bread, delicious toasted and served with a cheese course or as part of a bacon, lettuce and tomato sandwich. The bread can be made, start to finish, in just under 3 hours.

———○———

MAKES 1 LOAF
(ABOUT 12 SLICES)

EQUIPMENT:
One 1-litre (1¾-pint)
rectangular loaf tin,
preferably non-stick

1 teaspoon active dry yeast
1 teaspoon sugar
330ml (12fl oz) lukewarm water
2 tablespoons extra-virgin olive oil
2 teaspoon fine sea salt
About 500g (1lb 2oz) strong flour
90g (3oz) freshly grated Parmigiano-
Reggiano cheese
1 large egg beaten with 1 tablespoon
cold water, for egg wash

1. In the bowl of a heavy-duty electric mixer fitted with a dough hook, combine the yeast, sugar and lukewarm water, and stir to blend. Let stand until foamy, about 5 minutes. Stir in the oil and the salt.

2. Add the flour and the cheese all at once, mixing at the medium speed until most of the flour has been absorbed and the dough forms a ball. Continue to knead until soft and satiny but still firm, 4 to 5 minutes, adding additional flour as necessary to keep the dough from sticking. Transfer the dough to a clean work surface and knead by hand for 1 minute. The dough should be smooth and spring back when indented it with your fingertip.

3. Cover the bowl with plastic wrap. Let the dough rise until doubled in bulk, about 1 hour. Punch down the dough and shape it into a tight rectangle. Place the dough in a non-stick 1 quart (1 litre) rectangular loaf tin. Cover with a clean cloth and let rise until doubled in bulk, about 1 hour.

4. Preheat the oven to 220°C/425°F/gas mark 7.

5. Brush the top of the dough with the egg wash. With the tips of a scissors snip the top of the dough all over about 15 times to allow it to expand regularly during baking. Place the loaf tin on the bottom shelf of the oven. Bake until firm and golden brown, 35 to 40 minutes, or until an instant-read thermometer plunged into the centre of the bread reads 100°C/200°F.

6. Transfer the bread to a rack to cool.

Rye Water Crackers
Biscuits au Seigle

———◦———

The dense flavour of rye has always appealed, and I love nothing better than crunchy crackers with my cheese. Try these with an assortment of blue cheeses, or a rustic farm cheddar.

———◦———

MAKES ABOUT 40 CRACKERS

EQUIPMENT:
One 5.5cm- (2.25in-) scalloped cookie cutter; a garden mister

150g (5oz) rye flour
140 g (4oz) unbleached, plain flour
1 teaspoon fine sea salt
80ml (3fl oz) vegetable oil (peanut, or safflower oil)
125ml (4½floz) cold water
1 teaspoon coarse sea salt
1 teaspoon caraway or cumin seeds

PREHEAT THE OVEN TO
200⁰C/400⁰F

1. Combine the flours and salt into the bowl of a food processor. Add the oil and water and pulse until the mixture comes together. The dough should not form a ball.

2. With a pastry scraper, transfer the dough to a floured work surface. With the palms of your hands, gently work the mass of dough into a round. Cut into two pieces. Roll about 3mm (⅛in) thick. Cut out the dough with the cookie cutter. Transfer the rounds to non-stick baking sheets. Pierce each round 4 or 5 times with the tines of a fork to create an attractive design. With a garden mister, generously spray the crackers. This will make them even more crisp and will help the salt and seeds to adhere to the crackers. Sprinkle with salt and caraway or cumin seeds.

3. Place the baking sheets in the oven and bake until firm in texture and lightly browned around the edges, 20 to 25 minutes. If your oven has a tendency to bake unevenly, rotate the baking sheets from top to bottom, and front to back halfway through the baking period.

4. Remove from the oven and let cool on the baking sheets for 1 minute, to firm up. With a metal spatula, transfer the crackers to wire racks to cool completely. The crackers can be stored in an airtight container at room temperature for 1 week.

Chickpea-Flour Crêpes from Nice
Socca

———○———

On those many grey and rainy days in Paris, I often light up the oven and make these delicious crêpes from Nice as an appetiser to a warming cold-weather meal. While these golden treats can be found on the market streets of Nice, they are very easy to make at home and I find that they are always a great hit with guests. They can be cut into wedges, rolled up, and eaten by hand.

———○———

MAKES FOUR 30CM- (12IN-) CRÊPES, OR ENOUGH FOR ABOUT 16 SERVINGS

EQUIPMENT:
One 30cm- (12in-) paella or pizza pan

250g (9oz) chick pea flour
500ml (18fl oz) water
4 tablespoons extra-virgin olive oil, plus additional for cooking
1 teaspoon fine sea salt
Freshly ground black pepper to taste

PREHEAT THE OVEN TO 230°C/450°F/GAS MARK 8.

1. In a large bowl, combine the flour and water and stir to blend. Stir in the oil and sea salt.

2. Brush the paella or pizza pan with oil and place in the oven until the oil sizzles, 3 to 4 minutes. Pour about a quarter of the batter into the bottom of the hot pan, tipping and swirling it to evenly coat the pan. The batter should be about 3mm (⅛in) thick. Place in the centre of the oven and bake until the batter is firm and just begins to brown around the edges, 4 to 5 minutes.

3. Remove from the oven, drizzle with additional oil if desired, and season generously with freshly ground black pepper. Serve immediately, cutting the socca into wedges. Guests can roll the slices like a crêpe and eat the socca by hand. Serve with plenty of paper napkins!

I love these crêpes with a glass of chilled rosé de Provence.

Brioche

Brioche

———◇———

I have never counted the number of versions of brioche one finds in Paris, but over time I have developed a recipe that I love and share with you here. Once you get hooked on making brioche, you are set for life! There is nothing more satisfying than removing a pair of shiny, golden-brown crowns from your oven on a chilly day. You will say to yourself: 'I made this?' Although brioche is a traditional breakfast treat in France, usually served toasted with butter and jam, I like to serve it as a rich dinner bread, sliced and toasted and served as a first course with smoked salmon or foie gras.

———◇———

EQUIPMENT:

Two 1-litre (1¾-pint) rectangular loaf tins, preferably non-stick

FOR THE SPONGE:
185ml (6½fl oz) warm whole milk
1 package (2¼ teaspoons) active dry yeast
1 teaspoon sugar
1 large egg, lightly beaten
280g (10oz) unbleached, plain flour (divided into two batches)

FOR THE DOUGH:
65g (2½oz) sugar
1 teaspoon fine sea salt
4 large eggs, lightly beaten
Approximately 210g (7½oz) unbleached, plain flour
180g (6oz) unsalted butter, at room temperature

1. To make the sponge: In the bowl of a heavy-duty mixer fitted with a dough hook, combine the milk, yeast and sugar and stir to blend. Let stand until foamy, about 5 minutes. Stir in 140g (5oz) of flour and the egg and stir to blend. The sponge will be sticky and fairly dry. Sprinkle with the remaining 140g (5oz) of flour to cover the sponge. Set aside to rest, uncovered, for 30 to 40 minutes. The sponge should erupt slightly, cracking the flour.

2. To make the dough: Add the sugar, salt, eggs and 140g (5oz) of the flour to the sponge. With the dough hook attached, mix at low speed for 1 or 2 minutes, just until the ingredients come together. Still mixing, sprinkle in 70g (2½ oz) more of flour. When the flour is incorporated, increase the mixer speed to medium and beat for 15 minutes, scraping down the hook and bowl as needed.

3. To incorporate the butter into the dough you need to work the butter until it is the same consistency as the dough. To prepare the butter, place it on a flat work surface and, with a

dough scraper, smear the butter bit by bit across the surface. When it is ready, the butter should be smooth, soft and still cool.

4. With the mixer on medium-low, add the butter a few tablespoons at a time. When all of the butter has been added, increase the mixer speed to medium-high for 1 minute, then reduce the speed to medium and beat the dough for 5 minutes. The dough will be soft and sticky.

5. First rise: Cover the bowl tightly with plastic wrap. Let rise at room temperature until doubled in bulk, 2 to 2½ hours.

6. Second rise and chilling: Punch down the dough. Cover the bowl tightly with plastic wrap and refrigerate the dough overnight, or for at least 4 to 6 hours, during which time it will continue to rise and may double in size again.

7. After the second chill, the dough is ready to use. If you are not going to use the dough after the second rise, deflate it, wrap it airtight, and store in the freezer. The dough can remain frozen for up to 1 month. Thaw the dough, still wrapped, in the refrigerator overnight and use it directly from the refrigerator.

TO MAKE TWO
RECTANGULAR LOAVES:

One recipe brioche dough, chilled
Butter, for buttering loaf tins
1 large egg beaten with 1 tablespoon
cold water, for wash

PREHEAT THE OVEN TO
190°C/375°F/GAS MARK 5.

8. Divide the dough in 12 equal pieces, each weighing about 75g (2½oz). Roll each piece of dough tightly into a ball and place 6 pieces side-by-side in each of the two rectangular loaf tins. Cover the pans with a clean cloth and let rise until double in bulk, about 60 to 90 minutes (1 to 1½ hours).

9. Lightly brush the brioche with the egg wash. Working quickly, use the tips of a pair of sharp scissors to snip several

crosses along the top of dough. This will help the brioche to rise evenly as it bakes.

10. Place in the centre of the oven and bake until deeply golden and an instant-read thermometer plunged into the centre of the bread reads 100°C/200°F, 30 to 35 minutes. Remove from the oven and place on a rack to cool. Turn out once cooled.

> NOTE:
>
> The brioche is best eaten the day it is baked. It can be stored for a day or two, tightly wrapped. To freeze, wrap tightly and store for up to 1 month. Thaw, still wrapped, at room temperature.

Menu·Carte

An Easter Feast

—◦—

Chez Benoît's Spring Salad

—◦—

Jean-Guy's Basque-Spiced Leg of Lamb

—◦—

L'Ambroisie's White Beans with Mustard
and Sage

—◦—

Eight-Grain Bread and Brie

—◦—

Benoît's Prize-Winning Tarte Tatin

Vegetables

Vegetables
Les Légumes

Richard Lenoir Market Courgette-Tomato Gratin
Gratin de Courgettes aux Tomates Marché Richard Lenoir

Fresh Almonds, Courgettes, Curry and Mint
Étuvée de Jeunes Courgettes aux Amandes Fraîches

Oven-Roasted Tomatoes
Tomates Confites

Aubergine, Tomato and Parmesan Gratin
Gratin d'Aubergine, Tomates et Parmesan

Sautéed Asparagus with Spring Herbs
Asperges Sautées à Cru aux Herbes de Printemps

Asparagus, Morels and Asparagus Cream
Les Morilles Étuvées à la Crème et Pointes Vertes

Rich and Poor: Asparagus and Baby Leeks
Riche et Pauvre: Asperges et Poireaux

Gérard Mulot's Green Beans with Snow
Peas and Chives
Haricots Verts et Pois Gourmands

Gallopin's Green Bean, Mushroom
and Hazelnut Salad
Haricots Verts, Champignons et Noisettes Gallopin

Courgettes Stuffed with Goat's Cheese and Mint
Courgettes et Fromage de Chèvre à la Menthe

Wild Morel Mushrooms in Cream and Stock
Morilles à la Crème et Bouillon

Frédéric Anton's Twice-Cooked Mushrooms
Les Champignons de Frédéric Anton

Pierre Gagnaire's Jerusalem Artichoke Purée
Purée de Topinambours Pierre Gagniare

Benoît's Carrots with Cumin and Orange
Carottes au Cumin et Orange

Alain Passard's Turnip Gratin
Gratin de Navets Alain Passard

Richard Lenoir Market Courgette-Tomato Gratin
Gratin de Courgettes aux Tomates Marché Richard Lenoir

———o———

In the summer months, Paris' roving markets are filled with blindingly beautiful fresh fruits and vegetables, many of them grown just on the outskirts of Paris. On Sunday mornings I can often be found on the Boulevard Richard-Lenoir near the Bastille, shopping for tiny, tender courgettes with the blossoms still attached. The golden blossoms give the dish an almost Asian flavour.

———o———

SERVES 4

EQUIPMENT:
One 1-litre (1¾-pint) gratin dish

30g (1oz) fresh breadcrumbs
500g (1lb) fresh courgettes, scrubbed and cut into thin rounds
Fine sea salt
12 courgette blossoms (optional)
500ml (18fl oz) Tomato Sauce (page 269)
75g (2½oz) freshly grated Italian Parmigiano-Reggiano cheese

PREHEAT THE OVEN TO 220°C/425°F/GAS MARK 7.

1. In the gratin dish, layer half of the breadcrumbs, half of the courgettes, a fine sprinkling of sea salt, half of the courgette blossoms, if using, half of the tomato sauce, the remaining breadcrumbs, half of the cheese, the remaining courgettes, a fine sprinkling of sea salt, the remaining blossoms, if using, the remaining tomato sauce, and the remaining cheese.

2. Place in the centre of the oven and bake until bubbling and crispy, 20 to 25 minutes. Serve warm or at room temperature.

Richard Lenoir Market

Boulevard Richard-Lenoir, beginning at Rue Amelot

Paris 11

9am to noon, Thursday and Sunday

Fresh Almonds, Courgettes, Curry and Mint
Etuvée de Jeunes Courgettes aux Amandes Fraîches

———◦———

During the last days of chef Joël Robuchon's reign on Avenue Raymond Poincaré, this was one of the final dishes he served during the spring of 1996 before finally closing on 5 July of that year. I make it often, especially when I come across fresh almonds from Provence in the market in springtime.

———◦———

SERVES 6

500g (1lb) young courgettes, scrubbed, ends trimmed (but not peeled) and cut into pieces roughly the size of an almond
90g (3oz) whole fresh almonds (or substitute whole shelled and blanched almonds)
2 teaspoons Curry Powder or to taste (see page 268)
Fine sea salt
Freshly ground white pepper
2 tablespoons extra-virgin olive oil
24 fresh mint leaves, cut into a fine chiffonnade (fine ribbons)

1. In a large bowl, combine the courgettes, almonds, curry powder, salt and pepper. Cover securely with plastic wrap and set aside for 15 minutes for the almonds and courgettes to absorb the seasonings.

2. In a large, non-stick frying-pan, heat the oil over high heat until hot but not smoking. Transfer the almond-courgette mixture to the pan and cook, shaking the pan frequently, until golden, 3 to 4 minutes. The courgettes should remain crunchy. Add the mint and toss to blend evenly. Taste for seasoning.

3. To serve, place a dome of the warm almond-courgette mixture on a small plate. Serve as an accompaniment to roast pigeon, lamb or goat.

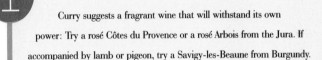

Curry suggests a fragrant wine that will withstand its own power: Try a rosé Côtes du Provence or a rosé Arbois from the Jura. If accompanied by lamb or pigeon, try a Savigny-les-Beaune from Burgundy.

Oven-Roasted Tomatoes
Tomates Confites

Nothing can match the pure, wholesome flavour of tomatoes and no method amplifies tomato essence like reduction. These are the sun-dried tomatoes of the 2000s, fresh tomatoes that are baked for hours in a very slow oven until much of their moisture evaporates, creating tomatoes with a dense, haunting, rich and pleasantly tangy flavour. Be sure to adjust the oven to the lowest possible heat, so that the tomatoes actually melt more than bake. I use the tomatoes in soups and salads, on sandwiches, for pasta, or anywhere I want a rich, pure tomato flavour. Although fresh herbs have a tendency to burn when baked, the liquid provided by the oil and the low oven temperature will prevent this from happening.

MAKES 500ML (18FL OZ)

1kg (2lb) fresh plum tomatoes, peeled, cored, seeded and quartered lengthways
Fine sea salt
Freshly ground black pepper
A pinch of icing sugar
2 sprigs fresh thyme, stemmed
4 plump, fresh garlic cloves, slivered
2 tablespoons extra-virgin olive oil

PREHEAT THE OVEN TO THE LOWEST POSSIBLE SETTING, ABOUT 80ºC/75ºF/GAS MARK ¼.

1. Arrange the tomato quarters side by side on a baking sheet. Sprinkle each side lightly with salt, pepper and icing sugar. Scatter the thyme leaves over the tomatoes and place a garlic sliver on top of each quarter. Drizzle with olive oil.

2. Place in the oven and cook until the tomatoes are very soft, about 1 hour. Turn the tomatoes, baste with the juices and cook until meltingly tender, and reduced to about half their size, about 2 hours in total. Check the tomatoes from time to time; they should remain moist and soft. Remove from the oven and allow to cool thoroughly.

3. Transfer the tomatoes to a sterilised jar, cover with the cooking juices and oil, cover securely, and refrigerate for up to 1 week.

Aubergine, Tomato and Parmesan Gratin
Gratin d'Aubergine, Tomates et Parmesan

———◦———

The classic trio of shiny black aubergine, brilliant red tomato sauce and nutty freshly grated Parmesan cheese remains one of my very favourite combinations. Come August, when the city of Paris empties out and seems more like a village than a big city, and we have delightfully generous hours of daylight, this is a favourite weeknight main-dish dinner, often served with a green salad and a nice, spicy red wine from the Rhône valley.

———◦———

SERVES 6

6 small, fresh aubergines, each weighing about 250g (8oz), rinsed and dried
Sea salt
Freshly ground white pepper to taste
Several teaspoons extra-virgin olive oil
About 250ml (9oz) Tomato Sauce (page 269)
3 tablespoons freshly grated Parmigiano-Reggiano cheese

PREHEAT THE OVEN TO 220ºC/425ºF/GAS MARK 7.

I serve this with a favourite red from the Rhône, such as the spicy Domaine de l'Oratoire Saint-Martin from the charming hilltop village of Cairanne.

1. Prick the aubergines all over with a two-pronged fork. Place the aubergines directly on the oven rack, to allow air to circulate as the aubergines cook. The aubergines will roast rather than steam, giving them a richer, more dense and slightly smoky flavour. Place another rack with a baking sheet beneath the oven rack to collect any juices. Cook until the aubergine is soft and collapsed, about 25 minutes.

2. Remove from the oven. Trim off the stem end and discard. Cut in half lengthways, without cutting all the way through the bottom skin. Open like a book and flatten. Repeat for remaining aubergines. Season with salt and pepper. Drizzle with oil. Spoon tomato sauce over the aubergine. Sprinkle with the cheese.

3. Return to the oven and bake until sizzling and fragrant, about 25 minutes more. Serve warm or at room temperature.

Sautéed Asparagus with Spring Herbs
Asperges Sautées à Cru aux Herbes de Printemps

———○———

Next to artichokes, I think asparagus is my favourite spring vegetable. Each year I try to add one or two new recipes to my repertoire. This one was inspired by a visit to the Richard Lenoir market one April weekend. Serve it as a first course or as a vegetable accompaniment to a simple roast chicken.

———○———

SERVES 6

3 tablespoons extra-virgin olive oil
12 spears fresh green asparagus,
cleaned and peeled
6 tablespoons Homemade Chicken
Stock (page 274)
Several drops freshly squeezed
lemon juice
2 tablespoons (15 g) unsalted butter
1 small shallot, very finely chopped
Fine sea salt
Freshly ground white pepper
Chopped fresh chives, chervil and
parsley leaves, to garnish

Marché Richard Lenoir,
Boulevard Richard-Lenoir, beginning at
rue Amelot
Paris 11
Thursday and Saturday mornings
Métro: Bastille or Richard Lenoir.

1. In a frying-pan large enough to hold the asparagus in a single layer, heat the oil over moderate heat until hot but not smoking. Add the asparagus and carefully roll them to coat evenly with oil. Add the chicken stock. Reduce heat to low, cover, and cook until the asparagus is tender but still firm when pierced with the tip of a knife, about 5 minutes. Drizzle with lemon juice.

2. Meanwhile, in a small saucepan, combine the butter, chopped shallot and a pinch of salt. Sweat – cook gently until soft but not browned – over moderate heat, about 2 minutes. Taste for seasoning. Cover and set aside.

3. Transfer three spears of asparagus to each of four warmed individual dinner plates. Sprinkle with herbs and serve.

Try this with a Muscat sec from Alsace, a much under-rated wine that is a great palate opener.

Asparagus, Morels and Asparagus Cream
Les Morilles Etuvées à la Crème et Pointes Vertes

———◦———

Guy Savoy, one of Paris' most creative and talented chefs, serves these delicate spears of green asparagus with a colourful and creamy purée of asparagus and wild morel mushrooms steeped in cream – a classic French combination that never fails to attract raves.

———◦———

SERVES 8

500g (1lb) thin green asparagus, trimmed
Coarse and fine sea salt
Freshly ground white pepper
2 tablespoons unsalted butter
500ml (18fl oz) Wild Morel Mushrooms in Cream and Stock (page 86)

1. Trim the asparagus, discarding the tip of the woody end. Trim the tender tips to about 10cm (4in). Reserve the less tender ends for the creamy asparagus purée.

2. Prepare a large bowl of iced water.

3. Fill a large pot with 3 litres (5 pints) of water and bring to a boil over a high heat. Add 3 tablespoons of salt and the asparagus tips. Boil, uncovered, until the tips are crisp-tender, about 3 minutes. Cooking time will vary according to the size of the asparagus tips. Immediately drain the asparagus tips (reserving the cooking water) and plunge them into iced water so that they cool down as quickly as possible and retain their crispness and bright green colour. The asparagus will cool in 1 to 2 minutes. After that, they will soften and begin to lose crispness and flavour.

4. Transfer the asparagus to a colander, drain and wrap in a thick towel to dry. The asparagus can be cooked up to 2 hours in advance. Keep them wrapped in the towel and hold at room temperature.

5. Bring the water back to a boil, add the asparagus ends and boil, uncovered, until very tender, about 8 minutes. Drain the

asparagus and transfer to the bowl of a food processor. Process to a smooth purée. Pass the purée through the finest grid of a food mill to remove any tough fibres. Taste for seasoning. The purée can also be prepared up to 2 hours in advance. Transfer to a container, cover and hold at room temperature.

6. At serving time, melt the butter in a large frying-pan and gently reheat the asparagus. Arrange the morels in a dome on warm salad plates. Spoon the asparagus purée around the morels. Arrange the asparagus teepee fashion over the morels and serve immediately.

Restaurant Guy Savoy

18, rue Troyon

Paris 17

Telephone: 01 43 80 40 61 Fax: 01 46 22 43 09

Métro: Charles de Gaulle-Etoile

Rich and Poor: Asparagus and Baby Leeks
Riche et Pauvre: Asperges et Poireaux

———————◦———————

Come early March, the markets of Paris explode with a flourish of green. Pencil-thin spring leeks arrive like lithe young ladies, while Provence steps in to provide the slimmest of green asparagus. The match is one made in heaven, for the common leek is often called 'the asparagus of the poor'. In this recipe, inspired by a version offered by Alain Ducasse deputy Frank Cerutti, the two are anointed with a touch of butter and then a few drops of balsamic vinegar to 'wake them up'. If slim leeks are not available, prepare with green asparagus only.

———————◦———————

SERVES 4

EQUIPMENT:
One 6-litre (10-pint) pasta pan with colander

8 baby leeks, white portion only; trimmed to about 18cm (7in)
8 spears green asparagus (about 250g/8oz trimmed weight)
About 500ml (18fl oz) Homemade Chicken Stock (page 274)
30g (1oz) unsalted butter
3 tablespoons freshly grated Parmigiano-Reggiano cheese
About ½ teaspoon balsamic vinegar
Fleur de sel (see page 100)
Chopped fresh chives, to garnish

1. Trim the leeks at the root. Rinse well under cold running water. Transfer to a bowl of cold water and soak for 5 minutes to get rid of any remaining dirt. When all the grit has settled to the bottom of the bowl, remove the leeks and dry thoroughly. Place the leeks in a frying-pan that will hold them in a single layer. Cover with chicken stock, cover and simmer until tender, about 8 minutes. Drain. Set aside and keep warm.

2. Trim the asparagus, discarding the tip of the woody end. Trim the tender tips to about 18cm (7in). (Reserve the less tender ends for an asparagus purée or a velouté.)

3. Prepare a large bowl of iced water.

4. Fill the pasta pan fitted with a colander with 5 litres (9 pints) of water and bring to a boil over high heat. Add 3 tablespoons of salt and the asparagus to the colander. Boil, uncovered, until the tips are crisp-tender, 3 to 4 minutes. Cooking time will vary according to the size of the asparagus. Immediately drain the asparagus and plunge them into the iced water so that they cool down as quickly as possible and

retain their crispness and bright green colour. The asparagus will cool in 1 to 2 minutes. After that, they will soften and begin to lose crispness and flavour. Transfer the asparagus to a colander, drain and wrap in a thick towel to dry.

5. In a frying-pan large enough to hold both the leeks and asparagus in a single layer, warm the butter over moderate heat just until it begins to foam. Add the two vegetables, interlaying them, side by side. Sprinkle all over with the cheese, being careful to keep the vegetables in place.

As the cheese melts into the vegetables and the butter, it should form a thick emulsion. Cook gently just until warmed through – being careful not to burn the butter – for 2 to 3 minutes. Drizzle with a few drops of balsamic vinegar. Immediately transfer the vegetables to a salad plates. Season with fine fleur de sel and garnish with chopped chives.

While the slight bitterness of asparagus can make wine a difficult choice, there are solutions. I enjoy this with a young Chardonnay, any Sauvignon Blanc, an Alsatian Pinot Gris or a Jurançon sec.

Restaurant Alain Ducasse au Plaza Athenée

25, avenue Montaigne

Paris 8

Telephone: 01 53 67 65 00 Fax: 01 53 67 65 00

Métro: Franklin D. Roosevelt

Gérard Mulot's Green Beans with Snow Peas and Chives
Haricots Verts and Pois Gourmands

———◦———

Paris' boulangeries have also become great spots for picking up a take-away lunch of sandwiches and salads. This spring-fresh salad, from the excellent bakery-pastry shop run by Gerard Mulot, is a favourite of mine. Crisp green beans are combined with equally crunchy snow peas and tossed with a touch of vinaigrette. The chives here are a welcome addition, adding a gentle hint of fresh onion. The combination of flavours is at once grassy, fresh and spring-like. The addition of chopped shallots adds an almost sweet counterpoint. Toss with your favourite vinaigrette or add sliced tomatoes for a flavour and colour contrast.

———◦———

SERVES 4

EQUIPMENT:
A large pot fitted with a colander

Sea salt
250g (8oz) green beans, rinsed and trimmed at both ends
250g (8oz) snow peas, rinsed and trimmed and both ends
2 tablespoons fresh chopped chives
2 shallots, peeled and finely chopped
Several tablespoons Classic Vinaigrette (page 260)

1. Prepare a large bowl of iced water.

2 Fill a large pot fitted with a colander with 3 litres (5 pints) of water and bring to a boil over a high heat. Add 4 tablespoons of salt and the beans, and cook until crisp-tender, about 5 minutes. Cooking time will vary, according to the size and tenderness of the beans. Immediately remove the colander from the water, allow the water to drain from the beans, and plunge the colander with the beans in it into the ice water so that they cool down as quickly as possible. The beans will cool in 1 to 2 minutes. If you leave them longer, they will become soggy and begin to lose flavour. Transfer the beans to a strainer, drain and wrap in a thick towel to dry. The beans can be cooked up to 4 hours in advance. Keep them wrapped in the towel and refrigerate, if desired.

3. Repeat with the snow peas: Bring the water back to the boil over a high heat. Add 4 tablespoons of salt and the peas, and cook until the snow peas are crisp-tender, 2 to 3 minutes. Cooking time will vary, according to the size and tenderness of

the peas. Immediately drain the peas and plunge them into the iced water so they cool down as quickly as possible. The peas will cool in 1 to 2 minutes. If you leave them longer, they will become soggy and begin to lose flavour. Transfer the peas to a strainer, drain and wrap in a thick towel to dry. The peas can be cooked up to 4 hours in advance. Keep them wrapped in the towel and refrigerate, if desired.

4. Combine the beans, peas, chives and chopped shallots in a large salad bowl. Toss gently. Add the vinaigrette and toss to coat evenly. Taste for seasoning.

5. Serve immediately, as a main course salad with toasted country bread, or as a side vegetable to accompany a simple fish, meat or poultry dish.

Boulangerie-Patisserie Gérard Mulot

76, rue du Seine

Paris 6

Telephone: 01 43 26 85 77

Métro: Mabillon

Gallopin's Green Bean, Mushroom and Hazelnut Salad
Haricots Verts, Champignons et Noisettes Gallopin

———○———

I last sampled this classic bistro vegetable salad at the colourful Gallopin, just across the street from the Paris bourse, or stock market. This is the sort of dish that depends upon freshness and care all around. It's hearty enough to serve as an entire luncheon meal, or as a first course as part of a major bistro feast.

———○———

SERVES: 2 AS A MAIN COURSE;

4 AS A FIRST COURSE

EQUIPMENT:
A large pot fitted with a colander

FOR THE SALAD:
250g (8oz) green beans, rinsed and trimmed at both ends
4 tablespoons fine sea salt
250g (8oz) fresh mushrooms, wiped clean, stems removed, thinly sliced
About 3 tablespoons chopped fresh chives
1 small shallot, peeled and finely chopped
3 tablespoons freshly toasted hazelnuts, coarsely chopped (see note overleaf)

FOR THE HAZELNUT VINAIGRETTE:
1 tablespoon best-quality sherry wine vinegar (or best-quality red wine vinegar)
Fine sea salt to taste
3 to 4 tablespoons best-quality hazelnut oil (or extra-virgin olive oil)

1. Prepare a large bowl of iced water.

2. Fill a large pot fitted with a colander with 3 litres (5 pints) of water and bring to a boil over a high heat. Add the 4 tablespoons of salt and the beans and cook until crisp-tender, about 5 minutes. Cooking time will vary according to the size and tenderness of the beans. Immediately remove the colander from the water, allow the water to drain from the beans and plunge the colander with the beans into the iced water so they cool down as quickly as possible The beans will cool in 1 to 2 minutes. If you leave them longer, they will become soggy and begin to lose flavour. Drain the beans and wrap in a thick towel to dry. The beans can be cooked up to 4 hours in advance. Keep them wrapped in the towel, refrigerated, if desired.

3. In a large bowl, combine the green beans, mushrooms, shallots, chives and toasted hazelnuts. Set aside.

4. Prepare the vinaigrette: In a small bowl, combine the vinegar and salt. Whisk to blend. Add the oil, whisking to blend. Taste for seasoning.

NOTE

Toasting nuts imparts a deep, rich flavour. To toast nuts, spread them on a baking sheet. Toast in an oven preheated to 175°C/350°F/gas mark 4 until fragrant and evenly browned, about 10 minutes.

5. At serving time, pour the vinaigrette over the salad. Toss gently to blend. Serve.

Gallopin

40, rue Notre-Dames-des-Victoires

Paris 2

Telephone: 01 42 36 10 32

Métro: Bourse

Courgettes Stuffed with Goat's Cheese and Mint
Courgettes et Fromage de Chèvre à la Menthe

I confess that during the summer months, I am thoroughly addicted to this preparation: tender round courgettes stuffed with goat's cheese and mint. Sometimes I serve abundant portions as a vegetarian main course, along with a huge green salad. When I can find the tiny round courgettes in the markets, that's what I use, as they are truly made for stuffing. If they are not available, use the smallest and freshest standard elongated courgettes you can find, cutting them in half lengthways and proceeding as you would for round courgettes.

SERVES 8

About 1 kg (2lb) round small courgettes (about 8)
2 tablespoons extra-virgin olive oil
1 small onion, peeled and cut into thin rounds
Curry powder to taste

1. Cut the tops off the courgettes. With a small spoon, carve out the pulp of the courgettes. Chop the pulp. Reserve both the pulp and the courgettes and set aside.

2. Bring a large pot of water to a boil. Add the courgettes and the tops and blanch until softened but still firm, about 5 minutes. Transfer them to a bowl of iced water to refresh, firm

*About 250g (9oz) fresh
goat's cheese
Several tablespoons cream or milk
4 tablespoons fresh mint, cut into a
chiffonnade (fine ribbons)*

....

*PREHEAT THE OVEN TO
200°C/400°F/GAS MARK 6*

and help the vegetable remain a bright green colour. Drain.

3. In a small, heavy-duty frying-pan, combine the onions, oil and a pinch of salt. Sweat, covered, over low heat until soft and cooked through, about 5 minutes. The onions should not brown. Add the courgette pulp and curry powder to taste and cook until softened, about 5 more minutes. Set aside.

4. In the bowl of a food processor combine the goat's cheese and 1 tablespoon of cream or milk. Process to a purée. If necessary, add additional cream or milk to form a smooth mixture. Set aside.

5. Place the courgettes side by side in a large gratin dish. Spoon the curried mixture into the courgettes, filling about two-thirds full. Sprinkle with about half the mint. Spoon the cheese over the curried mixture, filling all the way to the top. Sprinkle with the rest of the mint. Place the top on the courgette.

6. Place in the centre of the oven and bake until the courgettes are soft, about 15 minutes. Serve warm or at room temperature.

Wild Morel Mushrooms in Cream and Stock
Morilles à la Crème et Bouillon

Rare, fresh morels arrive in Paris markets in early March, just as the last crop of the equally rare black truffle says its farewell for the season. But I depend upon wild morel mushrooms year round, always keeping a supply for making this rich and elegant vegetable sauce, great for tossing with pasta or rice. I also serve it with Benoît's Fricassée of Chicken with Morels (page 184).

SERVES 6 TO 8

60g (2oz) dried morel mushrooms
30g (1 oz) unsalted butter,
at room temperature
Fine sea salt to taste
2 shallots, peeled and finely chopped
500ml (18fl oz) double cream
About 2 teaspoons freshly squeezed
lemon juice, or to taste
Freshly ground white pepper to taste

1. If any of the morels are extremely large, halve them lengthways. Place the morels in a colander and rinse well under cold running water to rid them of any grit. Transfer them to a heatproof measuring jug. Pour boiling water over the mushrooms to cover. Set aside for 20 minutes to plump them up. With a slotted spoon, carefully remove the mushrooms from the liquid, leaving behind any grit that may fall to the bottom. Place a piece of dampened cheesecloth in a colander set over a large bowl. Carefully spoon the soaking liquid into the colander, leaving behind any grit at the bottom of the measuring jug. You should have 375ml (about 13fl oz) of mushroom bouillon (stock). Set it aside.

2. In a medium-sized frying-pan, combine the butter, a pinch of salt and shallots and sweat over moderate heat without colouring the shallots, 2 to 3 minutes. Add the drained morels and about 125ml (4½fl oz) of the drained mushroom bouillon. Cook, uncovered, over moderate heat until the liquid is reduced to 2 to 3 tablespoons, about 5 minutes. Add the cream and remaining 250ml (9fl oz) of mushroom bouillon.

3. For Fricassée of Chicken with Morels (page 184) transfer the morels and liquid at this point.

4. Simmer, still uncovered, over low heat until the morels have lost most of their firmness, 8 to 10 minutes. Add lemon juice to taste. Season generously with white pepper. Taste for seasoning. Serve.

TRUC

If mushrooms are gritty, blanch in salted water for 3 minutes and drain under cold running water. This suggestion comes from the departed Parisian chef Jean-Claude Ferrero, a passionate mushroom lover and expert.

VARIATION

For a richer dish, to use in the recipe for Asparagus, Morels and Asparagus Cream (page 77), or to serve as a side vegetable dish to roast poultry, prepare Morels in Cream. For this variation, prepare as for the Cream and Stock recipe but add only 125ml (4½ fl oz) of the mushroom bouillon. The remaining bouillon can be frozen to enhance a mushroom soup.

Frédéric Anton's Twice-Cooked Mushrooms
Les Champignons de Frédéric Anton

———○———

I have worked with chef Frédéric Anton since the early 1980s, when he was assistant to chef Joël Robuchon. As a Robuchon acolyte, Anton was responsible for ordering – then accepting or rejecting – every leaf of lettuce, every grain of caviar and every wriggling langoustine that entered the kitchen. A perfect dish, as any cook knows, begins with absolutely fresh, flawless ingredients. In the kitchens of the Pré Catelan, where he is now the chef, Anton practises all he learned in the school of the master, then adds his own uncanny ability to nudge ingredients, create combinations that sing on the palate and, most of all, satisfy. I love spending time with him, and always learn a trick or two to take home to my own kitchen.

———○———

SERVES 4 TO 6

2 tablespoons extra-virgin olive oil
500g (1lb) large cèpe or porcini mushrooms (or substitute chanterelles, girolles, portobello or standard cultivated mushrooms), cleaned, trimmed and sliced
Sea salt
Finely ground white pepper
2 tablespoon unsalted butter
2 tablespoons chopped chervil leaves (or substitute chopped tarragon or parsley leaves)
Coarsely ground white pepper

1. Heat the oil in a large non-stick frying-pan over moderate heat until hot but not smoking. Add the mushrooms, season lightly with salt, and sauté just until they begin to give up their juices, 1 to 2 minutes. Using a slotted spoon, transfer the mushrooms to a platter to drain. With kitchen roll, wipe out the frying-pan. Melt the butter over moderate heat and return the mushrooms to the frying-pan. Season lightly with salt and pepper. Cook for 2 minutes more. Off the heat, sprinkle the mushrooms with chervil and toss to coat with the herb. Season with freshly ground white pepper and serve.

Le Pré Catelan

Route de Suresnes

Bois de Boulogne

Paris 16

Telephone: 01 44 14 41 14

Fax: 01 45 24 43 25

Métro: Porte Dauphine

> **FREDERIC ANTON SAYS**
> *Always cook mushrooms twice. Once to release their liquid. Then again to intensify their flavour.*

Pierre Gagnaire's Jerusalem Artichoke Purée
Purée de Topinambours Pierre Gagniare

———————○———————

I have had the good fortune of knowing and working with chef Pierre Gagnaire since his early restaurant days in the mid 1980s. Now his restaurant is just around the corner from our apartment, and when I need some spectacular culinary inspiration, I spend a morning watching the activity in his kitchens on Rue Balzac. Gagnaire is known to offer us some of the zaniest, tastiest and most astonishing combinations of ingredients, yet the kitchen itself is one of the most classic operations, and oh so calm, quite a contrast to Gagnaire's seemingly theatrical ways. This purée was served as part of a complex truffle dish one winter several years ago, and I have made this sublime combination of nutty Jerusalem artichokes – one of my favourite winter vegetables – brilliantly seasoned with a touch of vanilla, on many occasions. Serve it as a side dish to roast poultry.

———————○———————

SERVES 4

750ml (1¼ pints) whole milk
1kg (2lb) Jerusalem artichokes
Sea salt
1 fresh vanilla pod, split in half lengthways, seeds carefully scraped out

WHAT I LEARNED

There are purées and there are purées. If you want a perfectly silky and smooth purée, allow your mixture to purée in the food processor for 10, 15, even 20 minutes, until perfectly smooth.

1. Pour the milk into a large saucepan. Peel the Jerusalem artichokes, chop coarsely and drop instantly into the milk. This will prevent the vegetable from turning brown when it is exposed to the air. When all the Jerusalem artichokes are prepared, place over moderate heat and cook gently until soft, about 25 minutes. Watch carefully so the milk does not boil over.

2. Transfer the mixture in small batches to the bowl of a food processor. Purée. Do not place the plunger in the feed tube of the food processor or the heat will create a vacuum and the liquid will splatter. Purée continuously, until the mixture is perfectly smooth and silky. Professional chefs will purée for as long as 20 minutes at a time!

3. Return the purée to the saucepan and reheat gently. At serving time, stir in the vanilla seeds. Taste for seasoning. Using an immersion mixer (wand blender), froth the purée. Transfer to a warmed sauceboat and serve.

Benoît's Carrots with Cumin and Orange
Carottes au Cumin et Orange

———————◦———————

This beautifully seasoned carrot dish was on the menu when Benoît Guichard took over Jamin in the autumn of 1996. The chef's secret weapons are orange juice (which add a point of fruity acidity to the carrots as they cook) and cumin seed, a traditional accompaniment.

———————◦———————

SERVES 8 TO 10

2 tablespoons cumin seeds
3 tablespoons extra-virgin olive oil
750g (1½lb) carrots, peeled and thin-ly sliced
1 plump, fresh clove garlic
1 teaspoon sugar
BOUQUET GARNI:
2 bay leaves and a bunch of thyme, fastened with household twine
Sea salt to taste
125ml (4½fl oz) freshly squeezed orange juice (juice of 3 oranges)
1 tablespoon unsalted butter

1. To toast the cumin seeds, heat a small, non-stick frying pan over medium heat for 2 minutes. Add the cumin and toast over medium heat, stirring and shaking the pan constantly to prevent burning. Watch carefully, for the cumin will brown quickly. Toast just until the cumin fills the kitchen with its fragrance and turns dark brown, about 4 minutes. Transfer the cumin to a plate to cool.

2. In a large frying-pan, heat the oil over moderately high heat until hot but not smoking. Add the carrots, garlic, sugar and toasted cumin. Add enough water to cover the carrots by half. Add the bouquet garni. Butter a piece of wax paper, pierce it with holes and place on top of the carrots. Bring to a boil over high heat. Reduce to a simmer and cook for 25 minutes. Remove and discard the wax paper and the bouquet garni. Add the orange juice and cook over low heat, uncovered, until almost all the liquid has evaporated, stirring from time to time. At serving time, stir in a little butter. Taste for seasoning. Serve.

Jamin

32, rue de Longchamp

Paris 16

Telephone: 01 45 53 00 07

Métro: Trocadéro

Alain Passard's Turnip Gratin
Gratin de Navets Alain Passard

———o———

Each Saturday morning in Le Figaro *chef Alain Passard offers an incredible assortment of recipe ideas, each revolving around one ingredient. One day in February the subject was the rich golden cheese of the Auvergne mountains, Cantal. He suggested this preparation, which I promptly recreated. This vegetable gratin is delicious on its own, with a tossed green salad, or as a vegetable accompaniment to roast chicken, roast pork or veal.*

———o———

SERVES 4 TO 6

EQUIPMENT:
One 2-litre (3½-pint) gratin dish.

Butter for buttering the gratin dish
750g (1½lb) round spring turnips, peeled and cut into thin rounds
Sea salt
Freshly ground black pepper
125g (4½oz) cow's milk cheese, such as Cantal or Cheddar, coarsely grated
375ml (13fl oz) whole milk
½ teaspoon thyme leaves

PREHEAT THE OVEN TO
200°C/400°F/GAS MARK 6.

1. Butter the gratin dish, and layer half the turnips, half the cheese, the remaining turnips, and then the remaining cheese. Season well after each layer.

2. Add milk just to cover. Sprinkle with thyme, salt and pepper.

3. Place in the centre of the oven and bake until the turnips are soft and have absorbed most of the milk, about 1 to 1 ¼ hours. Serve immediately.

Arpège

84, rue de Varenne

Paris 7

Telephone: 01 45 51 47 33 Fax: 01 44 18 98 39

Métro: Varenne

Menu·Carte

A Springtime Parisian Party

———◇———

Boulevard Raspail Cream of Mushroom Soup

———◇———

Guy Savoy's Asparagus, Morels and
Asparagus Cream

———◇———

Manu's Grilled and Roasted Squab

———◇———

Joël Robuchon's Salade Pastorale

———◇———

Rue Poncelet Cherries in Sweet Red Wine

———◇———

Alléosse Fromage Blanc Ice Cream

Potatoes

Potatoes

Les Pommes de Terre

———○———

La Fontaine de Mars Crispy Sautéed Potatoes

La Fontaine de Mars Pommes de Terre Sautées à Cru

———○———

David van Laer's Potatoes Anna

Pommes de Terre Anna David van Laer

———○———

Chez Henri's Sautéed Potatoes

Pommes de Terre Sautées Chez Henri

Spring Noirmoutier Potatoes with Fleur de Sel

Pommes de Terre de Noirmoutier au Fleur de Sel

———○———

The Astor's Warm Potato, Tomato, Parmesan and Truffle Salad

Salade de Pommes de Terre Truffée à la Tomate Confite et au Parmesan

La Fontaine de Mars Crispy Sautéed Potatoes
La Fontaine de Mars Pommes de Terre Sautées à Cru

———○———

While some potatoes are pre-cooked by blanching before they are sautéed in fat, others are cooked raw or à cru, such as these. The recipe for these golden cubes of potato comes from one of my old-time favourite bistros, La Fontaine de Mars on the Left Bank, which is run by the outgoing Christiane Boudon and her husband, Jacques. If you go on a sunny day, try to secure a table on the terrace. If you look up in the right direction, you will see the very tip of the Eiffel Tower. These rich potatoes often accompany the bistro's confit de canard – duck that has been cooked in its own fat. I actually love these all on their own, with a nice simple green salad alongside. I cook them in a deep cast-iron pan with a lid to avoid splattering fat.

———○———

SERVES 4

EQUIPMENT:
One 6-litre (10-pint) cast-iron pan with lid; a wire mesh skimmer

1kg (2lb) russet potatoes
250ml (9fl oz) melted goose or duck fat
45g (1½oz) unsalted butter
Fleur de sel or fine sea salt
Freshly ground black pepper

1. Peel the potatoes, rinse well, cut into 1.25cm (½in) cubes and place in a bowl of cold water. At cooking time, pat them dry with a clean towel.

2. Line a baking sheet with kitchen towel. Set aside.

3. Place the goose or duck fat in the cast-iron pan and heat over high heat until very hot. Add the potatoes, stir to prevent them from sticking together, and sauté uncovered over a high heat, stirring regularly, until the potatoes are a deep, golden brown, 3 to 4 minutes.

4. With a wire skimmer, carefully transfer the potatoes to a platter. Carefully transfer the hot fat to a large dry container, such as an empty metal can. Be careful, the fat will be very hot.

5. Return the potatoes to the pan, add the butter, and continue cooking over moderate heat, taking care not to burn the butter, just until potatoes are evenly dark brown, 2 minutes more.

Transfer to paper towels to drain.

6. Season with fleur de sel and black pepper. Serve immediately.

> ❝ CHRISTIANE BOUDON SUGGESTS
>
> You may also want to make these potatoes 'bonne femme', a French term used to denote any dish prepared in a simple, family or rustic manner. These dishes are often served in the container in which they are cooked, such as a casserole dish, plate or pan. To make these potatoes 'bonne femme', sprinkle them with a mixture of 2 tablespoons chopped parsley mixed with 1 tablespoon chopped garlic just before sautéing in butter. ❞

Restaurant La Fontaine de Mars

129, rue Saint-Dominique

Paris 7

Telephone: 01 47 05 46 44

Métro: Ecole Militaire.

David van Laer's Potatoes Anna
Pommes de Terres Anna David van Laer

This crusty, crunchy, golden potato cake comes from David van Laer, and I first sampled it during the early years of his first Left Bank restaurant Le Bamboche. He has since moved to a new address with a new restaurant name, Maxence, but the rich cake still figures on the menu in the winter months.

SERVES 8

EQUIPMENT:
One 25cm-(10in-) round non-stick cake pan

1kg (2lb) Yukon Gold or russet potatoes
200g (7oz) unsalted butter, clarified
Sea salt
Freshly ground white pepper

PREHEAT THE OVEN TO 220ºC/425ºF/GAS MARK 7.

1. Peel and thinly slice the potatoes, dropping them in cold water as they are sliced. Wash the potatoes, drain and pat dry.

2. Brush the cake pan with the butter. Starting at the centre of the pan, arrange the potatoes, overlapping, in a single layer. Brush with butter. Season lightly with salt and pepper. Continue layering until all the potatoes and butter have been used, pushing down the layers with the back of a spatula to form a compact cake. Cut out a piece of aluminium foil to fit on top of the potatoes exactly. Place the foil over the potatoes.

3. Place the cake pan in the centre of the oven and bake for 30 minutes. Remove the foil and continue baking the potatoes until golden brown, 25 to 30 minutes more. Run a small sharp knife around the edge of the pan to loosen the potatoes. Invert the cake pan onto a large round serving platter with a lip to catch any excess butter. Serve immediately, cutting into wedges.

Le Maxence

9, bis Boulevard du Montparnasse

Paris 6

Telephone: 01 45 67 24 88 Fax: 01 45 67 10 22

Métro: Falguière

Chez Henri's Sautéed Potatoes

Pommes de Terres Sautées Chez Henri

———○———

When I spent an afternoon chatting with Josette and Gérard Gélaude at their 1940s bistro Chez Henri, Monsieur Gélaude immediately flinched at the thought of sharing this recipe. He would, in fact, not tell me everything. And since he swears that part of their charm is that they are cooked on his 50-year old coal-fired stove, by a chef who has cooked them for 14 years, there is no way we can duplicate them exactly. But I think I have made a pretty good stab at a home version of his sautéed potatoes. And they are, in fact, not sautéed at all, but deep-fried. The difference here is that he fries them with the pan covered, which makes for potatoes that have a beautifully crunchy exterior and a potato-rich, moist interior, since the humidity rests inside the potato as it cooks. Chef Gélaude uses the traditional French potato, bintje, similar to a long, waxy-fleshed baking potato, such a russet.

———○———

SERVES 4

EQUIPMENT:
One 6-litre (10-pint) heavy-duty saucepan with lid; a deep-fry thermometer; a wire skimmer

1kg (2lb) russet or Yukon Gold potatoes
1 litre (1¾ pints) vegetable oil (peanut or safflower)
Fine sea salt

Au Moulin à Vent (Chez Henri)

20, rue des Fossés Saint-Bernard

Paris 5

Telephone: 01 43 54 99 37

Métro: Jussieu or Cardinal Lemoine

1. Peel the potatoes, rinse well, cut into 1.25cm (½in) cubes and place in a bowl of cold water. At cooking time, pat them dry with a clean towel.

2. Line a baking sheet with paper towels. Set aside.

3. Place the oil in the saucepan or use a deep-fat fryer. The oil should be at least 2.5cm (1in) deep. Place a deep-fry thermometer in the oil and heat the oil to 190°C/375°F.

4. Add the potatoes, stir to prevent them from sticking together, cover the saucepan, and cook until the potatoes are a deep, golden brown, 3 to 4 minutes. You may need to do this in batches. If so, keep the cooked potatoes warm in a low oven.

5. Remove with a wire skimmer and transfer to paper towels to drain. Season with fine sea salt. Serve immediately.

Spring Noirmoutier Potatoes with Fleur de Sel
Pommes de Terre de Noirmoutier au Fleur de Sel

———◦———

One spring Thursday at the Avenue de Saxe market, the first of season baby potatoes (smaller than a golf ball) appeared at one stall. Each sack of precious potatoes came with a tiny bag of the equally noble fleur de sel, the fine crystals of sea salt that are hand-harvested on the island of Noirmoutier, not far from Nantes on the Atlantic coast. Noirmoutier potatoes are famed for their organic, earthy flavour, with a faint hint of the ocean and the salty soil in which they are grown. The merchant offered this recipe, nothing more than potatoes cooked slowly in butter and coarse salt, then seasoned with the fleur de sel. A few weeks later, another merchant offered the exact same recipe, warning, 'Avec les pommes de terre de Noirmoutier, surtout pas de huile d'olive.' – with Noirmoutier potatoes, definitely no olive oil. I confess to loving the potatoes cooked in butter when I am in Paris, and cook spring potatoes in olive oil when in Provence. Garlic is allowed, just a few cloves in their skins to perfume the potatoes.

———◦———

SERVES 4

1kg (2lb) baby potatoes (fingerlings or Yukon Gold), rinsed
Sea salt
3 tablespoons unsalted butter (or substitute extra-virgin olive oil)
4 plump, fresh, garlic cloves, in the skins (optional)
Fleur de sel, to taste (see page 100)

1. Place the potatoes in a large pot. Add the butter (or oil), garlic if using and coarse sea salt. Cover and cook over lowest possible heat, turning from time to time, until the potatoes are tender when pierced with a fork and are browned in patches, about 20 minutes. Cooking time will vary according to the size of the potatoes.

2. Using a slotted spoon, transfer the potatoes to a serving bowl. Serve, passing a small dish of fleur de sel at the table.

Breteuil Market

Avenue de Saxe, from Avenue de Segur

to Place Breteuil

Paris 7

9am to noon, Thursday and Sunday

FLEUR DE SEL, CAVIAR OF THE OCEAN
It is an essential ingredient that is as old as the Romans, but how is it that elementary sea salt – really nothing more than seawater evaporated by the sun and the wind – has become one of the modern world's gastronomic treasures?

The story of *fleur de sel* begins in the windswept Guérande peninsula in the Brittany region of France. Since the Middle Ages, here on this jagged body of marshy land jutting out into the Atlantic Ocean, man has captured the saline water in an intricate series of winding canals and tiny ponds until it is decanted and evaporated into one of the world's most precious commodities, *sel marin*, or sea salt. This Breton practice had all but died out a few decades ago, and the ports and salt marshes were in poor repair. To rescue their dying craft, a small number of salt marsh workers – called *paludiers* and *paludières* – banded together in the late 1970s and today there are about 220 artisans harvesting a total of 10,000 tons of sea salt each year in Brittany.

Trapping the ocean water at high tide, the salt marsh workers store the sea water in giant reservoirs for up to a month. The increasingly saline water is then directed into a labyrinth of smaller and smaller pools or basins, square reservoirs known as *oeillets*. The salt that crystallises on the surface of the water is carefully raked off and piled into giant mounds, what we know commonly as *sel gris*, or coarse grey salt, sel de mer. On a good day, a paludier working with as many as 60 to 80 *oeillet*, can gather up to 45kg (100lb) of salt. This natural product – a source of sodium, potassium, calcium, magnesium, copper and zinc – is totally unrefined and unwashed.

At certain times of the year, when the temperature is just right and a dry wind blows in from the east, a very, very fine film of crystals settles at the very edge of those small pools. This, the 'caviar of the ocean', fleur de sel, is traditionally harvested by the wives of the workers, and it is their painstaking job to rake off the fleur de sel, taking none of the larger crystals of *gros sel* with it. The practice is delicate and precarious, for the entire day's harvest can be destroyed by a change in the weather. With a faint aroma of iodine – some even say violets – this precious commodity accounts for only 5 percent of the total Brittany sea salt production, which is why it is prized. In France, it costs some four times the price of the coarse salt. The French like to call it *la fille du vent et du soleil*, 'daughter of the wind and the sun', for the delicate, shiny crystals are set in wicker baskets to dry naturally, in the sun.

Fleur de sel is the darling of chefs and bakers, as well as home cooks. The famed chef Joël Robuchon likes to use both *gros sel* and *fleur de sel* to season his homemade French-fried potatoes, since each salt imparts its own flavour and texture on the palate. However one utilises this gift from the sea, there is one solid rule: fleur is sel is never actually cooked, it is only added as a last-minute seasoning, to everything from a green salad to resting roasted leg of lamb.

While the *fleur de sel* from Brittany's Guérande peninsula is the most famous in France, there are also other excellent small-production salts that come from both the Ile de Noirmoutier and the Ile de Ré on the Atlantic Coast, and from the Camargue region along the Mediterranean. Today, creative packaging (some are even dated and signed by the salt rakers) has rocketed sea salt into the realm of rare French gastronomic treasures.

Both coarse and fine sea salt are essential to any cook's larder. To my palate, sea salt makes food taste seasoned, while regular table salt (refined and plumped up with additives to prevent clumping) makes food just taste salty.

The Astor's Warm Potato, Tomato, Parmesan and Truffle Salad
Salade de Pommes de Terre Truffée à la Tomate Confite et au Parmesan

---

Joël Robuchon first offered a version of this dish during the last days in his restaurant on Avenue Raymond Poincare in 1996. It has become a family favourite, with or without truffles. When preparing with the truffles, omit the herb garnish. Without truffles, the herb garnish serves to provide a fresh herbal note. The dish must be served hot, and I find that a last-minute warming in the microwave creates the perfect amount of required heat.

SERVES 4

500g (1lb) tiny yellow-flesh potatoes, such as ratte
About 1 tablespoon extra-virgin olive oil
Sea salt
Freshly ground white pepper
12 Oven-Roasted Tomatoes (page 74)
About 60g (2oz) Parmigiano-Reggiano cheese (in a chunk)
2 fresh black truffles (about 75g/2½oz; optional)
Coarse sea salt
Freshly ground white pepper
A mix of fresh chopped herbs, such as tarragon, dill and chives, to garnish (optional)

1. Scrub the potatoes, but do not peel them. Bring 1 litre (1¾ pints) of water to a simmer in the bottom of a steamer. Place the potatoes on the steaming rack. Place the rack over simmering water, cover and steam until a knife inserted in a potato comes away easily, 20 to 30 minutes. Drain the potatoes.

2. As soon as they are cool enough to handle, peel them. Slice the potatoes thinly and transfer them to 4 small individual microwave-safe serving bowls. Drizzle with olive oil and toss gently to coat with the oil. Season lightly with salt and pepper.

3. With a vegetable peeler, sharp knife or a mandolin, very thinly slice the truffle. Transfer the slices to a large plate. If using a fresh truffle, cover the slices with a damp cloth or plastic wrap to prevent the truffles from drying out. Set aside.

4. Place 3 Oven-Roasted Tomatoes on top of each serving of potatoes. Using a vegetable peeler, shave the Parmesan into long thin strips. Arrange half of the cheese shavings on top of the tomatoes. If using, arrange the truffle slices on top of the cheese. Arrange the rest of the cheese on top of the truffles. Drizzle with oil just to moisten. Cover with plastic wrap.

5. Place the bowls in a microwave oven and microwave at high until just warmed through, but not cooked, about 30 seconds. Remove from the oven. Remove the plastic wrap. Drizzle with a few drops of oil. Sprinkle with the coarse sea salt and pepper. Garnish with the herbs (if you are not using truffles). Serve immediately.

I enjoy a sturdy white with this. Why not a Châteauneuf-du-Pape Beaucastel Cru du Coudelet Côtes-du-Rhône? This powerful, rich, dry white is a complex and successful blend of Viognier, Marsanne, Bourboulenc and Clairette grapes.

Menu·Carte

Winter in the City

———o———

Gallopin's Green Bean, Mushroom and
Hazelnut Salad

———o———

Monge Market Guinea Hen with Sauerkraut
and Sausages

———o———

Bonbonnerie de Buci's Fresh Lemon Juice Tart

Pasta, Rice and Grains

Pasta, Rice and Grains

Les Pâtes, le Riz et Les Céréales

Flora's Polenta Fries
Frites de Polenta

Hélène's Polenta with Sheep's Milk Cheese
Escaoutoun Landais

Monsieur Lapin's Polenta Savoyarde
Polenta Savoyarde Monsieur Lapin

Joël Robuchon's Macaroni with Fresh Truffles
Macaroni aux Truffes Noires JR

Benoît Guichard's Macaroni Gratin
Gratin de Macaroni Benoît Guichard

Penne with Mustard and Chives
Penne à la Moutarde

Frédéric Anton's Risotto with Pancetta, Wild Mushrooms and Parmesan
Risotto Crèmeux aux Pancetta, Girolles et Parmesan

Spelt 'Risotto' d' Epeautre
Risotto d' Epeautre

William's White Bean Salad with Mushrooms and Cheese
Salade de Cocos de Paimpol, Champignons et Mimolette

L'Ambroisie's White Beans with Mustard and Sage
Cocos Blancs, Moutarde et Sauge l'Ambroisie

Guy Savoy's Lentil Ragoût with Black Truffles
Petit Ragoût de Lentilles et Truffes Noires Guy Savoy

Ambassade d'Auvergne Lentil Salad with Walnut Oil
Salade de Lentilles à l'Huile de Noix
Ambassade d'Auvergne

Flora's Polenta Fries
Frites de Polenta

———o———

Flora Mikula – chef-owner of the Left Bank Les Olivades – is one of my favourite Paris chefs, and one of the few authentically Provençal cooks in the capital. She is a native of Nîmes, a southern French capital that straddles the regions of Provence and the Languedoc. Flora trained in Provence, studied in London and New York, was sous-chef to Alain Passard at Arpège, and finally flew off on her own. Her international approach to food is reflected in her menus. Flora served us these amazing, not very French 'fries' one spring afternoon, teamed up with her Spicy Spare Ribs (page 200). The flavours are explosive: a perfect marriage of the rich corn essence of polenta and the creamy, lactic pungency of Parmigiano-Reggiano cheese. The fries offer three qualities we tend to crave in our foods: crusty, crunchy and salty. These are such a hit, I often serve them as an appetiser at room temperature,

———o———

SERVES 8

EQUIPMENT:
An electric deep-fat fryer (optional); a roulade pan

Oil for oiling the roulade pan
About 1 litre (1¾ pints) whole milk
1 tablespoon finely chopped fresh rosemary leaves
1½ teaspoons fine sea salt, plus more for seasoning at end
250g (8oz) coarse-grained yellow cornmeal (polenta)
80ml (3fl oz) extra-virgin olive oil
85g (3oz) freshly grated Italian Parmigiano-Reggiano cheese
3 litres (5 pints) vegetable oil (peanut or safflower) for frying
Fleur de sel, to garnish (or substitute fine sea salt)

1. Lightly oil the roulade pan. Set aside.

2. In a large, heavy-duty saucepan, bring the milk, rosemary and salt to a boil over high heat. Watch carefully, for milk will boil over quickly. Add the polenta in a steady stream, stirring constantly with a wooden spoon. Cook until thickened and until the polenta leaves the side of the pan as it is stirred, about 20 minutes. Remove from the heat. Stir in the oil and the cheese, stirring to blend thoroughly. If the mixture appears too thick, thin it out with additional milk. Pour the polenta onto the oiled pan. Even it out with a spatula. The mixture should be about 1.25cm (½in) thick. Refrigerate until firm, about 1 hour.

3. Remove the polenta from the refrigerator and cut into rectangles about 9 x 2.5cm (3½ x 1in).

4. Place the vegetable oil in an electric deep-fat fryer (or use a large, heavy-duty saucepan.) The oil should be at least 5cm (2in) deep. Place a deep-fry thermometer and a wire skimmer in the oil and heat the oil to 190ºC/375ºF. Fry the polenta in batches, about four at a time, until crisp and a deep, golden brown, about 2 minutes. Be careful as you drop the polenta in, and always allow several seconds before adding another, to prevent the fries from sticking together.

5. Remove and transfer to paper towels to drain. Sprinkle with fleur de sel. Serve warm or at room temperature.

TRUC

While I am a firm believer in chopping as many ingredients as I can by hand (for better control and authenticity of flavour and texture), there are some items that do better chopped by mechanical means. Rosemary is one of those, for I love the flavour the pungent, aromatic herb emits when it is chopped very very finely. I strip all the leaves off of a fresh rosemary branch and chop the leaves in my spice grinder, ending up with a fine green powder with a crisp, woodsy perfume.

Les Olivades

41, avenue de Ségur

Paris 7

Telephone: 01 42 83 70 09 Fax: 01 42 73 04 75

Metro: Ségur

Hélène's 'Polenta' with Sheep's Milk Cheese
Escaoutoun Landais

---○---

We tend to forget that two important regions of France – the Savoy and the Landes in the southwest – are great producers and consumers of corn and corn products. This recipe comes from young Parisian chef Hélène Darroze, a native of the Landes. It is a luscious corn flour preparation, lavishly laced with Basque sheep's milk cheese and Italian mascarpone. The first time I sampled this I dreamed that I had just a few bites of this for dinner every night. While Hélène prepares this with her local corn flour, not cornmeal, I have found the dish works beautifully with imported Italian cornmeal, or polenta.

---○---

SERVES 4

900ml (1½ pints) Homemade
Chicken Stock (page 274)
125g (4½oz) fine-grained yellow
cornmeal (polenta)
200g (7oz) French Basque sheep's
milk cheese, freshly grated
250g (9oz) mascarpone

This is delicious paired with Alain Brumont's fruity and elegant red Madiran Domaine de Bouscassé.

Restaurant Hélène Darroze

4 rue d'Assas

Paris 6

Tel: 01 42 22 00 11 Fax: 01 42 22 25 40

Métro: Sèvres-Babylone

1. Reduce the chicken stock by bringing 500ml (18fl oz) of chicken stock to a boil over high heat. Make sure you use a large saucepan, to prevent the stock from boiling over. Reduce until the mixture is thick and syrupy, to about 125ml (4½ fl oz), 10 to 12 minutes. Transfer the liquid to the top of a double boiler (*bain marie*), set over simmering water. Cover and keep warm.

2. In a large heavy-duty saucepan, combine the cornmeal and the remaining chicken stock and stir with a wooden spoon to blend. Cook the mixture over high heat, stirring until it is thickened and leaves the side of the pan as it is stirred, about 2 minutes. Reduce heat to low, add the sheep's milk cheese and the mascarpone and stir to blend. Cook, stirring to melt the cheese and thoroughly combine the mixtures, about 2 minutes more. The mixture should be soft and pourable. If it is not, thin it out with additional chicken stock.

3. Pour the mixture into warmed, shallow soup bowls. Drizzle with the reduced chicken stock and serve.

Monsieur Lapin's Polenta Savoyarde
Polenta Savoyarde Monsieur Lapin

―――――◦―――――

Monsieur Lapin is the name of a sweet Montparnasse restaurant run by the professional and outgoing Yves Plantard and his partner, chef François Ract. Their specialities, of course, include lapin, or rabbit, but also rotisserie-grilled rack of lamb with preserved lemons, and a rich bitter chocolate cake. Also available are several dishes from Chef Ract's childhood village in the mountainous Savoy region of France, known for its yellow cornmeal dishes (polenta), the food that feeds the skiers and mountain climbers of the area. In this dish, Chef Ract uses instant polenta, which he insists is as good as the one his mother used to make standing at the stove for hours on end.

―――――◦―――――

SERVES 4 TO 6

EQUIPMENT:
One l-litre (1¾-pint) gratin dish

750ml (1.25 pints) whole milk
1 teaspoon fine sea salt
Freshly grated nutmeg
170g (6oz) instant polenta
(yellow cornmeal)
125ml (4½fl oz) double cream
125g (4½oz) freshly grated Swiss
Gruyère cheese
About 500ml (18fl oz) Tomato Sauce
(page 269), warmed

PREHEAT THE GRILL. SET THE
RACK ABOUT 7.5CM (3IN) FROM
THE HEAT.

A light, soft white from the
shores of Lake Geneva, such as
a Crépy from the Savoy.

1. In a large, heavy-duty saucepan, bring the milk, salt and nutmeg to a boil over high heat. Watch carefully, for milk will boil over quickly. Add the polenta in a steady stream and, stirring constantly with a wooden spoon, cook until thickened and until the polenta leaves the side of the pan as it is stirred, about 2 minutes.

2. Remove from the heat. Stir in the cream and half the cheese, stirring to blend thoroughly. Pour into the gratin dish. Even out the top with a spatula. Sprinkle with the remaining cheese.

3. Place the gratin dish on an oven rack. Grill until the cheese is golden and bubbling, 1 to 2 minutes. Serve, with tomato sauce.

Monsieur Lapin

11, rue Raymond-Losser

Paris 14

Telephone: 01 43 20 21 39 Fax: 01 43 21 84 86

Métro: Gaîté

Joël Robuchon's Macaroni with Fresh Truffles
Macaroni aux Truffes Noires Joël Robinson

———o———

Revered chef Joël Robuchon may have closed his restaurant in Paris, but his presence is evident in many of the city's kitchens. Two lieutenants – Benoît Guichard at Jamin and Frédéric Anton at Le Pré Catelan – are following admirably in his footsteps. This elegant macaroni dish was on the menu at Robuchon's final restaurant along the Avenue de Raymond-Poincaré, served with a simple but sublime roast chicken.

———o———

SERVES 4

EQUIPMENT:
A 6-litre (10-pint) pasta pan fitted with a colander.

500ml (18 fl oz) Homemade Chicken Stock (page 274)
300ml (10fl oz) whole milk
3 tablespoons sea salt
3 tablespoons extra-virgin olive oil
16 large macaroni (zitoni) about 150g/5oz
3 tablespoons Black Truffle Butter (page 270)
90g (3oz) freshly grated Swiss Gruyère cheese
4 fresh black truffles (about 90g/3oz) sliced into thick rounds
Fresh chopped chives to garnish
Sea salt
Freshly ground white pepper

1. Prepare the reduced chicken stock: In a large saucepan, bring the chicken stock to a boil over high heat. Make sure you use a large pan, to prevent the stock from boiling over. Reduce until the mixture is thick and syrupy, to about 125ml (4½ fl oz), 10 to 12 minutes. Transfer the liquid to the top of a double boiler (bain marie), set over simmering water. Cover and keep warm.

2. Bring 3 litres (5 pints) of water, the milk, salt and oil to a gentle simmer over moderate heat in the pasta pan. Do not allow the liquid to boil or it will boil over. Add the macaroni and cook just until tender, 8 to 10 minutes. Lift the colander from the pot and shake gently to drain well, eliminating as much water as possible. Reserve the cooking water. Set the pasta aside.

3. In a large, non-stick frying-pan, melt the truffle butter over moderate heat. When melted, add the macaroni, taking care not to break the pasta. Add a few ladlefuls of the cooking liquid to create a sauce. Sprinkle the cheese evenly over the macaroni and cook, without turning, for 2 minutes.

4. Transfer four pieces of the macaroni to warmed individual dinner plates. Season with pepper. Arrange the truffles in between them and spoon the butter over the pasta. Spoon the chicken stock around the border of the pasta. Sprinkle with chives, season and serve immediately.

I enjoy this dish with a lovely Burgundy, such as a Savigny-les-Beaune.

Variations on this dish can often be found at:

Jamin

32, rue de Longchamp

Paris 16

Telephone: 01 45 53 00 07 Fax: 01 45 53 00 15

Métro: Trocadéro

Le Pre Catelan

Route de Suresnes

Bois de Boulogne

Paris 16

Telephone: 01 44 14 41 14 Fax: 01 45 24 43 25

Métro: Porte Dauphine

TRUC

Reduced chicken stock has become my secret weapon in the kitchen. Often there is a need for a glossy, rich yet light sauce to accompany a roast, a pasta or a risotto. A swirl of beautiful reduced chicken stock is the answer. My freezer is always well stocked with chicken stock, which I thaw and reduce as required.

Benoît Guichard's Macaroni Gratin
Gratin de Macaroni Benoît Guichard

———————◇———————

This rich macaroni gratin – a far cry from the macaroni and cheese of my youth – is deliciously moist. Benoît Guichard, Joël Robuchon protégé and chef at the famed Jamin restaurant, cooks the pasta in milk, then cools the cooking liquid down with ice cubes, which prevents the macaroni from drying out, and plumps it with milk rather than ordinary water. Like so many French dishes, this one is embellished with a golden cheese crust and the added sharpness of fresh chives and coarsely ground black pepper. This can be served as a main pasta course accompanied by a salad, or as an accompaniment to grilled or roasted meats or poultry.

———————◇———————

SERVES 8

EQUIPMENT:
One 6-litre (10-pint) pasta pan fitted with a colander; a 1.5-litre (2½-pint) gratin dish

FOR THE WHITE SAUCE:
250ml (9fl oz) whole milk
2 fresh or dried bay leaves
1 tablespoon plain flour
1 tablespoon unsalted butter
Fine sea salt
Freshly grated nutmeg
Freshly ground white pepper
185ml (6½fl oz) double cream

FOR THE PASTA:
3 litres (5 pints) whole milk
4 plump, fresh garlic cloves, peeled
4 tablespoons sea salt
500g (1lb) dried penne

125g (4oz) freshly grated Swiss Gruyère cheese
Coarsely ground white pepper,
4 tablespoons chopped fresh chives

1. To prepare the white sauce, or *béchamel*: In a large saucepan scald the milk over high heat, bringing it just to the boiling point. Turn off the heat. Add the bay leaves, cover and set aside to infuse for 10 minutes. Strain the milk through a fine-mesh sieve into measuring cup with pouring spout. Discard the bay leaves.

2. In a large saucepan, melt the butter over moderate heat. Whisk in the flour and cook, stirring constantly, for 1 minute. Do not let the flour brown. Remove the saucepan from the heat and whisk in the hot strained milk a few tablespoons at a time, stirring constantly until all of the milk has been incorporated into the flour and butter.

3. Return the saucepan to the heat. Add the salt and pepper and generous gratings of nutmeg. Cook over low heat, whisking constantly, until the sauce thickens, 1 to 2 minutes. Continue to cook over the lowest possible heat, whisking constantly, until the sauce is thick and any taste of raw flour is eliminated, about 5 minutes total. Set aside.

Once cooled, stir in the double cream. Set aside.

4. Preheat the grill.

5. To prepare the pasta: Combine the milk and garlic in the pasta pan. Scald the milk over high heat, bringing it just to bubbling point. Remove from the heat, cover and set aside to infuse for 10 minutes. Remove and discard the garlic. Bring the milk back to a simmer, add the pasta and salt and cook at a gentle simmer until still firm but *al dente* (you should just be able to cut the pasta with a knife), about 8 minutes.

6. Remove the pasta and milk from the heat and add about 12 ice cubes to stop the cooking. Once cooled, transfer the pasta with a slotted spoon to a large bowl. Discard the milk. Toss the drained pasta with the white sauce/cream mixture and transfer the mixture to the gratin dish. Sprinkle with the cheese.

7. Place the gratin dish on an oven rack about 7.5cm (3in) from the heat. Grill until the cheese is melted and golden, 2 to 3 minutes. Remove the gratin dish from the oven and season generously with coarsely ground white pepper. Garnish with chopped chives, and serve immediately.

BENOÎT SAYS
A white sauce is not made in two minutes! It must be cooked until no flavour of raw flour remains.

This gratin is delicious on its own, or could be served with a simple roast lamb or veal. In this case, Benoît Guichard suggests a Sociando-Mallet Bordeaux with a few years of age or a similar cru grand bourgeois from the Haut Medoc

Jamin
32, rue de Longchamp
Paris 16
Tel: 01 45 53 00 07 Fax: 01 45 53 00 15
Métro: Trocadéro

Penne with Mustard and Chives
Penne à la Moutarde

Years ago I clipped a version of this recipe that appeared in a French magazine article on the history of mustard. It seemed implausible, but since I love pasta and mustard I gave it a try. I love it! This is definitely a French touch with pasta. You might also be tempted to toss in bits of cubed smoked bacon, ham or mushrooms, or to play around with different mustards to go with different dishes. This is a rich dish, so don't plan on it as a main course, but rather as a side dish that goes well with roast chicken or lamb.

SERVES 6 TO 8

EQUIPMENT:
One 6-litre (10-pint) pasta pan fitted with a colander.

250g (8oz) dried penne
3 tablespoons coarse sea salt
250ml (9fl oz) double cream
1 large egg yolk, lightly beaten
2 tablespoons French Dijon mustard
Sea salt
Freshly ground white pepper
2 tablespoons freshly grated Italian Parmigiano-Reggiano cheese
3 tablespoons chopped fresh chives
Freshly grated Italian Parmigiano-Reggiano cheese, to serve

The best address in Paris for mustard is:

Boutique Maille

6, place de la Madeleine,

Paris 8

Telephone: 01 40 15 06 00

Métro: Madeleine

1. In the pasta pan, bring 5 litres (9 pints) of salted water to a rolling boil over high heat. Add the pasta, stirring to prevent it sticking. Cook until tender but firm to the bite, 11 minutes.

2. Meanwhile, in a large covered saucepan large enough to hold the pasta later on, combine the cream, egg yolk and mustard. Whisk to blend. Season to taste. Bring to a simmer over low heat. Turn off the heat and cover to keep warm while cooking the pasta. Remove the pasta pan from the heat. Remove the colander and drain over a sink, shaking to remove excess water. Immediately transfer the drained pasta to the sauce in the saucepan. Toss to evenly coat the pasta. Cover and let rest for 1 to 2 minutes to allow the pasta to thoroughly absorb the sauce.

3. Transfer to plates and serve immediately, garnished with chopped chives and freshly grated Parmesan.

This simple pasta dish calls out for a cru Beaujolais – a Brouilly, Morgon or Fleurie

Frédéric Anton's Risotto with Pancetta, Wild Mushrooms and Parmesan
Risotto Crèmeux aux Pancetta, Girolles et Parmesan

———————○———————

Rarely does a French chef get the point of risotto, but Joël Robuchon's protégé Frédéric Anton understands it in a way that only a pro can. One bite of his smooth, alabaster, creamy risotto layered with parchment-thin slices of pancetta, a good dose of Parmesan, and powerfully intense tiny fresh girolles mushrooms, and you almost want to stop right there. For a second bite means you'll be on your way to finishing this ingenious, ephemeral dish, a meal all on its own. The texture, flavour, aroma and essence of each ingredient shines through, yet each plays an essential note in a minor culinary symphony. The first time I sampled this dish – during one of Frédéric Anton's first months at Le Pré Catelan in 1997 – I was in ecstasy. The risotto has all the Robuchon trademarks of full flavours and complexity, yet remains faithful to its Italian heritage.

Textures here are paramount: the salty crunch of the pancetta serves as a palate-pleasing counterpoint to the tooth-tenderness of the mushrooms, while the risotto serves as a midpoint between the two. The reduced chicken stock adds that extra attentive touch that is now one of chef Anton's signatures.

———————○———————

SERVES 4 TO 6

EQUIPMENT:
One 6-litre (10-pint) saucepan

FOR THE PANCETTA:
8 paper-thin slices of pancetta or bacon, measuring about 2.5 x 12.5cm (1 x 5in) each

FOR THE MUSHROOMS:
1 tablespoon extra-virgin olive oil
4 large, fresh cèpe or porcini mushrooms (or substitute chanterelles or girolles, cremini, portobello, or standard cultivated mushrooms), cleaned, trimmed and sliced
Sea salt
Finely ground white pepper

1. Preheat the gill. Set a rack 7.5cm (3in) from the heat.

2. Place the slices of pancetta side by side on a baking sheet. Place the baking sheet on the rack. Grill until the pancetta is golden and sizzling, 1 to 2 minutes. Transfer to a double thickness of kitchen towels to drain. Turn off the oven. Return the pancetta to the oven to keep warm.

3. Heat the oil in a large non-stick frying-pan over moderate heat until hot but not smoking. Add the mushrooms, season lightly with salt and sauté just until they begin to give up their juices, 1 to 2 minutes. Transfer the mushrooms to a fine-mesh sieve to drain. With kitchen towel, wipe out the frying-pan. Melt the butter over moderate heat and return the mushrooms

1 tablespoon unsalted butter
Chopped fresh chervil leaves (or
substitute chopped fresh tarragon or
chopped fresh parsley leaves)

....

FOR THE SAUCE
500ml (18fl oz) Homemade Chicken
Stock (page 274)

....

FOR THE RICE:
About 1.25 litres (2.25 pints)
Homemade Chicken Stock (page 274)
1 tablespoon goose fat or
unsalted butter
1 plump, fresh clove garlic, peeled,
halved lengthways and degermed
Sea salt
1 shallot, peeled and chopped
270g (about 10oz) Italian
Arborio rice
60g (2oz) freshly grated Italian
Parmigiano-Reggiano cheese
1 tablespoon extra-virgin olive oil
2 tablespoons double cream

....

FOR THE GARNISH:
A chunk of Italian Parmigiano-
Reggiano cheese, for grating
as garnish
Coarsely ground white
pepper, to garnish

TRUC

When boiling any liquid over
high heat to reduce it, always
use an extra-large saucepan to
prevent it from boiling over.

---

to the frying-pan. Season lightly with salt and pepper. Cook for
2 minutes more. Off the heat, sprinkle the mushrooms with
chervil, and toss to coat with the herb. Transfer the mushrooms
to the turned-off oven to keep warm.

4. To reduce the chicken stock, bring it to a boil over high heat
in the large saucepan. Make sure you use a large saucepan, to
prevent the stock from boiling over. Reduce until the mixture is
thick and syrupy, to about 250ml (4½fl oz), 10 to 12 minutes.
Transfer the liquid to the top of a double boiler (*bain marie*), set
over simmering water. Cover and keep warm.

5. In a large saucepan, heat the stock for the rice and keep it
simmering, at barely a whisper, while you prepare the risotto.

6. In a large, non-stick frying-pan melt the goose fat or butter
over low heat. Add the halved garlic to perfume the fat. Add the
shallot and salt and sweat – cook, covered, over low heat
without colouring until soft and translucent – 3 to 4 minutes.
Remove and discard the garlic.

7. Add the rice and stir until it is well coated with the fats, glistening and semi-translucent, 1 to 2 minutes. This step is
important for good risotto; the heat and fat will help to
separate the grains of rice, ensuring a creamy consistency in the
end.

8. When the rice becomes glistening and semi-translucent, add
a ladleful of the stock. Cook, stirring constantly until the rice
has absorbed most of the stock, 1 to 2 minutes. Add another
ladleful of the simmering stock, and stir regularly until all the
stock is absorbed. Adjust the heat as necessary to maintain a
gentle simmer. The rice should cook slowly and should always

be covered with a veil of stock. Continue adding ladlefuls of stock, stirring frequently and tasting regularly, until the rice is almost tender but firm to the bite, about 17 minutes total. The risotto should have a creamy, porridge-like consistency.

9. Remove the saucepan from the heat and stir in the cheese, olive oil and cream, tasting regularly, seasoning with salt and pepper to taste. To serve, transfer the risotto to warmed, shallow soup bowls. Garnish with the mushrooms, shavings of fresh Parmesan and the pancetta. Carefully spoon the reduced chicken stock around the border of the risotto. Season with coarsely ground white pepper. Serve immediately.

THE GLORIES OF GOOSE FAT

Nothing replaces goose fat for a luxurious feel on the tongue, a richness that neither oil nor butter can supply. Goose fat (which can be refrigerated for a year in a well-sealed container) can be used in place of just about any fat, although it is most often used with starchy dishes such as potatoes or rice. Since fat actually 'fixes' the flavour of foods – makes them come alive in a way they can't on their own – using more than one kind of fat in a dish, as Frédéric Anton does here, only intensifies flavours.

The wild mushrooms in this dish suggest a good red, such as an Italian Barolo or Chianti, or a fine Bordeaux, such as a St-Estèphe or a Paulliac.

Le Pré Catelan

Route de Suresnes

Bois de Boulogne

Paris 16

Telephone: 01 44 14 41 14 Fax: 01 45 24 43 25

Métro: Porte-Dauphine

Spelt 'Risotto'
Risotto d'Épeautre

———◇———

During the 1990s, as Mediterranean cuisine became the rage all over France, Parisian chefs took a fancy to épeautre, the Provençal grain that resembles spelt. Epeautre is always referred to as 'the poor man's wheat', for it will grow in the poor, rocky soil of the south. Parisian chefs cook épeautre much like risotto, resulting in a grain that is chewy, wholesome and creamy. This recipe was given to me by Emmanual Leblay, a talented chef who has worked in the best restaurants in Paris, London and Provence. I love his idea of adding whipped cream, which has a soufflé-like effect in aerating this elegant dish of simple, peasant origins.

———◇———

SERVES 6 TO 8

EQUIPMENT:
A large, deep frying-pan with lid; a heavy-duty mixer fitted with a whisk

500g (1lb) épeautre or spelt
3 tablespoons extra-virgin olive oil
2 tablespoons unsalted butter
2 onions, peeled and chopped
1 shallot, peeled and chopped
Fine sea salt
1.5 litres (about 2½ pints) Homemade Chicken Stock (page 274)
2 fresh or dried bay leaves
250ml (9fl oz) double cream
Freshly ground white pepper

1. Place the épeautre in a large, fine-mesh sieve and rinse thoroughly. Transfer to a large bowl, cover with cold water and soak for 2 hours. Rinse again and set aside.

2. In a large, deep frying-pan, combine the oil, butter, onions, shallots and a pinch of salt, and sweat – cook, covered, over low heat without colouring until soft and translucent – about 5 minutes. Add the épeautre, the chicken stock, the bay leaves, and 1 teaspoon of salt. Bring to a boil over high heat, then reduce heat to simmer. Cook, uncovered, until tender, about 30 minutes, stirring from time to time to keep the grain from sticking to the pan. Place a large sieve over a large bowl and drain the épeautre in the sieve, discarding the cooking liquid.

3. While the épeautre is cooking, whip the cream in the bowl of a heavy-duty mixer fitted with a whisk at moderate speed until soft peaks form. Gradually increase the speed to high, whisking until stiff peaks form. Scrape down the sides of the bowl. Set aside.

4. At serving time, return the cooked épeautre to the frying-pan

and sauté over moderate heat to toast it lightly, 2 to 3 minutes. Taste for seasoning. Stir in the whipped cream. Serve as an accompaniment to roast chicken, lamb or squab.

Épeautre can be found in most fine supermarkets, as well as at the Provençal oil shop:

Oliviers & Co.

28, rue de Buci

Paris 6

Telephone: 01 44 07 15 43

Métro: Saint-Germain des Prés or Odéon

William's White Bean Salad With Mushrooms and Cheese
Salade de Cocos de Paimpol, Champignons et Mimolette

———o———

I have known chef William Ledeuil since the late 1980s when he was chef at Guy Savoy's first bistro, Le Bistro de l'Etoile across from Savoy's elegant restaurant near the Arc de Triomphe. I would follow him anywhere – and have – and I am a regular customer at Les Bookinistes, where he cooks some of the most inventive and modern bistro fare in the world. This dish – complex in its evolution but not in execution – is typical of his full-flavoured, imaginative fare. For years, the sweet and almost caramel-like cheese from the north of France, mimolette, was known only to the aficionados from the north of France, and wrongly neglected by everyone else. Today, chefs are finding that its richness, colour and sweet edge make it a brilliant cheese to be used in place of the more common Italian Parmigiano-Reggiano. If you can secure fresh shell beans (fresh cranberry or borlotti beans, fresh white cannellini or white kidney beans) by all means buy them. They can be shelled and frozen, then cooked like fresh beans. Their smooth, rich, nuttiness and firm sweet flavour will make you a convert forever. Note here that chef Ledeuil, like many French chefs, loves to use Italian balsamic vinegar as a last-minute seasoning.

———o———

FOR THE BEANS:
1 tablespoon extra-virgin olive oil
3 plump, fresh garlic cloves, peeled
and halved lengthways
Several bay leaves, preferably fresh
Sea salt
500g (1lb) fresh small white (navy)
beans or red (cranberry) beans in the
pod, shelled, or 250g (8oz) dried
small white beans (such as
cannelloni, Great Northern
or marrow beans)
500ml (9fl oz) Homemade Chicken
Stock (page 274)
60g (2oz) smoked bacon, cut into
matchsticks

FOR THE MUSHROOMS:
500g (1lb) meaty mushrooms, rinsed
and trimmed
2 tablespoons extra-virgin
olive oil
Sea salt
Freshly ground white pepper
2 tablespoons thyme leaves

45g (1½oz) rocket leaves, stemmed,
washed and dried
Balsamic vinegar
Several drops of pistachio, walnut or
olive oil
1 shallot, peeled and finely chopped
About 1 tablespoon finely-chopped
fresh chives
An 85g (3oz) chunk of French
Mimolette cheese or Italian
Parmigiano-Reggiano, shaved
Celery salt

1. In a large saucepan, combine the oil, garlic, bay leaves and salt. Stir to coat with the oil. Sweat – cook, covered, over low heat until the garlic is fragrant and soft – about 2 minutes. Add the fresh or prepared dried beans (see note) and stir to coat with the oil. Add the chicken stock and bacon. Simmer gently, uncovered, until the beans are tender, about 35 minutes. (Cooking time will vary according to the freshness of the beans. Add additional stock or water if necessary.) Let the beans cool in the cooking liquid.

2. Preheat a gas, electric or ridged, cast-iron, stovetop grill. Or, prepare a wood or charcoal fire. The fire is ready when the coals glow red and are covered with ash.

3. Cut each mushroom lengthways into 3mm (⅛ in) slices. Brush both sides of each mushroom slice with oil. Season with salt, pepper and thyme. Place each mushroom on the grill at a 45-degree angle to the ridges of the grill. Grill for 1 minute, pressing firmly down on the mushrooms with a baking sheet, to accentuate the impression of the grill marks. Still grilling the same side of the mushroom, reposition each mushroom at the alternate 45-degree angle. Grill for 1 minute more, pressing firmly down on the mushrooms with a baking sheet. This will form a very even and attractive grill mark on the mushrooms. Turn each mushroom over and grill on the other side, positioning the mushrooms again at the two angles, pressing firmly down on the mushrooms with a baking sheet, grilling for a total of 2 minutes more. Season lightly with salt and pepper. Set aside.

4. Using a vegetable peeler, shave the cheese into long thin strips. If the chunk of cheese becomes too small to peel, grate the remaining cheese and place in a bowl. Set aside.

5. Arrange the rocket leaves in a small bowl. Season to taste with balsamic vinegar, salt and olive oil. Toss to evenly coat the greens. Set aside.

6. Using a slotted spoon, transfer the beans to the centre of four warmed, shallow soup bowls and drizzle with balsamic vinegar, oil, the shallot and chives. Spoon several teaspoons of the bean cooking liquid around the edge of the beans. Top the beans with the mushrooms. Arrange several shavings of cheese on top of the mushrooms. Arrange several dressed rocket leaves all around the edge of the bowl. Sprinkle with celery salt and serve.

> NOTE
>
> If using dried beans, rinse the beans, picking them over to remove any pebbles. Place the beans in a large bowl, add boiling water to cover and set aside for 1 hour. Drain the beans, discarding the water. Proceed with the recipe as for fresh beans.

THE REGAL FRENCH BEAN

Students in my cooking school are always amazed at the quality and variety of France's fresh white beans. From May until October, one finds the creamy white cocos blanc encased in their pale celadon-green pods. Come September Brittany's prized AOC Haricots de Paimpol appear in the market, and find their way onto many of the city's menus. Whichever variety I find in the market, I use them the day they are purchased, carefully shelling them just before cooking to preserve their moisture and freshness.

One November day I found them freshly shelled at a vegetable stand at the Left Bank market along the Avenue de Saxe. The merchant suggested that they could be frozen, for a real treat come Christmas time. A revelation and a 'truc' I followed and will never forget. And once there are no fresh white beans at all, I can still find the incomparably creamy dried haricots blanc Tarbais, beans from the southwestern city of Tarbes, whose beans are honoured with a Label Rouge.

I find the beans at:

La Grande Epicerie de Paris

38 rue de Sèvres

Paris 7

Telephone: 01 44 39 81 00

Be prepared to pay the price of these luxurious beans. At last purchase, they cost a good 160 francs (about £25) a kilo.

Les Bookinistes

53, Quai des Grands-Augustins

Paris 6

Tel: 01 43 25 45 94 Fax: 01 43 25 23 07

Métro: RER Saint-Michel

L'Ambroisie's White Beans with Mustard and Sage
Cocos Blancs, Moutarde et Sauge l'Ambroisie

———————○———————

One November evening at a celebratory birthday dinner at L'Ambroisie – Paris' most romantic dining room – we feasted on roasted lamb and these wholesome white beans, touched with a hit of sharp mustard and a hint of fresh sage. The dish is typical of chef Bernard Pacaud's light and subtle touch: That trace of mustard transforms what could be a ho-hum dish into one that elevates the lowly bean into an ingredient of elegance and sophistication. If you can find fresh white beans in the market, by all means use them; they will reward you with a creaminess and nutty flavour that dried beans cannot match.

———————○———————

SERVES 8

3 tablespoons extra-virgin olive oil
20 plump, fresh garlic cloves, peeled and halved lengthways
1kg (2lb) fresh small white (cocos blancs) beans in the pod, shelled; or 500g (1lb) dried white cocos blancs, flageolets, cannelloni, navy, or Great Northern beans
1 litre (1¾ pints) Homemade Chicken Stock (page 274)
2 fresh or dried bay leaves
Large bunch of fresh sage
2 teaspoons fine sea salt, or to taste
About 3 tablespoons French coarse-grain mustard
A cruet of extra-virgin olive oil for seasoning at table

1. In a large, heavy-bottomed saucepan, combine the olive oil and garlic and stir to coat the garlic with the oil. Place over moderate heat and cook – stirring from time to time – until the garlic is fragrant, about 2 minutes. Do not let the garlic brown.

2. Add the fresh or soaked dried beans (see note), stir to coat with oil, and cook for 1 minute more. Add just enough stock to cover the beans. Add the bay leaves, sage and 2 teaspoons of fine sea salt. Cover and bring to a simmer over moderate heat. Simmer gently until the beans are tender, about 30 minutes for fresh beans, about 1 hour for soaked dried beans. Cooking time will vary according to the freshness of the beans. Stir from time to time to make sure the beans do not stick to the bottom of the pan. The beans should just be covered with liquid. Add additional stock or water if necessary.

3. Taste for seasoning. Remove and discard the bay leaves and sage. Add mustard to taste, stirring to distribute it evenly throughout the beans. Taste for seasoning. Serve piping hot. Pass a cruet of extra-virgin olive oil to drizzle over the beans.

NOTE

To prepare dried beans, rinse them, picking them over to remove any grit. Place the beans in a large saucepan. Cover with boiling water by 5cm (2in). Cover and let stand until the beans swell to at least twice their size and have absorbed most of the liquid, about 1 hour. Drain the beans in a colander, discarding the soaking liquid. Proceed with the recipe.

MEMORY LANE

Bernard and Danielle Pacaud opened their first incarnation of L'Ambroisie along the Left Bank Quai de la Tournelle in the early 1980s, just after my arrival in Paris. These were heady days of culinary minimalism and Nouvelle Cuisine, when diners flocked to l'Ambroisie for Pacaud's ethereal red pepper mousse, skate with cabbage and feather-light *mille-feuilles*, or puff pastry. I remember one evening in this contemporary, nine-table restaurant, when my friend Susy Davidson and I swooned over a particular white Burgundy served that night. Susy remarked, 'I wish I could bathe in Meursault.' Later on, it became a custom to stop by L'Ambroisie at the end of the evening, for a nightcap and a chat about the Parisian food world. We once stopped with Chicago food writer, Bill Rice, after dining at the renowned Tour d'Argent down the street. Now that the Pacauds have moved to the grand Place des Vosges, my husband Walter and I continue the tradition, stopping in for a sip of champagne and a chat after a late-night stroll around the Marais.

L'Ambroisie

9, place des Vosges

Paris 4

Telephone: 01 42 78 51 45

Métro: Saint-Paul

Guy Savoy's Lentil Ragoût with Black Truffles
Petit Ragoût de Lentilles et Truffes Noires Guy Savoy

The flinty, dusty flavour of peasant-like lentils creates a remarkable alliance with the elegantly earthy essence of the truffle. This unforgettable, haunting dish has long been on the menu at one of my favourite Paris restaurants, Guy Savoy. I sample this each winter, as part of his memorable truffle feast, one that generally includes his famed artichoke soup with truffles.

SERVES 4

250g (8oz) French lentils, preferably lentilles du Puy
500ml (9fl oz) Homemade Chicken Stock (page 274)
1 carrot, peeled
1 onion, peeled and stuck with a clove
Sea salt
Freshly ground black pepper
60g (2oz) unsalted butter, chilled and cut into small cubes
2 fresh black truffles (about 45g/1½oz) one-third chopped; two-thirds cut into small triangles

1. Place the lentils in a large, fine-mesh sieve and rinse under cold running water. Transfer them to a large, heavy-duty saucepan, cover with cold water, and bring to a boil over high heat. When the water boils, remove the saucepan from the heat. Transfer the lentils to a fine-mesh sieve and drain over a sink. Rinse the lentils under cold running water. Return the lentils to the saucepan, add the chicken stock, and bring just to a boil over a high heat. Reduce the heat to a simmer.

2. With a slotted spoon, skim any impurities that rise to the surface. Once the liquid is clear of impurities, add the carrot and onion, and simmer gently, uncovered, over a low heat, until the lentils are just cooked yet still firm in the centre, about 30 minutes. Cooking time will vary according to the freshness of the lentils: the fresher they are, the more quickly they will cook. Remove and discard the onion and carrot.

3. Transfer the lentils to a fine-mesh sieve set over a bowl. Drain, reserving the cooking liquid. Transfer the reserved liquid and a ladleful of lentils to the bowl of a food processor and purée. Return the lentils and the purée to the saucepan. Taste for seasoning.

4. Add the butter and the chopped truffle and warm over low heat just until the flavours are blended. Taste for seasoning, adding truffle oil or truffle essence if desired. Transfer to small, warmed plates and sprinkle with the truffle triangles. Serve immediately.

THE MYSTERIOUS BLACK TRUFFLE

Why make such a fuss over a rather gnarled and unprepossessing black mushroom? Because of its rarity, its unpredictable nature, its overwhelming and unique fragrance and its clean, crisp texture. The black truffle has also played an essential role in the history French gastronomy, finding its way into the menus of the most renowned and memorable tables. The fact that production in France has declined over the past hundred years, that man has not been able to reproduce it in laboratories, and that its sale remains a rather clandestine and secret affair, all add an air of mystery and excitement.

Guy Savoy

18, rue Troyon

Paris 17

Telephone: 01 43 80 40 61 Fax: 01 46 22 43 09

Métro: Charles de Gaulle-Etoile

THE FAMED LENTILLE DU PUY

The best lentils in the world are a deep green, almost black, and have a mysteriously flinty, sometimes peppery flavour. And when they are cooking on top of the stove, they fill the house with an almost pungent earthiness. These qualities are no surprise, for the lentils are grown on the volcanic soil of the rocky Auvergne region in centre of France, a soil that transmits all of its qualities into the well-known lentilles vertes du Puy. It's a lentil with an Appellation d'Origine Contrôlée, a quality standard recognised by the French government and given only to products grown according to certain standards and traditions on certain soils.

Ambassade d'Auvergne's Lentil Salad with Walnut Oil
Salade de Lentilles à l'Huile de Noix Ambassade d'Auvergne

———o———

When I moved to Paris in 1980, L'Ambassade d'Auvergne was one of my favourite early haunts, serving as a spot for gastronomic discovery. Then, so many dishes – such as giant platters of sausages, warming platters of flinty green lentils from the heart of France – were a revelation. I can't make lentils without thinking of this lively family restaurant, where such regional favourites as this one remain a cornerstone. I like to serve this as a main-course accompanied by a tossed green salad.

———o———

SERVES 8

FOR THE LENTILS:
2 tablespoons goose fat or extra-virgin olive oil
1 onion, peeled and chopped
60g (2oz) smoked ham, diced
500g (1lb) French lentils, preferably lentilles du Puy
1 litre (1¾ pints) Homemade Chicken Stock (page 274)
Sea salt
Freshly ground black pepper

FOR THE VINAIGRETTE:
1 tablespoons French Dijon mustard
2 tablespoons best-quality red wine vinegar or sherry vinegar
170ml (6fl oz) best-quality walnut oil or extra-virgin olive oil
1 shallot, peeled and finely chopped
Sea salt
Freshly ground black pepper

120g (4oz) lean slab bacon, rind removed and cubed
3 tablespoons chopped fresh chives

1. In a large, heavy-duty saucepan, melt the goose fat over medium-high heat. Add the onions and ham and sweat – cook, covered, over a low heat without colouring until soft and translucent – about 5 minutes. Transfer the mixture to a small bowl. Set aside.

2. Place the lentils in a large, fine-mesh sieve and rinse under cold running water. Transfer them to the same heavy-duty saucepan. Cover with cold water, and bring to a boil over high heat. When the water boils, remove the saucepan from the heat. Transfer the lentils to a fine-mesh sieve and drain over a sink. Rinse the lentils under cold running water. Return the lentils to the saucepan, add the chicken stock, and bring just to a boil over high heat. Reduce heat to a simmer. With a slotted spoon, skim any impurities that rise to the surface. Once the liquid is clear of impurities, add the carrot and onion and simmer gently, uncovered, over low heat until just cooked yet still firm in the centre, about 30 minutes. Cooking time will vary according to the freshness of the lentils: the fresher they are, the more quickly they will cook.

3. Meanwhile, prepare the vinaigrette. In a large salad bowl, combine the mustard and vinegar and whisk to blend. Add the walnut or olive oil and shallot and whisk again. Taste for seasoning. Set aside.

4. Cook the bacon. Place the bacon in a large, dry, non-stick frying-pan. Pan-fry over moderate heat until golden brown, 5 to 6 minutes. Remove with a slotted spoon to a plate covered with a double-thickness of kitchen towels.

5. Once cooked, transfer the lentils to a fine-mesh sieve, draining and discarding any remaining liquid. Transfer the lentils to the salad bowl with the vinaigrette, tossing with the vinaigrette until evenly and thoroughly coated. Let sit until the lentils have absorbed the vinaigrette, about 10 minutes. Sprinkle with the cubed bacon. Taste for seasoning. Serve warm.

A young, chilled Beaujolais.

WHAT I LEARNED

Nut oils such as walnut and hazelnut are far more perishable than cold-pressed olive oils. And there is a reason. No heat is necessary when pressing an olive to obtain oil. Nuts, on the other hand, need to be gently nudged to give up their precious oils. So heat is applied when pressing nuts to obtain oil. Unfortunately, heat also destroys a natural preservative in the oil, which is why nut oils go rancid more quickly than olive oil. There are also other reasons why oils go rancid: the fruit could have been spoiled from the beginning; the materials used to press the fruit, or the container in which the oil was stored may not have been totally sanitary. When you bring a bottle of nut oil home, keep it stored in the refrigerator and use within a year.

Ambassade d'Auvergne

22, rue du Grenier Saint-Lazare

Paris 3

Tel: 01 42 72 31 22 Fax: 01 42 78 85 47

Métro: Rambuteau

Menu · Carte

Rib-Sticking Fare

———o———

Flora's Polenta Fries

———o———

Flora's Spicy Spare Ribs

———o———

Blood Orange Ice Cream Le Jardin
de Courcelles

———o———

Jean-Luc Poujauran's Shortbread Cookies

Soups

Soups
Les Soupes

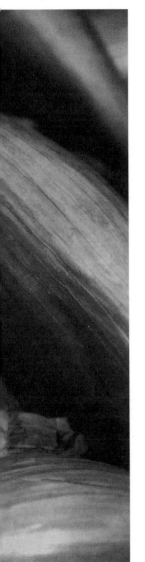

The Market Gardeners' Courgette and Curry Soup
Soupe de Courgettes au Curry Les Maraîchers

Boulevard Raspail Cream of Mushroom Soup
Crème de Champignons Boulevard Raspail

Taillevent's Cream of Watercress Soup
with Caviar
Crème de Cresson au Caviar Taillevent

Summer Tomato and Vegetable Soup
Gaspacho: Arpège and Port Alma

Mustard Ice Cream
Crème Glacé à la Moutarde

Tante Louise's Caramelised Cauliflower Soup
with Foie Gras
Soupe de Chou-Fleur Caramélisée au Foie Gras

Le Bookiniste's Cream of Corn Soup
Crème de Maïs, Champignons d'Automne

Oliviers & Co.'s Provençal Three-Grain Soup
Soupe Provençale aux Trois Céréales Oliviers & Co.

Joël Robuchon's Creamy White Bean Soup
Crème de Cocos Joël Robuchon

Brasserie Balzar's Midnight Onion Soup
Soupe à l'Oignon Gratinée Brasserie Balzar

Potato, Leek and Oyster Soup Le Maxence
Soupe Parmentier aux Huîtres Le Maxence

Pumpkin Soup for Halloween
Velouté de Potiron 'Halloween'

Spicy Langoustine Broth
Bouillon de Langoustines

Rue Bayen Fish Soup
Soupe de Poissons de Roche

Fresh Crab Soup
Soupe de Favouilles

The Market Gardeners' Courgette and Curry Soup
Soupe de Courgettes au Curry Les Maraîchers

———◦———

*Fragrant, with a gentle touch of curry, verdant as a vegetable garden in August
and as smooth as silk, this versatile courgette soup can be served piping hot or refreshingly
cold. The curry helps accentuate the sweet and almost grassy flavour of the courgette, and adds
an elegantly piquant touch. Firm, unblemished, top-quality courgettes are plentiful in the Paris
markets from June to September, when I make this soup regularly, freezing any extras for a quick
meal when I'm pressed for time. My husband Walter prefers a mild curry flavour
(about 2 teaspoons), while I crave a greater hit of spice (1 tablespoon). Season your
soup to meet your taste.*

———◦———

SERVES 6 TO 8

*EQUIPMENT:
One 6-litre (10-pint) stock pan*

*1 large onion, peeled, halved length-
ways, and cut into thin half-moons
2 tablespoons extra-virgin olive oil
2 teaspoons curry powder, or to taste
Fine sea salt to taste
4 small courgettes (about
350g/12oz), rinsed and cut into thin
rounds
1 litre (1¾ pints) homemade Chicken
Stock (page 274)*

1. In the stock pan, combine the onion, oil, curry powder and a pinch of salt. Stir to coat the onions. Sweat over low heat, stirring until the onions are soft, 3 to 4 minutes.

2. Add the stock and courgettes, and stir to blend. Place over a moderate heat, cover, and simmer gently for 20 minutes.

3. Blend the liquid in a food processor or with a hand-held immersion blender until emulsified into a smooth-textured mixture. The soup may be prepared ahead of time up to this point. Cool and refrigerate. At serving time, reheat the soup, serving in warm, shallow soup bowls.

Marché Carmes

Place Maubert

Paris 5

Open 7am to 1.30pm, Tuesday, Thursday and Saturday

Métro: Maubert-Mutualité

Boulevard Raspail Cream of Mushroom Soup
Crème de Champignons Boulevard Raspail

At once elegant and classic, this is a favourite come autumn, when every gastronome in France begins to think of mushrooms, no matter how humble. The famed Paris mushroom – champignon de Paris – was originally cultivated in underground caves located beneath the subways and the sewers of Paris, caves that were excavated for the stone with which many of Paris' buildings are constructed. Today, the mushrooms are more likely to be grown by farmers outside of Paris. I often find superbly fresh mushrooms at the organic produce market held each Sunday morning along the Boulevard de Raspail. While the French revere the variety of wild mushrooms found all over the nation's woods and forests, one should not underestimate the flavour and value of the common cultivated mushroom, used here for a simple but exquisite mushroom soup.

SERVES 6

EQUIPMENT:
One 6-litre (10-pint) stock pan; 6 warm shallow soup bowls

2 leeks, white and tender green parts
45g (1½oz) unsalted butter

1. To prepare the leeks, trim them at the root and split lengthways for easier cleaning. Rinse well under cold running water. Transfer to a bowl of cold water and soak for 5 minutes to rid any excess dirt. When all the grit has settled to the bottom of the bowl, remove the leeks and dry thoroughly. Chop coarsely and set aside.

750g (1¼lb) mushrooms, trimmed,
washed and thinly sliced
1.5l (2½ pints) Homemade Chicken
Stock (page 274)
750ml (1.25 pints) double cream (or
a mix of half double cream and half
whole milk)
Sea salt
Freshly ground white pepper

2. In the soup pot, combine the leeks, butter and a pinch of salt, and sweat, covered, over low heat – cook until soft but not brown – about 3 minutes.

3. Add the mushrooms and cook, stirring often, for another 5 minutes. Add the chicken stock. Cover and simmer gently for about 35 minutes. Taste for seasoning.

4. Blend the liquid in a food processor or with a hand-held immersion blender until emulsified into a smooth-textured mixture. The soup may be prepared ahead of time up to this point. Reheat at serving time.

5. At serving time, add the cream (or milk and cream mixture) and simmer gently, uncovered, over low heat until thickened about 5 minutes. To serve, ladle the soup into warmed soup bowls.

Marché Biologique

Boulevard Raspail

Between Rue de Cherche-Midi and Rue de Rennes

Sunday 9am to 1pm

Taillevent's Cream of Watercress Soup with Caviar
Crème de Cresson au Caviar Taillevent

———○———

For more than twenty years, Taillevent has been one of our favourite restaurants, a place that my husband Walter and I reserve for special occasions. Owner Jean-Claude Vrinat is one of the city's finest hosts, a model restaurateur if there ever was one. He kindly shared the recipe for this festive soup, one that seems like the perfect choice for a celebratory New Years' Eve dinner. Like so much of the fare at this august restaurant, this soup shines with simple elegance.

———○———

SERVES 6

EQUIPMENT
One 6-litre (10-pint) soup pot;
a 6-litre (10-pint) pasta pan fitted with
a colander; 6 warm, shallow soup
bowls

FOR THE LEEK AND
STOCK BASE:
45g (1½oz) unsalted butter
500g (1lb) leeks, white and tender
green parts, cleaned, halved and
thinly sliced
1 onion, peeled and finely chopped
Fine sea salt
1 litre (1¾ pints) Homemade
Chicken Stock (page 274)
500ml (18fl oz) double cream (or
substitute whole milk)

FOR THE WATERCRESS:
3 tablespoons coarse sea salt
4 bunches watercress, leaves only, rinsed

1. In the soup pot, combine the butter, leeks, onion and a pinch of salt, and sweat, covered, over low heat – cook until soft but not brown – about 3 minutes. Add the chicken stock and cream. Simmer gently, uncovered, for 30 minutes. Blend the liquid in a food processor or with a hand-held immersion blender until emulsified into a smooth-textured mixture. Return the mixture to the saucepan, increase the heat to high, and bring to a gentle boil. Using a slotted spoon, skim off any impurities that may rise to the surface. Set aside. This mixture can be prepared up to one day in advance. To store, cover and refrigerate.

2. Meanwhile, in the pasta pan fitted with a colander, bring 4 litres (7 pints) of water to a boil over high heat. Add the salt and the watercress. Blanch, uncovered, until soft and wilted, 2 to 3 minutes. Drain and refresh in a bath of ice water. Drain and purée in a food processor. Place in a fine mesh sieve and carefully press out any remaining liquid. Set aside.

FOR THE CREAM:
250ml (9fl oz) double cream
Juice of 1 lemon
Sea salt
Freshly ground white pepper

2 tablespoons caviar,
preferably Osetra

3. In the bowl of a heavy-duty mixer fitted with a whisk, whip the cream at high speed until stiff. Add the lemon juice, and season to taste with salt and pepper. Set aside.

4. At serving time, reheat the creamy soup mixture. Remove the mixture from the heat and add the watercress purée, stirring until thoroughly blended. Serve in warm, shallow soup bowls, placing a scoop of the cream in the centre of each bowl. Top with a spoonful of caviar. Serve.

Taillevent

15, rue Lamennais

Paris 8

Telephone: 01 44 95 15 01

Métro: Charles de Gaulle-Etoile or George V

Summer Tomato and Vegetable Soup
Gaspacho: Arpège and Port Alma

French chefs adore gaspacho, and this brilliant red summer soup can be found at many of the city's best tables in the warm months. At home, I like to make it with the giant Russian heirloom tomatoes for sale at farmer's markets in late summer. Russian heirloom tomatoes are huge, weighing up to 1kg (2lb) each, and are a brilliant, deep red, making for a truly colourful soup. Here I offer two variations, one from Le Pont Alma paired with delicious fresh lump crabmeat and another from Arpège, where it is served as an appetiser, with a dollop of rich mustard ice cream.

SERVES 8

1.5kg (3lb) ripe tomatoes, cored and quartered
1 red pepper, quartered
1 green pepper, quartered
1 medium cucumber, peeled, seeded and coarsely chopped
2 plump, fresh garlic cloves, peeled, quartered and degermed
60ml (2fl oz) best-quality sherry wine vinegar
3 tablespoons extra-virgin olive oil
Sea salt

1. In the bowl of a food processor, purée the tomatoes. Add the remaining ingredients and purée. Taste for seasoning.

2. Pass the mixture through a fine-mesh sieve, discarding the solids that remain in the sieve.

3. Transfer to a bowl, cover and refrigerate to chill for at least 3 hours and up to 24 hours. Serve in chilled bowls.

VARIATIONS:

From chef Paul Canal at Port Alma:
10, avenue de New York, Paris 16
Telephone: 01 47 23 75 11
Métro: Alma-Marceau.

Gaspacho with Crab Meat: Add several spoonfuls of fresh lump crabmeat, drained, picked over, and flaked into generous bite-sized pieces

From chef Alain Passard at Arpège: 84, rue de Varenne, Paris 7
Telephone: 01 45 51 47 33
Métro: Varenne

Gaspacho with Mustard Ice Cream (page 142): Add a dollop or a quenelle of mustard ice cream to the centre of the soup bowl. Garnish with a chiffonnade (thin ribbons) of fresh basil.

Mustard Ice Cream
Crème Glace à la Moutarde

———◦———

It was a steamy day in July when my good friend Susan Loomis and I lunched at Arpège, home of Alain Passard, one of France's most creative chefs. When the waiter set before us a tiny bowl of gaspacho laced with this golden mustard ice cream, we were first taken by surprise, then joy, as we devoured this original, creative combination. Wacky, you say? Try it, you will be an instant convert!

———◦———

SERVES 8

EQUIPMENT:
An ice cream maker

6 large egg yolks
500ml (18fl oz) whole milk
250ml (9fl oz) double cream
1½ tablespoons French mustard

Arpège

84, rue de Varenne

Paris 7

Telephone: 01 45 51 47 33

Métro: Varenne

1. Place the egg yolks in a medium size bowl and whisk to blend.

2. In a medium, heavy-duty saucepan, cook the milk over a medium heat until bubbles form around the edges. Slowly whisk the hot milk into the egg yolks. Return this mixture to the saucepan. Rinse out and dry the mixing bowl, then set a fine-mesh sieve on top. Set aside.

3. Place the saucepan over a low heat. Using a wooden spoon, stir the sauce gently but constantly, sweeping the entire pan bottom and reaching into the corners. As soon as the sauce is slightly thickened, remove the pan from the heat and stir gently for 2 minutes to complete the cooking. The sauce should be the consistency of double cream and register around 75°C/170°F on an instant-read thermometer.

4. Remove from the heat and immediately stir in the cream to stop the cooking. Stir in the mustard. Pass through the fine-mesh sieve. Cool completely. When thoroughly cooled, transfer to an ice cream maker and freeze according to manufacturer's instructions.

Tante Louise's Caramelised Cauliflower Soup with Foie Gras

Soupe de Chou-Fleur Caramélisée au Foie Gras

———○———

Several years ago, chef Bernard Loiseau from Burgundy expanded his holdings by adding Tante Louise – a cosy, old-fashioned bistro near the Madeleine – to his empire. There, chef Arnaud Magnier has a fine hand, and produces classic bistro fare as well as such modern dishes such as this soup. Come the cold grey days of November in Paris, this hearty soup is there to cheer me up. The fresh cauliflower, enhanced by the nutty flavour of brown butter, pairs perfectly with the richness of the foie gras. You can, of course, prepare it without the foie gras garnish, but why deprive yourself?

———○———

SERVES 6

EQUIPMENT:
One 6-litre (10-pint) pasta pan with colander; a 6-litre (10-pint) soup pot; 6 warm individual soup bowls

1 large head cauliflower (about 1.3kg/2¾lb)
Sea salt
Juice of 1 lemon
60g (2oz) unsalted butter
125g (4oz) fresh duck liver (foie gras), cut into tiny cubes
1 litre (1¾pints) Homemade Chicken Stock (page 274)
Freshly ground white pepper

1. Prepare the cauliflower: cut the head in quarters, removing the core from each piece. Cut or break the florets into small pieces. In the pasta pan, bring 4 litres (7 pints) of water to a boil over high heat. Add 2 tablespoons salt and the lemon juice. Add the cauliflower, and cook, uncovered, for 15 minutes. Drain. Transfer to a food processor and purée until smooth.

2. To prepare the brown butter, melt the butter in the soup pot over a moderately high heat. Watch it carefully. The butter will go through several stages, from a foamy white liquid to one that is almost clear and golden, with big airy bubbles. When the butter begins to brown and gives off a nutty aroma, about 2 minutes, add the cauliflower purée (do not delay or the butter could burn) and stir to blend. Add the chicken stock and stir to blend. Simmer, covered, for 5 minutes.

3. Process the liquid in a food processor or with a hand-held immersion blender until emulsified into a smooth-textured mixture. Taste for seasoning. The soup may be prepared ahead of time up to this point. Reheat at serving time.

141

4. At serving time, ladle the soup into warmed, shallow soup bowls. Sprinkle with the cubed foie gras and serve immediately.

Restaurant Tante Louise

41, rue Boissy d'Anglas

Paris 8

Telephone: 01 42 65 06 85

Métro: Madeleine

Les Bookinistes's Cream of Corn Soup
Crème de Maïs, Champignons d'Automne

The first time chef William Ledeuil proposed this creamy, fragrant, endearing soup, I wanted to say 'You've got to be kidding.' Cream of corn soup seemed so American, I couldn't imagine it on a French bistro table. But leave it to the talented William to come up with a sophisticated, elegant soup, embellished with a trio of wild mushrooms and the unforgettable grilled peanut oil from the house of Leblanc in southern France.

SERVES 8

EQUIPMENT:
A food mill, fitted with the finest blade; a hand-held immersion blender; 8 warm, shallow individual soup bowls

1. With a sharp knife, scrape the kernels from the cob. Place the corn and the scraped cobs in a large, shallow pan big enough to hold the corn in two layers. Cover with milk. Cover, bring to a simmer over moderate heat and simmer for 90 minutes. Remove the corn from the pan. Reserve the milk. Drain and refresh the kernels and discard the scraped cobs. Set aside the kernels.

6 ears of fresh corn on the cob (about
2kg/4lb)
2 litres (3½ pints) whole milk
150g (5oz) unsalted butter
80ml (3fl oz) double cream
Sea salt
Freshly ground white pepper
1 tablespoon extra-virgin olive oil
90g (3oz) shitake mushrooms, cleaned
and dried
90g (3oz) trompette mushrooms,
cleaned and dried
90g (3oz) chanterelle mushrooms,
cleaned and dried

2 shallots, peeled and finely chopped
1 tablespoon finely-chopped
fresh chives
About 2 teaspoons grilled peanut oil
(or substitute hazelnut or walnut oil)
Celery salt

2. Transfer the corn kernels and cooking liquid in batches to a food processor and purée. Place a food mill fitted with the finest blade over a large saucepan. Pass the purée through the food mill into the saucepan. Stir in 120g (4oz) of the butter and all of the cream. Taste for seasoning. Keep warm over the lowest possible heat.

3. Toss the shitakes with olive oil. Grill, turning regularly. Season with salt and pepper. Set aside.

4. Sauté the chanterelles and trompettes in remaining 30g (1oz) of the butter. Add the shallots and the chives. Toss to blend thoroughly.

5. Process the corn soup with a hand-held immersion blender until emulsified into a smooth-textured mixture.

6. Arrange the mushrooms in the bottom of warmed, shallow soup bowls. Pour the soup over the mushrooms. Drizzle with grilled peanut oil and season with celery salt.

Chef William suggests a Domaine de la Passière Blanc Corbières.

Les Bookinistes

53, quai des Grands-Augustins

Paris 6

Telephone: 01 43 25 45 94 Fax: 01 4325 23 07

Métro: RER Saint-Michel

Oliviers & Co.'s Provençal Three-Grain Soup
Soupe Provençale aux Trois Céréales Oliviers & Co.

———o———

Like a wintry Mistral wind blowing down the Rhône valley, this cold-weather soup sings of the wholesomeness of Provence. This soup is inspired by the beautiful products found in Oliviers & Co., a Left Bank shop that offers an extraordinary array of olive oils from all over the Mediterranean, as well as a fine line of organic grains. Here a trio of grains – pearl barley, lentils and the Provençal épeautre, the poor man's wheat known to us as 'spelt' – team up with tomatoes and leeks, carrots and garlic, making for what the French call 'la bonne cuisine de famille'.

———o———

SERVES 8

EQUIPMENT:
A soup pot; 8 warm individual soup bowls

60g (2oz) spelt or épeautre
60g (2oz) pearl barley
60g (2oz) dark green imported lentils, preferably lentilles de Puy (page 126)
4 tablespoons extra-virgin olive oil
2 fresh or dried bay leaves
½ teaspoon fresh or dried thyme leaves
3 leeks, white portion only, chopped
2 carrots, peeled and cubed
Fine sea salt to taste
One 765g (28oz) can peeled Italian plum tomatoes in juice
1.25 litres (2¼ pints) water
1 head garlic, cloves peeled, halved and degermed
1 cruet of olive oil for the table

1. Place the grains in a fine-mesh sieve and rinse under cold running water. Set aside.

2. In a soup pot, combine the oil, bay leaves, thyme, leeks, carrots and 1 teaspoon salt. Sweat – cook, covered, over low heat without colouring – until soft, about 5 minutes. Add the tomatoes and cold water. Bring to a boil over moderate heat.

3. Add the grains, stir and simmer, covered, until the grains are tender, about 45 minutes. Cooking time will depend upon the freshness of the grains – older grains take longer to cook. Remove and discard the bay leaves. Taste for seasoning. This soup is even more delicious the second day, after the flavours have had time to ripen. Serve piping hot, drizzled with olive oil.

Oliviers & Co.

28, rue de Buci

Paris 6

Telephone: 01 44 07 15 43

Métro: Saint-Germain des Prés or Odéon

Joël Robuchon's Creamy White Bean Soup
Crème de Cocos Joël Robuchon

———○———

During the last years of his chiefdom on the famed Rue de Longchamp, Joël Robuchon served this rich, soul-warming, white bean cream as part of his all-truffle menu. With a faintly smoky flavour and that creamy richness of good white beans, this should be served in small portions. I like to serve it as a small first course, which can be drunk from a simple white demitasse cup. The final soup can be anointed with finely-chopped truffles or with a drizzling of hazelnut oil.

I only recently learned that fresh white beans, such as the French cocos blanc, which can be found from May to September, can easily be frozen. So when you find the beans in your farmer's market, freeze them for one of those cool winter days when bean soup is all that will do!

———○———

SERVES 6

EQUIPMENT:
One 6-litre (10-pint) stock pan; 6 warm individual demitasse cups, or small soup bowls

500g (1lb) small white (navy) beans
2 carrots, peeled and halved
1 onion, peeled and stuck with a clove
3 cloves garlic, peeled
Bouquet garni: several springs of parsley, thyme and several bay leaves wrapped in cotton twine
90g (3oz) smoked bacon, in one piece
500ml (18fl oz) Homemade Chicken Stock (page 274)
250ml (9fl oz) double cream
90g (3oz) unsalted butter
1 clove garlic, very finely chopped
Sea salt
Freshly ground white pepper
1 fresh black truffle (about 25g/1oz), cleaned and chopped (optional)

1. If using dried beans: Place the beans in the pot and cover with cold water. Bring to a boil over high heat, reduce heat to simmer and blanch for 2 minutes. Drain the beans through a fine-mesh sieve, discarding the liquid. Return the beans to the pot. Add the carrots, onion, garlic, bouquet garni, bacon and 1 teaspoon of salt. Cover with cold water, bring to a boil, and put the lid on the pot. Simmer gently over low heat, until the beans are very tender, about 30 minutes for fresh beans, 90 minutes for dried beans.

2. Drain the beans. Remove and discard the carrot, onion, garlic, bouquet garni and bacon. Transfer the beans to a food processor. Purée. Pass the purée through the finest grid of a food mill. The soup can be prepared ahead of time up to this point. Cool and refrigerate.

3. At serving time, reheat the purée, add the chicken stock and cream, stir to blend and bring just to a simmer. Stir in the butter and the chopped garlic. Taste for seasoning. Serve piping

Several teaspoons best-quality hazelnut oil (optional)

hot, in very small soup bowls or in small demitasse cups. Sprinkle with chopped truffles or drizzle with hazelnut or pistachio oil.

A Guigal Condrieu or a Goubert Viognier.

Brasserie Balzar's Midnight Onion Soup
Soupe à l'Oignon Gratinée Brasserie Balzar

There are few Parisian traditions as solid as the late-night onion soup feast at the Left Bank Brasserie Balzar. Unlike many heartier versions that call for deep, dark, caramelised onions and rich beef stock, this is a very delicate, highly digestible soup. Here, the onions are cooked to a golden pale colour, and enriched with a mixture of veal stock, white wine and water. Be sure to use the best-quality imported Swiss Gruyère you can find. You won't regret it.

SERVES 8 TO 10

EQUIPMENT:
One 10-litre (17-pint) soup pot; oven-proof soup bowls

1.5kg (3lb) onions
90g (3oz) unsalted butter
100ml (4fl oz) peanut oil
1 tablespoon fine sea salt
40g (1½oz) plain flour
500ml (18fl oz) Homemade Chicken Stock (page 274)

1. Peel the onions and halve them vertically. Cut the halves lengthways into thin slices. In a large soup pot, melt the butter over low heat. Add the oil, onions and salt, and stir to coat the onions. Cook, covered, over low heat – stirring occasionally so the onions do not scorch – just until the onions are soft but still pale, about 15 minutes.

2. Sprinkle the flour over the onions and stir to coat the onions. Immediately add the stock, wine, water, pepper, thyme and bay leaves. Bring just to the boil. Immediately reduce the heat to

150ml (5fl oz) dry white wine, such
as Sancerre
4 litres (7 pints) water
1½ teaspoons freshly ground
white pepper
Several branches fresh thyme,
wrapped in cheesecloth
Several fresh or dried bay leaves
8 slices baguette cut into thin slices
and toasted
500g (1lb) Swiss Gruyère, freshly
grated

low. Simmer, partially covered, for 30 minutes. Taste for seasoning. The soup can be prepared up to this point one day in advance. Refrigerate in a covered container. Reheat gently at serving time.

3. Preheat the grill.

4. Ladle the soup into individual ovenproof soup bowls. Top each serving with a slice of toasted baguette. Cover the bread with a thick coating of grated Gruyère cheese. Place under the grill. As soon as the cheese begins to bubble, serve the soup.

While most soups don't call out for wine, I do like a sip of the same young Sancerre (from the house of Sautereau) I use to make this soup. It comes from my favourite Paris wine merchant, Juan Sanchez, at the Left Bank La Dernière Goutte.

Brasserie Balzar

49, rue des Ecoles,

Paris 5

Telephone: 01 43 54 13 67

Metro: Odéon or Cluny-La-Sorbonne

La Derniere Goutte

6, rue Bourbon-le-Château

Paris 6

Telephone: 01 43 29 11 62

Métro: Saint-Germain des Prés or Odéon

Potato, Leek and Oyster Soup Le Maxence
Soupe Parmentier aux Huîtres Le Maxence

———◦———

Potato soups have long been a French favourite, and the classic combination of leeks and potatoes – named after eighteenth-century agronomist Antoine-Auguste Parmentier, who popularised the potato in France – is one of the most obvious winter warm-ups. I sampled this restorative soup one October evening at the diminutive Bamboche, then the newly created Left Bank restaurant of chef David van Laer. That evening, we ordered a brisk white Burgundian Marsannay wine: the circle of flavours was complete, with the briny oysters, the creamy warm soup and the chilled white wine. Chef van Laer has since moved to new quarters a few blocks away, but you can still find this soup on the menu at Le Maxence.

———◦———

SERVES 4

EQUIPMENT:
A 6-litre (10-pint) soup pot;
4 warm, shallow soup bowls

2 tablespoons unsalted butter
2 leeks, white and tender green part, cleaned, halved lengthways and thinly sliced
Fine sea salt to taste
250g (8oz) baking potatoes, such as russets, peeled and thinly sliced
1 litre (1¾ pints) whole milk
80ml (3fl oz) double cream
Freshly grated nutmeg
8 large, fresh oysters, freshly shucked and removed from their shells

1. In the soup pot, combine the butter, leeks and 1 teaspoon fine sea salt, and sweat over low heat – cook, covered, until soft but not brown – about 3 minutes. Add the potatoes, milk, cream and several gratings of nutmeg. Simmer, covered, stirring often to prevent the starchy soup from sticking to the bottom of the pot, about 20 minutes more. Taste for seasoning.

2. Process the liquid in a food processor or with a hand-held immersion blender until emulsified into a smooth-textured mixture. (The soup may be prepared ahead of time up to this point. Cool and refrigerate.) At serving time, reheat the soup. Transfer to soup bowls and float 2 fresh oysters in each soup bowl. The oysters will cook slightly in the heat of the soup.

Le Maxence

9 bis, Boulevard du Montparnasse

Paris 6

Telephone: 01 45 67 24 88 Fax: 01 45 67 10 22

Métro: Falguière

Pumpkin Soup for Halloween
Velouté de Potiron 'Halloween'

———○———

In recent years, the French have gone crazy over Halloween. Pumpkins carved with wonderfully expressive faces can now be found piled high at my market on Rue Poncelet. A vegetable merchant suggested this simple soup to celebrate what has become an international holiday. This soup of few ingredients looks and tastes as though you have been working for days on the ultimate pumpkin soup.

———○———

SERVES 4

EQUIPMENT:
One 6-litre (10-pint) soup pot; 4 warm shallow soup bowls

1kg (2lb) pumpkin, cubed
1 litre (1¾ pints) Homemade Chicken Stock (page 274)
1 tablespoon sugar
3 tablespoons crème fraîche or double cream
Sea salt
Freshly ground white pepper

1. In the soup pot, combine the pumpkin, chicken stock and sugar, and bring to a boil over high heat. Cover and boil for 18 minutes, counting from the time the liquid comes to a boil. The pumpkin should cook quickly to avoid any bitterness.

2. Process the liquid in a food processor or with a hand-held immersion blender until emulsified into a smooth-textured mixture. The soup may be prepared ahead of time up to this point. Cool and refrigerate.

3. At serving time, return the mixture to the stockpot and bring to the boil again. With a flat-mesh sieve, skim off any scum that rises to the top. Add the cream and bring back to the boil. Taste for seasoning. Serve immediately, in warm, shallow soup bowls.

VARIATION

At Guy Savoy's bistros, they often serve pumpkin soup with very thin slices of Forme d'Ambert – the blue cow's milk cheese from the Auvergne – floating on top.

Spicy Langoustine Broth
Bouillon de Langoustines

—◦—

*When I made this for my cooking class in Paris, the students declared this 'A Hummer',
meaning it's the kind of restorative broth that makes you hum with satisfaction. I serve this
whenever I make any dish with langoustines, since I hate the thought of tossing out the shells
that give up such a rich, elusive flavour. Like so many of what I call my 'little soups', I serve this
one in demitasse cups as people come in the door, or as we gather around the kitchen island
before sitting down to dinner. The best langoustines in Paris come from my favourite fish
market on Rue Bayen.*

—◦—

SERVES 8

EQUIPMENT:
*A large heavy-duty roasting pan or
large deep frying-pan; warm small
soup bowls or demitasse cups*

2 tablespoons extra-virgin olive oil
*1kg (2lb) langoustine shells, rinsed
but left whole (or substitute shrimp or
lobster shells)*
*2 whole oranges, preferably organic,
rinsed and quartered*
1 tablespoon fennel seeds
2 pieces star anise
4 litres (7 pints) cold water
*One 765g (28oz) can peeled Italian
plum tomatoes in juice*
Several fresh or dried bay leaves
*One plump, moist garlic head, halved
crosswise but not peeled*
*¼ teaspoon ground chilli peppers, or
piment d'Espelette*
1 teaspoon fine sea salt
1 tablespoon tomato paste

1. In a heavy-duty roasting pan or large, deep frying-pan, heat the oil over moderate heat until hot but not smoking. Add the shells and sear until they turn a bright pink, 2 to 3 minutes. Add all the other ingredients. Bring to a boil, uncovered, and boil vigorously, for 30 minutes. To extract maximum flavour from the shells, use a wooden mallet to crush and break up the shells while the soup is cooking.

2. Line a large colander with a double layer of dampened cheesecloth and place the colander over a large bowl. Ladle the broth into the colander, discarding the solids. Taste for seasoning. Serve warm in small cups as an appetiser or in warmed, shallow soup bowls as a first course.

Daguerre Marée

4, rue Bayen

Paris 17

Telephone: 01 43 80 16 29

Métro: Ternes

A fruity, chilled Chenin Blanc, such as a Cappellet Chenin Blanc with
the flavours of melon and citrus.

EVERYDAY IDIOM

While we say, 'Too many cooks spoil the broth', the French say, '*On
n'arrive à rien quand tout le monde s'en mêle*', meaning 'Nothing
happens when everyone gets involved'.

Rue Bayen Fish Soup
Soupe de Poissons de Roche

*There are as many versions of fish soup as there are cooks. At my fish market on the
Right Bank Rue Bayen, the fishmongers occasionally sell a varied selection of tiny, freshly
caught Mediterranean rockfish, called* poissons de roche. *When I see fresh, glistening,
oftentimes wriggling varieties of these fish and shellfish, I grab a kilo's worth and rush
them home for a quick luncheon soup. The tiny fish should neither be washed nor gutted.
The same soup can be prepared with larger fish (such as whiting, red mullet, small monkfish,
baby crabs and conger eel), which would need to be scaled, gutted and washed.*

SERVES 6

3 tablespoons extra-virgin olive oil
1 head plump, fresh garlic, halved
horizontally (do not peel)

1. In a 6-litre (10-pint) heavy-bottomed soup pot, combine the
oil, garlic, bouquet garni and salt. Soften the garlic over
moderate heat for 3 to 4 minutes. Add the fish, increase heat to
high and let the ingredients sweat for 5 minutes.

2 teaspoons sea salt, or to taste
1kg (2lb) very fresh rockfish: includ-
ing small rascasse, girelles,
galinettes, shore crabs (favouilles),
small crustaceans, conger eel
5 large ripe tomatoes, rinsed and
quartered (do not peel) or substitute
1 small can (490g/14 oz) peeled
tomatoes in their juice
⅛ teaspoon ground cayenne pepper,
or to taste (optional)
4 dried fennel branches (optional)
Fresh or dried peel of 1 orange
(optional)
1.5 litres (2½ pints) water
BOUQUET GARNI:
a generous bunch of flat-leaf parsley,
celery leaves, fresh bay leaves and
sprigs of thyme tied in a bundle
with cotton twine
sourdough bread, to serve

2. Add the tomatoes. If using, add the cayenne pepper, fennel branches and orange peel. Add the water. Bring to a vigorous boil and cook, uncovered, at a galloping boil for 25 minutes. Skim carefully to avoid any bitterness. Remove and discard the bouquet garni and fennel branches.

3. Pass the contents through the coarse blade of a food mill placed over another saucepan. Add the saffron. Bring just to a boil and serve. This soup does not need rouille or aioli or cheese, just a few thin slices of sourdough bread toasted and rubbed with garlic.

Any flowery, herbal Provençal white wine, such as Cassis, Côtes-de-Provence, Côtes-du-Rhône or Côstieres de Nîmes.

Poissonerie Daguerre Marée

4, rue Bayen

Paris 17

Telephone: 01 43 80 16 29

Métro: Ternes

Fresh Crab Soup
Soupe de Favouilles

In France, the tiniest of hard-shelled crabs – with a greenish back and measuring no more than 7.5cm (3in) in length – are prized for the delicious crab soup. The same crab, known in Italy as Grachio commune, *and in Spain as* Cangrejo de mar, *can be found in Paris markets in spring and autumn, sold live as favouilles. In this recipe, the tiny crabs (too small to eat on their own) are used to flavour the soup, and discarded after cooking. I think that this soup is brilliant in its simplicity, and wonderful when served with croûtons prepared from homemade Parmesan Bread (page 61).*

SERVES 6

EQUIPMENT:
One 6-litre (10-pint) cast-iron pan

3 tablespoon extra-virgin olive oil
2 leeks, tender white portion only, rinsed, halved lengthways and thinly sliced
1 bulb fennel, finely chopped
1 stalk celery, finely chopped
Sea salt
1kg (2lb) live baby crabs (rock crab or blue crab), rinsed but left whole
3 tomatoes, cored and chopped
125ml (4½fl oz) white wine
2 litres (3½ pints) hot water
⅛ teaspoon cayenne (or to taste)
⅛ teaspoon saffron threads
¼ cup small pasta, such as osmarino or orzo
BOUQUET GARNI:
several sprigs of parsley, fennel leaves, bay leaves and thyme, wrapped in the green part of the leek and secured with cotton twine

1. In the cast-iron pan, combine the oil, leeks, fennel, celery and a pinch of salt. Sweat, covered, over low heat until soft, stirring from time to time, about 5 minutes. Increase heat to high, add the crabs, and cover. Cook until coloured, about 2 minutes.

2. Add the tomatoes, wine, hot water and the bouquet garni. Season to taste with salt and cayenne. Bring to a rapid boil and boil, covered, for 20 minutes. To extract maximum flavour from the shells, use a wooden mallet to crush and break up the shells.

3. Remove from the heat and strain through a fine mesh sieve or food mill, pressing down on the crabs to extract as much liquid as possible. Return the liquid to the heat, taste for seasoning, and add the saffron and the pasta.

4. Cook until the pasta is cooked through, about 5 minutes. Taste for seasoning. Serve hot, with croûtons.

Menu·Carte

End of Summer Vegetable Festival

———○———

Summer Tomato and Vegetable Soup

———○———

Domaine St Luc's Cake aux Olives and
Tomato Sauce

———○———

Courgette Stuffed with Goat's Cheese and Mint

———○———

Aubergine-Tomato Gratin

———○———

Fig and Almond Gratin

Fish and Shellfish

Fish and Shellfish

Les Poissons et les Fruits de Mer

Le Dôme's Sole Meunière
Sole Meunière Le Dôme

Le Bistrot du Dôme's Clams with Fresh Thyme
Palourdes au Thym Bistrot du Dôme

Slow-Roasted Salmon
Saumon Confit

Le Bookinistes' Fresh Cod Brandade
Brandade Les Bookinistes

Memories of Brittany Lobster with Cream
Homard à la Crème

Clams in Vinaigrette
Palourdes au Vinaigrette

Le Duc's Hot Curried Oysters
Huîtres Chaudes Le Duc

The Taxi Driver's Wife's Secret Mussels
Moules Secrètes

La Cagouille's Sea Scallops with Warm Vinaigrette
Coquilles Saint-Jacques Vinaigrette Tiède

Langoustines Ledoyen
Langoustines Ledoyen

Le Dôme's Sole Meunière
Sole Meunière Le Dôme

———◦———

For years, I have travelled from Paris restaurant to Paris restaurant in search of the best sole à la meunière – literally 'sole in the style of the miller's wife'. As I sampled the sweet fish here and there, I studied the moistness and size at one restaurant, the colour and fragrance of the brown butter at another, the dexterity of the server in filleting the fish at yet another. I determined that the famous Montparnasse Art Deco brasserie Le Dôme – whose prized fish comes from the l'Ile d'Yeu on the Brittany coast – had the best of all worlds, so I set aside a morning to spend in the kitchen with the Dôme's chef, Frank Graux. I expected to pick up a few tips, but hardly expected him take all the classic ideas of the cooking of this delicate, prized fish and throw them out the window!

While traditional recipes for sole suggest you skin the fish, dust it with flour and cook it in clarified butter, Graux does none of the above. In fact, the idea for leaving the skin intact came from his children. One day he served them turbot with the skin, and one of the children cleaned his plate and asked if there was some more skin leftover! Here, then are some of the tips I learned at Le Dôme, which can be applied to the pan-frying of any flatfish. This is a simple preparation, but one that requires a bit of practice. The practice is worth it, and the rewards incredible.

———◦———

SERVES 4

EQUIPMENT:
An oval, heavy-duty non-stick frying-pan large enough to hold the fish

2 sole, or any firm, white-fleshed fish, such as flounder, trout, or perch, each about 375g (12oz)
About 125g (4oz) butter (slightly salted)
Finely-chopped curly parsley
Freshly squeezed lemon juice

1. Season the fish with salt. Heat a dry non-stick pan over high heat until smoking. Add the butter, let it begin to melt for about 10 seconds, then add the fish (if it is sole, place it light-skinned side down).

2. Reduce heat to low. Cook, undisturbed, until the skin near the tail portion begins to pull away from the flesh, about 4 minutes. During this time, the butter should turn brown and emit an aroma of grilled hazelnuts. If the butter is getting too brown, add more to cool it down and stop it burning. Should the butter burn, discard it and begin again with fresh butter.

3. With a flexible spatula, turn the fish over and cook for 4 minutes more.

4. Remove the pan from the heat. Transfer the fish to a serving platter and fillet. Transfer the fillets to warm dinner plates. Pour the butter from the frying-pan all over the fish. (For sole sèche, or dry sole without the butter sauce, delete this step, discarding the brown butter. Season with parsley and lemon and serve.)

WHAT I LEARNED

The most astonishing thing I learned from this recipe is that brown butter can cook for a long time, up to 10 minutes, without burning, as long as you carefully regulate heat.

CHEF FRANK GRAUX'S TIPS FOR PERFECT PAN-FRIED FLATFISH

Use the best-quality lightly salted butter you can find. Many cooks recommend using clarified butter (which removes the water and solids which burn and discolour when the butter is heated to a high temperature), but Graux feels that clarifying denatures the flavour of the butter, which is so important to this dish. He prefers using lightly salted butter, which burns less quickly than unsalted butter.

Do not skin the fish, only scale, gut and trim it. The skin acts as a natural preserving barrier, so you do not need the 'artificial' barrier of the commonly used coating of flour.

Use the right pan: he uses a heavy-duty, aluminium, non-stick, oval pan that leaves generous room for the fish. You need to seal the fish first to prevent the butter from saturating the inside of the fish. If the pan is too small or the heat too low, the fish will be soggy with fat, rather than crisp on the outside and juicy on the inside.

Begin at high heat and reduce heat to low: Once the fish is 'sealed' over high heat, reduce heat to low to finish cooking and to prevent the outside from burning.

Le Dôme

108, Boulevard du Montparnasse

Paris 14

Telephone: 01 43 35 25 81 Fax: 01 42 79 01 19

Métro: Vavin

The elegance of the fish, the sweetness of the flesh and nuttiness of the butter make me want a rich wine, such as a white Burgundy, a golden Meursault whose own nuttiness echoes the best elements of this classic dish.

The Bistrot du Dôme's Clams with Fresh Thyme
Palourdes au Thym Bistrot du Dôme

———○———

The first time I visited the bustling, all-fish Bistrot du Dôme in 1989, I fell in love with this dish. It is one of those simple, four-ingredient preparations that emerges with a multitude of flavours and aromas. The iodine-rich juices of the clams merge with the sweet tang of the cream, all punctuated with the herbal zest of fresh thyme. A hit of black pepper serves to wake up and round out the flavours.

———○———

SERVES 4 AS A FIRST COURSE;
2 AS A MAIN COURSE

1kg (2lb) small fresh littleneck or Manila clams, purged (see note)
1 teaspoon fresh thyme leaves
180ml (6fl oz) double cream
Freshly ground black pepper to taste

One of my favourite wines at Le Bistrot du Dôme is their lovely dry Vouvray from the house of Huet.

Le Bistrot du Dôme
1, rue Delambre
Paris 14
Telephone: 01 43 35 32 00
Métro: Vavin

1. In a large, shallow frying-pan, combine the purged clams, thyme and cream. Stir to coat the clam shells with the cream. Cover. Cook over a high heat, shaking occasionally, until all the clams are open, 2 to 3 minutes.

2. Transfer the clams in their shells and the sauce to warmed, shallow soup bowls. Discard any clams that do not open. Season with freshly ground black pepper. Serve with plenty of toasted country bread to absorb the sauce.

WHAT I LEARNED
Do not try to make this dish with low fat cream. There is not enough fat to bind the cream to the clam liquor, and the sauce will separate and curdle when heated.

TO PREPARE CLAMS
To prepare clams, scrub the shells under cold running water. Discard any broken shells or shells that do not close when tapped. In a large bowl combine 1.5 litres (2½ pints) cold water and 3 tablespoons of fine sea salt and stir to dissolve. Add the rinsed clams and refrigerate for 3 hours. Remove the clams with your fingers, leaving behind the sand and grit.

Slow-Roasted Salmon
Saumon Confit

———◇———

I first tasted a version of this dish while sampling the sublime, straightforward cuisine of Dominique Bouchet, who now mans the stoves at the Hôtel Crillon and one of the city's most romantic dining rooms, Les Ambassadeurs. In this recipe, the salmon is cooked in a low oven for 17 minutes. This makes for an extremely moist fish, one that tastes neither raw nor cooked, but rather a perfect stage in between. I like to serve it as a first course, with a chiffonnade of sorrel and a sorrel sauce.

———◇———

SERVES 4 AS A MAIN COURSE

500g (1lb) fresh salmon fillet, skinned
Several teaspoons extra-virgin olive oil
Fine sea salt
Freshly ground white pepper to taste
Sorrel Sauce (page 273)

PREHEAT THE OVEN TO
100°C/200°F/GAS MARK 1/2

1. Run your fingers over the top of the salmon fillet to detect any tiny bones that remain in the salmon. With a pair of tweezers, remove them. Cut the salmon into four serving pieces.

2. Place the salmon in an ovenproof dish that will hold the fish snugly. Using a pastry brush, brush the salmon on all sides with oil. Place the baking dish in the centre of the oven and roast until the fish is a bright pinkish-orange and flakes easily, 17 minutes. Remove from the oven and trim off and discard any white milky portions or darkened edges. Remove the dish from the oven and, with a wide spatula, transfer the fish to a small rack set on top of a plate to drain.

3. Serve at room temperature (never hot or cold or you will lose its essence). Serve with Sorrel Sauce (page 273) and a sorrel chiffonnade (thin ribbons of sorrel) or with Celeriac Rémoulade (page 26).

Les Ambassadeurs Hôtel Crillon 10, place de la Concorde Paris 8
Telephone: 01 44 71 15 02
Métro: Concorde

I enjoy this with a fresh and fragrant Viognier, such as one made by one of my favourite winemakers, Jean-Pierre Cartier in Gigondas.

Les Bookinistes Fresh Cod Brandade
Brandade Les Bookinistes

———◦———

Chef William Ledeuil is a truly talented chef in the employ of the gifted Guy Savoy. Ledeuil has been at the helm at the Left Bank Les Bookinistes – with its colourful modern decor mimicking old-time bistros – since it first opened in 1994. On one of my earliest visits, he offered us this delicious and simple first course of fresh cod and potatoes. I make it often, embellishing it with chives for a touch of green and the gentle bite of that versatile herb.

———◦———

SERVES 6 AS A MAIN COURSE

EQUIPMENT:
A food mill; a fine-mesh sieve; six 14cm- (5½in-) individual gratin dishes or a large gratin dish

500ml (18fl oz) double cream
500ml (18fl oz) whole milk
500g (1lb) skinned fresh cod, cut into 5cm (2in) cubes
5 garlic cloves, peeled, halved, germ removed
1 bay leaf
2 sprigs fresh thyme
1 teaspoon whole white peppercorns
2 tablespoons coarse sea salt
500g (1lb) waxy yellow-fleshed potatoes, peeled and cubed
Sea salt
Freshly ground white pepper to taste
10g (⅓ oz) chopped fresh parsley
10g (⅓ oz) chopped fresh chives
3 tablespoons fresh breadcrumbs
Chopped truffle peelings, to taste
Chopped chives and fine sea salt, to garnish

1. In a large saucepan, combine the cream, milk and the cod.

2. Wrap the garlic, bay leaf, thyme and peppercorns in a small piece of cheesecloth and tie in a bundle. Add the herb bundle to the saucepan. Add the coarse salt. Bring the liquid just to a boil over medium heat. Lower the heat and simmer, until fish flakes easily with a fork, 3 to 4 minutes.

3. Drain the fish. Transfer to a large bowl and set aside. Reserve the cream/milk cooking liquid, transferring it back to the large saucepan.

4. Prepare the potatoes: Place the potatoes in the cooking liquid used to poach the cod. Simmer, uncovered, over a moderate heat, stirring regularly, until a knife inserted into a potato comes away easily, 15 to 20 minutes. Watch carefully, for the liquid can easily boil over. Drain the potatoes as soon as they are cooked. Pass them through the coarse blade of a food mill into a large bowl. Reserve. Pass the cooking liquid through a fine-mesh sieve. Reserve.

5. Preheat the grill.

6. In a large bowl, combine the cooked, drained cod and the potatoes, stirring regularly, adding enough of the cooking liquid to make a soft, moist mixture. It should have the consistency of loose mashed potatoes. Keep adding the milk mixture, as the cod and potatoes will quickly absorb the liquid. Taste for seasoning, adding parsley, chives and chopped truffle peelings, to taste.

7. To serve, evenly divide the cod mixture into 6 gratin dishes or a single large gratin dish. Sprinkle lightly with the breadcrumbs. Place under the grill until lightly browned. Garnish with additional chopped chives and fine sea salt.

> ### NOTE
> If doubling the recipe, the cream and milk mixture need only be multiplied by 1½, not 2.

A Condrieu from Georges Vernay.

Les Bookinistes

53, quai des Grands-Augustins

Paris 6

Telephone: 01 43 25 45 94 Fax: 01 4325 23 07

Métro: RER Saint-Miche

Memories of Brittany Lobster with Cream
Homard à la Crème

---◦---

Often the memory of a dish plays as much of a role in enjoyment as the dish itself. One of my fondest food memories is the lobster I ate at l'Etrave, a casual fish restaurant in Brittany in the port town of Cléden Cap Sizun, where the lobster was halved and doused with cream and grilled under a fierce fire until golden and bubbly. In Paris, this is the only way I prepare lobster, often in the winter when we feast on the dish in front of a roaring fire with a glass of chilled, bubbling champagne.

---◦---

SERVES 2

EQUIPMENT:
One 6-litre (10-pint) pasta pan fitted with a colander

1 lobster, about 1kg (2lb)
3 tablespoons coarse sea salt
250ml (9fl oz) double cream

PREHEAT THE GRILL.

1. Parboil the lobster: Bring the pot of water to a boil over high heat. Add the salt and plunge the lobster head first into the pot, cover, and cook for 5 minutes for the first 500g (1lb) and 3 minutes for the additional 500g.

2. Remove the colander from the water, drain, and let the lobster cool for a few minutes. Transfer the lobster to a cutting board, laying it on its back. Split the lobster in half. Plunge a sturdy chef's knife through the back of the head. Cut forward through the head and back through the body and tail. Remove the head sac and intestines. Crack the claws and legs slightly with the back of a knife. Place the halves cut-side up, side by side, on a baking sheet. Pour the cream into the claws and the tail.

3. Place the baking sheet on an oven rack about 7.5cm (3in) from the heat. Grill until the lobster flesh is firm and the cream is brown and bubbling, 6 to 10 minutes. Transfer each lobster half to a warmed dinner plate and serve.

The rich combination of lobster and cream cries out for a rich and elegant wine. Why not a creamy vintage champagne? Other suggestions include a top California Chardonnay or a fine white Burgundy.

WHAT I LEARNED

This dish taught me not to be afraid of cooking lobster. It is a dish that is simple and clear. Once you have it down, it's the only lobster recipe you need in your repertoire.

Clams in Vinaigrette
Palourdes au Vinaigrette

Paris probably offers the best and freshest shellfish in France. Thanks to modern transportation and a ready enthusiasm for the abundance of food from the nation's waters, the capital offers an embarrassment of riches. Much of the year one can find tiny coques – miniature clams that are so so sweet, almondy, and satisfying – and when I want to prepare a quick meal I put coques on the menu. Although this dish is made in just 3 or 4 minutes, you do have to think ahead: clams tend to be sandy and must always be purged in a cold salt water bath.

SERVES 4 AS A FIRST COURSE;
2 AS A MAIN COURSE

EQUIPMENT:
2 to 4 warmed shallow soup bowls

THE VINAIGRETTE:
2 tablespoons balsamic vinegar
2 tablespoons best-quality sherry
wine vinegar
4 tablespoons extra-virgin olive oil
3 tablespoons chopped fresh chives
1 shallot, peeled and finely chopped
Sea salt
Freshly ground black pepper

1kg (2lb) small fresh littleneck or
Manila clams, purged (see note)

1. Prepare the vinaigrette: In a small bowl, combine the vinegar and salt, and stir to dissolve the salt. Add the oil, whisking to blend. Add the chives, shallot and pepper. Set aside.

2. Place the purged clams in a large, shallow frying-pan. Cover and cook over a high heat, shaking occasionally, until all the clams are open, 2 to 3 minutes. With a large, slotted spoon, transfer the clams in their shells and the sauce to warmed, shallow soup bowls. Discard any clams that do not open.

3. Whisk the vinaigrette one more time and pour the vinaigrette over the clams. Toss well to coat the clams with the dressing. Serve with plenty of toasted country bread to absorb the sauce.

TO PREPARE CLAMS

Scrub the shells under cold running water. Discard any broken shells or shells that do not close when tapped. In a large bowl combine 1.5 litres (2$\frac{1}{2}$ pints) cold water and 3 tablespoons of fine sea salt and stir to dissolve. Add the rinsed clams and refrigerate for 3 hours. Remove the clams with your fingers, leaving behind the sand and grit.

Any good, acidic white wine goes well here. Mardon's Quincy is one of my favourites, with its pure, distinctive grassiness.

Poissonerie: Bruno Gauvain

16, rue Dupin

Paris 6

Telephone: 01 42 22 46 65

Métro: Sèvres-Babylone

Le Duc's Hot Curried Oysters
Huîtres Chaudes Le Duc

———○———

Le Duc is one of Paris' finest fish restaurants, and this is one of its classic dishes. These hot oysters are great to pass as an appetiser or a first course palate-opener. The salt and the curry stimulate the appetite and get you ready for more!

———○———

SERVES 4 AS A FIRST COURSE;
2 AS A MAIN COURSE

About 250ml (9fl oz) coarse salt
8 ultra-fresh oysters, scrubbed, shucked, and the liquor strained and reserved
2 shallots, peeled and chopped
1 plump, fresh garlic clove, peeled and chopped
1 tablespoon unsalted butter
60ml (2fl oz) double cream
½ teaspoon cayenne
½ teaspoon powdered saffron
¾ teaspoon Curry Powder (page 268)
1 tablespoon freshly squeezed lemon juice
Freshly ground white pepper

PREHEAT THE GRILL.

Le Duc

243, boulevard Raspail

Paris 14

Telephone: 01 43 20 96 30 Fax: 01 43

20 46 73

Métro: Raspail

1. Sprinkle an ovenproof gratin dish with coarse salt to cover the bottom and form a cushion for the oysters. Arrange the oysters on the bed of salt. Set aside.

2. In a small saucepan combine the shallots, garlic and butter and sweat – cook, covered, over low heat without colouring until soft and translucent – 1 to 2 minutes. Stir in the cream and spices and cook until thick and creamy, 1 to 2 minutes. Stir in the lemon juice and reserved oyster liquor. Taste for seasoning.

4. Spoon the sauce over the oysters. Place the gratin dish under the grill and cook just until the sauce melts and begins to sizzle, about 45 seconds. Serve immediately.

Serve with champagne or a young, crispy, dry, almost sparkling (the French call it perlant) Muscadet de Sevre et Maine sur Lie, an underrated Atlantic coast wine made near the town of Nantes. Recommended makers include D. Maugis from the village of Vertou and the Domaine de la Louveière, in La Haie-Fouasière.

The Taxi Driver's Wife's Secret Mussels
Moules Secrètes

———○———

I feel as though I am a magnet for people wanting to reveal their most guarded secrets:
wherever I go in Paris, it seems that people want me to know about their special recipes. One day
while a taxi driver was taking me from restaurant to market to speciality shop, he confided that
his wife made the best mussels in the world. So delicious, he said, that everyone raved about
them and his wife never, ever revealed her secret. I did not even have to pop the question,
and pretty soon he had shared his spouse's most guarded recipe. The key is Gewürztraminer, the
aromatic wine from France's Alsace region. At first I was a bit doubtful, for acidic white wines,
such as those from the Loire, are most commonly used in mussels. Well, now I am a
convert. The faint sweetness of Gewürztraminer mirrors the sweetness of the finest mussels.
I always look for the tiniest mussels in the market for I find them the most flavourful.
Some of the best in Paris are the moules de bouchot from Le Baie St Michel.

———○———

SERVES 4 AS A FIRST COURSE;
2 AS A MAIN COURSE

EQUIPMENT:
A large, deep, covered frying-pan;
4 warm shallow soup bowls

1kg (2lb) fresh mussels
2 shallots, peeled and finely chopped
3 tablespoons unsalted butter
¼ teaspoon fine sea salt
500ml (9fl oz) Alsatian
Gewürztraminer wine
Freshly ground black pepper
2 teaspoons fresh or dried
thyme leaves
Handful of fresh, flat-leaf parsley
leaves, chopped

1. Thoroughly scrub the mussels and rinse with several changes of water. If an open mussel closes when you press on it, then it is good; if it stays open the mussel should be discarded. Beard the mussels. Do not beard the mussels more than a few minutes in advance or they will die and spoil. Note that in some markets mussels are pre-prepared, in that the small black beard that hangs from the mussel has been clipped off, but not entirely removed. These mussels do not need further attention. Set aside.

2. In a large, deep frying-pan, combine the shallots, butter and salt over low heat. Cover and sweat – cook until softened – about 3 minutes. Add the wine, bring to a boil over high heat and boil, uncovered, until reduced by half, about 5 minutes.

3. Add the mussels, sprinkle generously with pepper, and stir.

Cover and cook just until the mussels open, about 3 minutes. Remove the mussels as they open. Do not overcook. Discard any mussels that do not open.

4. Transfer the mussels and liquid to 4 warm shallow soup bowls. Sprinkle each with thyme, parsley and freshly ground pepper. Serve immediately, with finger bowls, as well as plenty of crusty baguette to soak up the memorable sauce.

I use an inexpensive Gewürztraminer when preparing this dish, and serve the same wine with the mussels.

One of the best places to buy fish in the Left Bank is:

Poissonerie de Bac

69, rue de Bac

Paris 7

Telephone: 01 45 48 06 64

Métro: Rue du Bac

WHAT I LEARNED

Years ago, a fishmonger warned me against taking mussels home in a plastic bag and storing them in the refrigerator. Mussels stored in a sealed bag will suffocate and die. Rather, when you get home from the market, either place the mussels on a shelf in the refrigerator with the bag opened or, better yet, transfer them to a large bowl and cover the bowl with a damp cloth.

La Cagouille's Sea Scallops with Warm Vinaigrette
Coquilles Saint-Jacques Vinaigrette Tiède

———○———

To my mind, this is one of the finest ways to cook scallops: simply seared in a hot pan, the rich, golden, nutty, almost caramelised sweet aroma and flavour of these rich muscles from the sea are allowed to shine, unadorned and unsmothered. The vinaigrette – here prepared with about half the amount of acid that is used in a classic vinaigrette – is there just to gently coat the scallop and add just the slightest touch of acid to balance the richness of the scallop's meat. In dictating this recipe, La Cagouille owner Gerard Allemandou noted: 'Delicate, subtle, with a meat that is dense and velvety, the scallop allows unlimited preparations, but the cook must always look to respect the delicacy of its smooth, soft sweet flavour.'

———○———

SERVES 4 AS A FIRST COURSE

8 large sea scallops (250g/8oz in total)
Sea salt
Freshly ground white pepper

FOR THE VINAIGRETTE:
1 tablespoon best-quality sherry wine vinegar
Fine sea salt
8 to 10 tablespoons grapeseed or a mild extra-virgin olive oil

About 2 tablespoons finely-chopped chives
About 2 tablespoons finely-chopped flat-leaf parsley leaves
About 2 tablespoons finely-chopped chervil leaves or tarragon leaves
Fleur de sel (see page 100)
Freshly ground white pepper

1. Rinse the scallops and pat them dry. Remove the little muscle on the side of the scallop and discard. Cut each scallop in half horizontally, and set aside.

2. Prepare the vinaigrette: in a small jar, combine the vinegar and salt and cover. Shake to dissolve the salt. Add the oil and cover. Shake to form an emulsion. Taste for seasoning. Set aside.

3. In a large, dry, non-stick frying-pan over a high heat, sear the scallops and cook just until they brown around the edges, 30 seconds to 1 minute on each side. Season each side after it has cooked. Cooking time will vary according to the size of the scallops. For scallops that are cooked all the way through, sear for 1 minute or more on each side.

4. Spoon 2 teaspoons of vinaigrette and a half teaspoon of finely-chopped herbs on each warmed dinner plate. Carefully transfer four scallop halves to each of the prepared plates.

Sprinkle the scallops with additional herbs. Season with fleur de sel and pepper. Serve, with Spring Noirmoutier Potatoes Cooked in Coarse Salt (page 100).

As chef Allemandou suggests, 'A great white wine will help this dish reach its apotheosis. A Condrieu from Georges Vernay, for example.'

WHAT I LEARNED

This is one of the simplest of dishes that must be followed to the letter. Be sure that your herbs are perfectly chopped, as finely as possible, so that they do not overwhelm the delicate scallops. Take your time in preparing the herbs and you will be justly rewarded.

La Cagouille

10-12 Place Brancusi

(across from 23, rue de l'Ouest)

Paris 14

Telephone: 01 43 22 09 01 Fax: 01 45 38 57 29

Métro: Gaîté

Langoustines Ledoyen

Langoustines Ledoyen

———○———

Chef Christian Le Squer, of the Paris Right Bank restaurant Ledoyen, considers langoustines
to be 'refined lobsters'. I agree with him, for they are one of my top ten favourite foods to eat, up
there with oysters, artichokes, asparagus and squab. Langoustines have a more delicate flavour
than lobster; they satisfy instantly in the way that only pure protein can. When properly cooked,
langoustines have a delicate texture that reminds me of plump down pillows. This is one
recipe that allows you to enjoy to the fullest their pure, unadulterated flavour and texture.
Where langoustines are not available, the dish is just as delicious prepared
with the freshest of giant, raw shrimp.

———○———

SERVES 6

FOR THE THREE-SPICE BLEND:
1 tablespoon whole coriander seeds
3 whole pieces star anise
1 tablespoon whole fennel seeds

FOR THE CITRUS EMULSION:
2 tablespoons freshly squeezed
lemon juice
Fine sea salt
125ml (4½fl oz) hazelnut or
extra-virgin olive oil

FOR THE LANGOUSTINES:
Several tablespoons extra-virgin
olive oil
4 tablespoons very finely-chopped
fresh basil leaves
90g (3oz) kadaif (shredded Greek
pastry found in speciality stores)
24 langoustines or extra-large shrimp
in the shell, shelled and deveined

Several tablespoons basil chiffonnade
(thin ribbons), to garnish

1. To prepare the three-spice blend, combine the coriander grains, star anise and fennel seed in a spice mill and grind until fine. Transfer to a spice jar and seal.

2. To prepare the citrus emulsion, combine the lemon juice and salt in a small bowl. Stir to dissolve the salt. Whisk in the oil. Taste for seasoning. Set aside.

3. Prepare three plates: one with about 2 tablespoons of olive oil, one with the chopped basil and one with the kadaif. Sprinkle the three-spice mix over the langoustines. Roll the seasoned langoustines in the oil to coat evenly. Roll them in the herbs, then the kadaif.

4. Heat 3 tablespoons of olive oil in a large, non-stick frying-pan. Add the langoustines, browning them evenly on all sides, about 1 minute per side.

5. Transfer 4 langoustines to the centre of a warm dinner plate. Drizzle the citrus emulsion over the langoustines. Repeat for the other three palates. Garnish with basil chiffonnade. Serve immediately.

> My choice is a Viognier, such as the regal white from the caves of Jean-Pierre Cartier, Domaine les Gouberts, in Gigondas.

Ledoyen

Carré Champs-Elysées,

Telephone: 01 53 05 10 01 Fax: 01 47 42 55 01

Métro: Champs Elysées-Clemenceau

Menu·Carte

A Seafood Celebration

———○———

Spicy Langoustine Broth

———○———

La Cagouille's Sea Scallops with Warm
Vinaigrette

———○———

Le Dôme's Sole Meunière

———○———

Joël Robuchon's Burnt Cream

Poultry

Poultry
La Volaille

Lemon Chicken
Poulet au Citron

Benoît's Fricassée of Chicken with Morels
Fricassée de Poulet aux Morilles Benoît

Chicken Fricassée with Two Vinegars
Fricassée de Poulet aux deux Vinaigres

Chicken Fricassée with Morels and Vin Jaune
Fricassée de Poulet aux Morilles et au Vin Jaune

Grilled Chicken with Mustard and Red Pepper
Poulet Grillé à la Diable

Place Monge Market Guinea Hen with Sauerkraut
and Sausages
Pintade au Choucroute, Marché Place Monge

Manu's Grilled and Roasted Pigeon
Pigeon Grillé et Rôti Manu

Parisian Roasted Turkey
Dinde Rôtie

Lemon Chicken
Poulet au Citron

———◦———

When I can't think of what to cook, I cook chicken. When there is chicken on a restaurant menu, I order chicken. I think that I could eat moist, healthy, chewy roast farm chicken almost every day of my life. There is something so simple and sublime about well-bred, free-range poultry. This is the simplest of recipes, and one I credit to my husband Walter. Actually, I cooked the chicken, he discovered the 'truc'. He walked in the door from work one evening as I was taking a roast chicken from the oven. The chicken was particularly small and so rather than putting a whole lemon in the cavity as is my custom, I quartered the citrus lengthways. As Walter carved the chicken he squeezed all the juices from the lemons over the poultry. The juice itself had become a rich, complex 'confit', thick, dense and fragrant.

We swooned over that little touch of genius. Ever since, this has become one of our weeknight treats, which we usually team up with a simple green salad, two or three kinds of cheese, some Poilâne bread and, of course, a glass or two of good French wine.

———◦———

SERVES 4 TO 6

EQUIPMENT:
One oval roasting pan, just slightly larger than the chicken (about 22 x 33cm/9 x 13in) fitted with a roasting rack

1 best-quality farm chicken, (about 2.5kg/5lb), with giblets
Sea salt
Freshly ground black pepper to taste
2 lemons, preferably organic, scrubbed, dried and quartered lengthways
Small bunch of thyme
75g (2½oz) unsalted butter, softened

PREHEAT THE OVEN TO
220ºC/425ºF/GAS MARK 7.

1. Generously season the cavity of the chicken with salt and pepper. Place the giblets, the lemons and bunch of thyme in the cavity. Truss. Rub the skin of the chicken with the butter. Season all over with salt and pepper.

2. Place the chicken on its side on the roasting rack in the roasting pan. Place in the centre of the oven and roast, uncovered, for 20 minutes. Turn the chicken to the other side, and roast for 20 minutes more. Turn the chicken breast-side up, and roast for 20 minutes more, for a total of 1 hour's roasting time. By this time the skin should be a deep golden colour.

3. Reduce the heat to 190ºC/375ºF/gas mark 5. Turn the chicken breast-side down, at an angle if at all possible, with its head down and tail in the air. (This heightens the flavour by

allowing the juices to flow down through the breast meat.)
Roast until the juices run clear when you pierce a thigh with a
skewer, about 15 minutes more.

4. Remove from the oven and season generously with salt and
pepper. Transfer the chicken to a platter, and place on an angle
against the edge of an overturned plate, with its head down
and tail in the air. Cover loosely with foil. Turn off the oven and
place the platter in the oven, with the door open. Let rest for a
minimum of 10 minutes and up to 30 minutes. The chicken
will continue to cook during this resting time.

5. Meanwhile, prepare the sauce: Place the baking dish over
moderate heat, scraping up any bits that cling to the bottom.
Cook for 2 to 3 minutes, scraping and stirring until the liquid is
almost caramelised. Do not let it burn. Spoon off and discard
any excess fat. Add several tablespoons cold water to deglaze
(hot water will cloud the sauce). Bring to a boil. Reduce the
heat to low and simmer until thickened, about 5 minutes.

6. While the sauce is cooking, remove the lemons from the
cavity of the chicken. Carve the chicken into serving pieces and
transfer to a warmed platter. Squeeze the lemons all over the
pieces of poultry, extracting as much juice as possible. Strain
the sauce through a fine-mesh sieve and pour into a gravy boat.
Serve immediately.

The lemony tang of this chicken suggests a simple white, such as an
Alsatian Riesling.

Benoît's Fricassée of Chicken with Morels
Fricassée de Poulet aux Morilles Benoît

———○———

This recipe was dictated to me one morning as I spent the day behind the stove with Benoît Guichard, at his Michelin two-star restaurant, Jamin. Despite the luxurious surroundings, Jamin has at its soul a very solid home-style of French cooking. I love this dish, because the mahogany tones of the morel sauce permeate the chicken as it cooks, resulting in a penetrating, welcoming colour. The recipe allows for plenty of sauce, so the dish is ideal for pairing with strands of fresh pasta or fluffy white rice.

———○———

SERVES 4

EQUIPMENT:
A large covered frying-pan

2 medium onions, peeled
4 tablespoons extra-virgin olive oil
30g (1oz) unsalted butter
4 chicken legs, thighs attached,
(about 1.5kg/3lb) at room
temperature
Sea salt and freshly ground white
pepper to taste
One recipe Wild Morel Mushrooms in
Cream and Stock (page 86)

1. Slice the onions in half lengthways. Place each half, cut-side down, on a cutting board and cut crosswise into very thin slices.

2. In a large frying-pan, combine 2 tablespoons of oil and 1 tablespoon of butter and a pinch of salt. Add the onions and sweat – cook, covered, over low heat without colouring – for about 5 minutes. With a slotted spoon, transfer the onions to a clean plate. Set aside.

3. Liberally season the chicken on all sides with salt and pepper. Add 2 more tablespoons of oil and 1 tablespoon of butter to the frying-pan over moderate heat. When hot, add the chicken, skin side down and brown until the poultry turns an even golden colour, about 5 minutes. Turn the pieces and brown them on the other side, 5 minutes more. Carefully regulate the heat to avoid scorching the skin. When all the pieces are browned, use tongs – to avoid piercing the meat – to transfer them to a platter.

4. Pour off and discard the fat in the pan. Return the chicken to the pan. Add the onions and the Morels in Cream and Stock.

Cover and simmer over the lowest possible heat for 20 minutes. Taste for seasoning. Serve with rice or fresh pasta.

This classic dish deserves a classic wine: If you can find it, try an Arbois vin jaune Côtes du Jura, a golden wine much like a fino sherry. Or, even better, is the rare Château-Chalon, a strong and dry sherry-like wine that is bottled only after six years of ageing.

Jamin

32, rue de Longchamp

Paris 16

Telephone: 01 45 53 00 07 Fax: 01 45 53 00 15

Métro: Trocadéro

Fricassée of Chicken with Two Vinegars
Fricassée de Poulet aux deux Vinaigres

———————○———————

This recipe, typical of the sort of traditional bistro fare that makes French food so appealing and satisfying, appeared in my shopping bag one day as part of a promotion for the delicate, creamy-fleshed poulet de Bresse, *the king of French chicken. The first time I made this for my husband Walter and myself, there were a few leftovers. The next day Walter asked what I did with the chicken. When I said I froze it, he replied, 'Oh, good, it makes me happy to know that I have it in my future.' Then he added, 'But I really think you need to test that again, soon.' I did, and it's been a family favourite ever since. At home, I serve this with steamed rice or fresh pasta.*

———————○———————

SERVES 4

EQUIPMENT:
A deep frying-pan with lid

1 fresh farm chicken (1.5 to 2kg/ 3 to 4lb), cut into 8 serving pieces
Sea salt
Freshly ground white pepper to taste
3 tablespoons extra-virgin olive oil
60g (2oz) unsalted butter
80ml (3fl oz) white champagne vinegar
80ml (3fl oz) red wine vinegar
80ml (3fl oz) white wine
2 shallots, peeled and finely chopped
185ml (7fl oz) Homemade Tomato Sauce (page 269)
400ml (15fl oz) Homemade Chicken Stock (page 274)
250ml (9fl oz) double cream

1. Liberally season the chicken on all sides with salt and pepper.

2. In a deep frying-pan, combine the oil and butter, and heat over moderate heat. When the fats are hot but not smoking, add the chicken, skin-side down and brown until the poultry turns an even golden colour, about 5 minutes. Turn the pieces and brown them on the other side, 5 minutes more. Carefully regulate the heat to avoid scorching the skin. This may have to be done in batches. When all the pieces are browned, use tongs – to avoid piercing the meat – to transfer them to a platter.

3. Pour off and discard the fat in the pan. Off the heat, deglaze with the two vinegars. Add the wine and the shallots and cook, covered, over a low heat until softened, 2 to 3 minutes. Return the chicken to the pan. Cover and simmer over low heat for 15 minutes more.

4. Transfer the chicken to a large, warmed platter and cover

with aluminium foil to keep warm. Add the tomato sauce and the stock to the pan; stir to blend thoroughly. Add the cream and cook, uncovered, over medium heat for 5 minutes. Return the chicken to the pan and cover. Cook over a low heat, turning from time to time to absorb the sauce, about 10 minutes more. Taste for seasoning. Serve with rice or fresh pasta.

THE PAMPERED BRESSE CHICKEN

On one of my early trips to France in the 1970s, I spent a day reporting on the life of the pampered Bresse chicken. I didn't speak a word of French at the time and my husband Walter served as my translator. As luck would have it, the sweet gentleman who took us around spoke about the fastest French I had ever heard. He would speak for about five minutes without taking a breath. When I would ask Walter to translate, these speeches would be condensed into a sentence or two! Thank goodness one can report with one's eyes as well as one's ears. What can I say about Bresse poultry? They are the crème de la crème of the poultry world. Delicate, meltingly tender, meat that is as white as alabaster. It is no surprise that Bresse poultry loves creamy sauces and delicate flavours. Bresse is a actually the name of a breed of poultry grown in the region just south of Lyon and can be detected in markets by their red, white and blue tricolour seal and a numbered leg band. A Bresse chicken lives freely – just as the name implies, free range – for the early part of its life, then rests indoors for one week to obtain that white white meat. But the quality of the poultry comes from what it is fed: cereal grains, corn and dairy products, not to mention all the insects it finds on its wanderings about the yard.

Bresse poultry can be found at any good Parisian butcher shop. I often buy mine at:

La Grande Epicerie de Paris Bon Marché

38, rue de Sèvres

Paris 7

Telephone: 01 44 39 81 00

Métro: Sèvres-Babylone

NOTE

Where Bresse poultry is not available, use a good, meaty, free-range chicken, organic if you can find it.

This dish from the Bresse region of France is tailor-made for a simple, fruity Beaujolais.

Fricassée of Chicken with Morels and Vin Jaune
Fricassée de Poulet aux Morilles et au Vin Jaune

My good friend Hervé Poron is the truffle king of Provence. Throughout the year, he also supplies me with extraordinary dried morels, which I use to prepare this luscious chicken dish. This is one of my husband Walter's favourite Sunday night suppers, perfect for sitting around the fire on chilly Paris nights.

SERVES 4

EQUIPMENT:
One deep-sided 30cm- (12in-) frying-pan with a lid

60g (2oz) dried morel mushrooms
60g (2oz) unsalted butter, at room temperature
Fine sea salt to taste
1 fresh farm chicken (1.5–2kg/3–4lb), cut into 8 serving pieces, at room temperature
Sea salt and freshly ground white pepper to taste
3 tablespoons extra-virgin olive oil
75g (2½oz) unsalted butter
2 shallots, peeled and finely chopped
2 plump, fresh garlic cloves, peeled and finely chopped
500ml (18fl oz) vin jaune from the Jura or sherry or an oaky Chardonnay
250ml (9fl oz) double cream

1. Prepare the morels: Place them in a colander and rinse well under cold running water to rid them of any grit. Transfer them to a heatproof measuring cup. Pour boiling water over the mushrooms to cover. Set aside for 20 minutes to plump them up. With a slotted spoon, carefully remove the mushrooms from the liquid, leaving behind any grit that may fall to the bottom. If any of the morels are extremely large, halve them lengthways.

You can save the soaking 'bouillon'. When making this dish I serve rice, so use the bouillon in place of water. I also like to freeze the remaining liquid to enhance a mushroom soup. Place a piece of dampened cheesecloth in a colander set over a large bowl. Carefully spoon the soaking liquid into the colander, leaving behind any grit at the bottom of the measuring cup.

2. Liberally season the chicken on all sides with salt and pepper.

3. In the frying-pan, combine the oil and 60g (2oz) unsalted butter over a moderate heat. When the fats are hot but not smoking, add the chicken, skin side down and brown until the poultry turns an even, golden colour, about 5 minutes. Turn the pieces and brown them on the other side, 5 minutes more.

Carefully regulate the heat to avoid scorching the skin. This may have to be done in batches. When all the pieces are browned, use tongs – to avoid piercing the meat – to transfer them to a platter. Season once again with salt and pepper.

4. Pour off and discard the fat in the frying-pan. Add the remaining butter, the shallots and the garlic. Sweat – cook, covered, over low heat – until soft but not brown, about 3 minutes.

5. Add the wine and boil, uncovered, over high heat, to burn off the alcohol, which could make the sauce bitter. Add the cream and the morels and stir to blend. Return the chicken and any cooking juices to the frying-pan. Cover, and cook over a low heat turning the chicken in the sauce once or twice, until the chicken is cooked through and has thoroughly absorbed the sauce, about 20 minutes more. Taste for seasoning. Serve with rice or fresh pasta.

There is no choice here, the wine must be the golden, sherry-like Vin Jaune from the Jura, the best being from Château Chalon.

Grilled Chicken with Mustard and Red Pepper
Poulet Grillé à la Diable

In French cooking, any meat or poultry seasoned with mustard and hot pepper, and coated with breadcrumbs, is called à la diable, *since the devil, or* diable, *is associated with anything hot and fiery. Cafés and bistros all over Paris offer versions of this classic. I like to make mine with a combination of sharp Dijon mustard and coarse-grain Dijon mustard, and a good hit of spice, usually what the French call* piments langues d'oiseaux, *or bird's tongue peppers. This is a great picnic dish as well, and I often make it for lunch on the train to Provence via the high-speed TGV. When we eat at home, I serve this chicken with steamed rice or sautéed potatoes and a green salad.*

SERVES 6

6 chicken legs, thighs attached
2 tablespoons Dijon mustard
1 tablespoon coarse-grain Dijon mustard
¼ teaspoon finely ground hot red pepper
2 eggs
60g (2oz) fine homemade breadcrumbs
45g (1½oz) unsalted butter

PREHEAT THE OVEN TO
180°C/375°F/GAS MARK 5

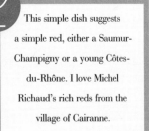

This simple dish suggests a simple red, either a Saumur-Champigny or a young Côtes-du-Rhône. I love Michel Richaud's rich reds from the village of Cairanne.

1. In a small bowl, combine the mustards and red pepper; stir to blend.

2. Place the eggs in a shallow platter and, with a fork, whisk lightly to blend.

3. With a pastry brush, brush the chicken legs and thighs all over with the mustard and pepper mixture. Dip them in the egg mixture, coating evenly on all sides. Sprinkle with the breadcrumbs, coating as evenly as possible.

4. Place the chicken pieces side by side in a roasting pan. Dot with butter. Place in the oven and bake for 30 to 35 minutes, basting frequently. The chicken is done when the juices run clear when pierced with a fork. Remove from the oven and transfer to a baking rack to help firm up the coating.

5. Serve hot or cold, with sautéed potatoes or steamed rice and a green salad.

Manu's Grilled and Roasted Squab
Pigeon Grillé et Rôti Manu

———————●———————

This classic squab preparation was taught to me by chef Emmanual Leblay – known as Manu – who has worked in some of Paris' best kitchens, from Guy Savoy to Arpège to Lucas Carton. He is a talented and exacting cook – follow this simple preparation to the letter and your palate will be richly rewarded! Since a whole squab can be awkward to eat, I find it is best to partially debone the bird (this can be done by your butcher). When prepared in this manner, the tender breast portion cooks quickly, while the firm dark meat retains all its natural flavour and moisture by being cooked on the bone. Be sure to offer finger bowls, so guests can enjoy every morsel.

———————●———————

SERVES 6

6 squabs (each about 500g/1lb), cleaned and partially deboned (see instructions), livers and carcasses reserved
1 large onion, peeled and chopped
About 6 tablespoons extra virgin olive oil
3 tablespoons best quality sherry wine vinegar
Sea salt and freshly ground white pepper to taste

1. Prepare the stock: In a large, deep frying-pan, heat 3 tablespoons of oil until hot but not smoking. Add the onion, reduce heat, and cook until lightly browned, about 5 minutes. Add the squab carcasses and cook until the bones are browned, about 5 minutes more. Cover with water and cook over moderately high heat for about 20 minutes, skimming out any impurities that rise to the surface. Strain the poultry stock through a fine-mesh sieve and set aside.

2. Place the poultry livers on a large plate and crush with a fork to a purée. Place in a bowl and, with a small whisk, beat until smooth. Set aside.

3. In a large frying-pan heat the remaining oil until hot but not smoking. Add the livers and cook, stirring regularly with a whisk, until cooked through, 3 to 4 minutes. Add the vinegar and cook 3 minutes more. Add the reserved poultry stock and cook over moderate heat until the mixture is reduced to a syrupy reddish-black sauce, about 15 minutes. Set aside and keep warm.

4. Preheat the grill, and preheat the oven to 220°C/425°F/gas mark 7.

5. Place the flattened and partially deboned squabs on a baking sheet and coat with olive oil. Season generously with salt and pepper. Place under the grill (or on a grill), skin side towards the heat. Grill just until the poultry begins to weep a bit, 3 to 4 minutes. Transfer the poultry, skin side up, to a baking sheet. Place under the grill or in a very hot oven until cooked through but still moist, about 5 minutes. Immediately season with salt and pepper. Turn off the oven and let rest for 5 minutes.

6. To serve, place a squab in the centre of the plate and spoon the sauce over the crevice in the centre of the bird. Serve immediately.

TIPS FOR SUCCESSFUL BONING

- Use a sharp, pointed knife, selecting knife size to suit the size of the bones
- Keep the knife blade against the bone to avoid cutting into flesh or skin
- Use the point of the knife to help locate the bones
- Scrape rather than cut the meat from the bones
- To see what you are doing, pull flesh away from bones with fingers as you work
- Work with short sawing or stroking movements of the knife. Avoid force.

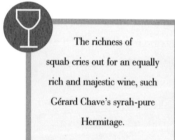

The richness of squab cries out for an equally rich and majestic wine, such Gérard Chave's syrah-pure Hermitage.

PARTIALLY DEBONING POULTRY

To cook poultry quickly and evenly, and make it easier to eat, it is best to partially debone the bird: The central carcass is removed, but the wing and leg bones are left in, to conserve the form of the bird while cooking. You can ask your butcher to do this for you, but it is also handy (and rewarding) to know how to do it yourself. The first bird may take 15 minutes to do correctly, so like everything else in life, you will be rewarded for your patience and perseverance! The French call this method 'a la crapaudine', for the flattened bird – especially pigeon – resembles a 'crapaud' or toad.

Place the bird on its back and pull the legs and wings to stretch them out and make the bird more malleable. With a large, sharp knife, cut off the head, leaving most of the neck. Cut off the wings (which tend to burn during cooking). Cut the legs at the ball joint just to the drumstick. Reserve the wings and legs for stock and set aside.

Place the bird breast side down and gently flatten with the palm of your hand. Using a small, sharp knife, make a slit – CUTTING THROUGH THE SKIN ONLY – down the backbone from the neck to the tail.

WORKING ON ONE SIDE OF THE BACKBONE ONLY, cut and scrape the flesh and skin away from the carcass, working evenly with short sharp stokes of the knife. After each stroke, carefully ease the flesh and skin away from the carcass with the fingers of your other hand.

Cut the flesh from the saber-shaped bone near the wing. Cut through the joint and remove. When you reach the ball and socket joints connecting the wing and thigh bones to the carcass, sever them. The wing and thigh are now separated from the carcass but still attached to the skin.

Using longer strokes of the knife, continue cutting the breast meat away from the bone until the ridge of the breastbone, where skin and bones meet, is reached.

Repeat on the other side of the backbone.

When the skin and meat have been freed from the carcass on both sides of the bird, they will remain attached to the carcass only along the breastbone.

Pull gently to remove the breastbone and the carcass from the flesh. Be careful because the skin here is easily torn. The bird is now partially boned.

Place Monge Market Guinea Hen with Sauerkraut and Sausages
Pintade au Choucroute, Marché Place Monge

———◦———

One chilly day in March at the Place Monge market in the student quarter of the 5th arrondissement, I happened to spy a variation of this warming winter dish. The poultry merchant had boned a plump farm guinea hen, stuffed it with sauerkraut and wrapped it with bacon. He advised me to brown the poultry, then braise it with beer. I knew I didn't have time to prepare his pintade that night, so a few days later created this version at home. It's now become one of our favourite winter dishes. The entire house takes on a beautifully smoky aroma from the meats, as appetites rise in anticipation of dinner. If you can, use fresh rather than canned sauerkraut. Fresh sauerkraut can usually be found in delicatessens or in the deli section of the supermarket.

———◦———

SERVES 4

EQUIPMENT:
One large cast-iron casserole with a lid

1 guinea hen, about 1.5kg (3lb), giblets reserved
Sea salt and freshly ground black pepper to taste
6 bay leaves
15 juniper berries
3 teaspoons cumin seeds
3 tablespoons extra-virgin olive oil
750g (1½lb) sauerkraut
500ml (9fl oz) beer
4 smoked pork sausages, such as keilbasa, each about 125g (4oz)
4 thick slices smoked bacon

1. Generously season the inside of the guinea hen with salt and pepper. Place the giblets, 2 bay leaves, 5 juniper berries and 1 teaspoon cumin seeds inside the guinea hen. Truss.

2. In a casserole large enough to hold the guinea hen, heat the oil until hot but not smoking. Add the poultry and brown evenly on all sides. Remove the guinea hen from the casserole. Discard the fat in the pan.

3. Generously season the poultry all over with salt and pepper. Return the guinea hen, breast side up, to the casserole. Spoon the sauerkraut all around the poultry. Sprinkle with the 4 remaining bay leaves, 10 juniper berries and 2 teaspoons of cumin seeds. Pour the beer all over the poultry and sauerkraut. Cover and braise over a low heat for about 1 hour, stirring from time to time. About ten minutes before the cooking time is over, add the sausages. Cover and cook until the poultry and sausages are cooked through.

4. Just before the guinea hen is finished cooking, grill the smoked bacon until crispy and cooked to desired doneness. Set aside.

5. To serve, remove and discard the bay leaves. Transfer the sauerkraut and sausages to a large, warmed platter. Carve the guinea hen and serve with the sausages and sauerkraut. Garnish each plate with a slice of grilled bacon.

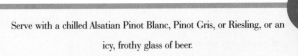

Serve with a chilled Alsatian Pinot Blanc, Pinot Gris, or Riesling, or an icy, frothy glass of beer.

Place Monge Market

Place Monge

Paris 5

Wednesday, Friday and Sunday mornings

Métro: Monge

Parisian Roasted Turkey
Dinde Rotie

———o———

When I first moved to Paris, turkeys were impossible to find at the end of November. Since the French do not celebrate the American Thanksgiving holiday, most birds were raised to be ready for the holiday table at Christmastime. Today, the French have adopted the autumn celebrations of Halloween and Thanksgiving, so finding a late November turkey is less of a trauma. I love to prepare it with this delicious sausage, rosemary and fennel stuffing, which keeps the bird beautifully moist as it roasts. By tenting the turkey with foil for the first hour of cooking, the stuffing cooks first, allowing the bird to cook evenly and slowly, from the inside out. It also avoids excessive browning. Rather than traditional American gravy, I serve this with a simple sauce prepared with the roasting juices.

———o———

SERVES 8 TO 10

1 free-range roasting turkey (3–4kg/6–8lb), heart, liver, gizzard and neck reserved
1½ tablespoons unsalted butter
Sea salt and freshly ground white pepper

FOR THE STUFFING:
The heart, liver and gizzard of the turkey, chopped into bite-sized pieces
500g/1lb bulk sausage meat
2 large eggs, lightly beaten
2 teaspoons fennel seeds
120g (4oz) very fine breadcrumbs
3 tablespoons fresh rosemary leaves, chopped
Freshly ground pepper

PREHEAT THE OVEN TO 220°C/425°F/GAS MARK 7.

1. In a large bowl, combine all of the stuffing ingredients. With your hands, blend the ingredients thoroughly, breaking up any remaining large pieces of sausage meat. Season with pepper and mix to blend. With your hands, pack the stuffing into the cavity of the turkey. Don't be afraid to push the stuffing slightly as you go, so there are no air pockets. Truss. Rub the skin of the turkey with the butter and season generously with salt and pepper.

2. Place the turkey breast-side up in the centre of a roasting pan. Add the neck to the pan. Lightly tent the turkey with aluminium foil to prevent the skin from browning before the turkey is fully cooked. Place the roasting pan in the centre of the oven and roast for 30 minutes.

3. Remove the pan from the oven and gently remove the foil. Baste the turkey thoroughly, cover with the foil and return the pan to the oven. Roast for an additional 30 minutes, basting

from time to time. By this time, the skin should be a deep golden colour. Reduce the heat to 190°C/375°F/gas mark 5 and baste again. Remove the foil and roast uncovered until the juices run clear when you pierce a thigh with a skewer, about 30 minutes more.

4. Remove from the oven and immediately season the turkey generously with salt and pepper. Transfer the turkey to a platter, and place it at an angle against the edge of an over-turned plate, with its head down and tail in the air. This heightens the flavour by allowing the juices to flow down through the breast meat. Cover the turkey loosely with foil. Turn off the oven and place the turkey in the oven, with the door ajar. Let it rest for at least 10 minutes or up to 30 minutes. The turkey will continue to cook as it rests.

5. Meanwhile, prepare the sauce: Remove and discard the turkey neck. Place the baking dish over a moderate heat, scraping up any bits that cling to the bottom. Cook for 2 to 3 minutes, scraping and stirring until the liquid is almost caramelised. Do not let it burn. Spoon off and discard excess fat. Add several tablespoons cold water to deglaze (hot water would cloud the sauce), and bring to a boil. Reduce the heat to low and simmer until thickened, about 5 minutes. Taste for seasoning.

6. While the sauce is cooking, carve the turkey and arrange it on a warmed platter. Spoon the stuffing into a warmed serving bowl. Strain the sauce through a fine-mesh sieve, and pour into a gravy boat. Serve immediately with the turkey and stuffing.

At our last Thanksgiving celebration, we sampled a rich white Rhône, the Châteauneuf-du-Pape from Château Beaucastel. The clean, fruity and floral flavours stand up nicely to the rich sausage stuffing.

Menu·Carte

Halloween, Paris Style

○

Toasty Salted Almonds

○

Pumpkin Soup for Halloween

○

Parisian Roast Turkey

○

Pierre Gagnaire's Jerusalem Artichoke Purée

○

Benoît's Carrots with Cumin and Orange

○

The Apple Lady's Apple Cake

○

La Maison du Miel's Heather Honey Ice Cream

Meats

Meats
Les Viandes

Flora's Spicy Spare Ribs
Travers de Cochon Fermier au Miel et Épices

Alsaco's Sauerkraut, Pork and Sausages
La Choucroute Alsaco

Frédéric Anton's Four-Hour Pork Roast
Rôti de Porc de Quatre Heures Frédéric Anton

Le Mauzac's Hanger Steak
Onglet de Boeuf Le Mauzac

Allobroges Braised Lamb Shanks with Garlic
Souris d'Agneau Braisée et Ail Confit

Eric Lecerf's Braised Leg of Lamb
Gigot d'Agneau Braisé Eric Lecerf

Jean-Guy's Basque-Spiced Leg of Lamb
Gigot d'Agneau Basquaise Jean-Guy

Veal Flank Steak Boucherie Duciel
Bavette de Veau Boucherie Duciel

Flora's Spicy Spare Ribs
Travers de Cochon Fermier au Miel et Epices

Frankly, the French are not very creative with spare ribs. In the twenty years that I have been in France, only once was I served them, and that was at Flora Mikula's charming Provençal restaurant Les Olivades. They were unfatty ribs, so meaty, chewy and tender, all bathed in a sweet glistening sauce of honey and spices, so shiny that you wanted to don ice skates and go for a spin! Later, I began researching what happens to all those ribs from French pigs. Then one day a butcher explained that this cut was traditionally reserved for terrines and pâtés. So, if you want ribs in France you need to ask the butcher to save you some the next time he butchers a pig. This recipe has become a favourite around our house. French ribs are moist, not too fatty (but not so lean that you think you are eating cardboard) and, oh, the sauce is a delight. Just enough spice, just enough of that elegant French touch. I love it when American traditions – such as Halloween, Thanksgiving and ribs – are embraced by the French and given a new twist and a French accent. Whenever I prepare these, which is often in the cool autumn and winter months, I always accompany the ribs with Flora's irresistible Polenta Fries (page 108).

SERVES 4

EQUIPMENT:
A large roasting pan

FOR THE SAUCE:
125ml (4½fl oz) honey
60ml (2fl oz) tomato paste
2 tablespoons Thai Curry Paste (page 267) or a commercial variety

2 baby back pork ribs, about 2kg (4lb)
250ml (9fl oz) dry white wine
3 tablespoons freshly squeezed lemon juice

PREHEAT THE OVEN TO
150°C/300°F/GAS MARK 2

1. Prepare the sauce: In a small bowl, combine the honey, tomato paste and curry paste, mixing with a fork to blend.

2. In a roasting pan large enough to hold the meat in a single layer, heat the oil until hot but not smoking. Add the pork ribs and sear – browning well on each side – about 2 minutes per side. With a pastry brush, brush the ribs with about half of the sauce, reserving the remaining sauce to serve at table. Sear for 1 minute more per side. Pour the wine and lemon juice over the ribs. Cover the roasting pan tightly with aluminium foil.

3. Place the roasting pan in the centre of the oven. Cook until the meat is very tender and you can just loosen, or wiggle the bone from the meat with little effort, about 1½ hours. Cut the

ribs into serving portions and serve, passing additional sauce.
These are delicious served with Flora's Polenta Fries (page 108)
as an accompaniment.

In honour of the chef, Flora Mikula, I would serve one of the
up-and-coming wines from her home region of Nimes, such as a Costières de
Nimes. Some good finds include wines from Château de la Tuileries, Mas des
Bressades or Domaine du Vieux Relais.

Les Olivades

41, avenue de Ségur

Paris 7

Telephone: 01 42 83 70 09 Fax: 01 42 73 04 75

Metro: Ségur

WHAT I LEARNED

While spare ribs are traditionally roasted, Flora has the brilliant idea of searing those ribs before roasting. It's
brilliant! In typical French style, the searing adds a dimension to the meat that roasting alone cannot impart.
The searing locks in a depth of flavour and a moistness that makes these ribs memorable.

Alsaco's Sauerkraut, Pork and Sausages
La Choucroute Alsaco

———○———

I admit to having had a passion for both sauerkraut and sausages from an early age. As a child I could easily eat an entire can of sauerkraut at a single sitting. It was, I am sure, the combination of salt and tang of the cured cabbage that pleased my palate. When I lived in New York City, my husband Walter and I even used to make homemade sauerkraut in our Central Park West apartment. As for sausages, well I confess that during my sojourn as a vegetarian, I still craved sausages and occasionally broke with my diet and dug into a plateful of earthy, smoked pork sausages.

This is the quintessential choucroute recipe. Use the finest sausages, pork products and sauerkraut and you and guests will be in for a real treat. Choucroute is a perfect dish for entertaining, for the most difficult part comes in securing the many kinds of smoked and salted pork, as well as sausages. This recipe comes from L'Alsaco, one of my favourite Parisian restaurants specialising in the food of the Alsace region of France. When the outgoing owner-chef Claude Steger shared this recipe with me, he noted, 'This is for ten people, with no first course, and all good eaters, or bons mangeurs!' Well, I have cut his recipe in half and I think that it would still feed an army. Use as many of the meats and sausages as you can find, and be sure to use all the seasonings. The result is crisp and fragrant sauerkraut that has mingled for a good hour with the essence of delicious cured meats, creating a harmonious and surprisingly light and digestible meal. Choucroute has, in fact, become one of our customary Thanksgiving day favourites in Paris. When I prepare this, I use a young (and usually less expensive) Alsatian Riesling wine in cooking and save an older, more mature Riesling for the meal. I might start the meal with a Winter Mesclun Salad (page 53) paired with little Ham and Goat's Cheese Wraps (page 13) as a first course. If you can, use fresh rather than canned sauerkraut. Fresh sauerkraut can usually be found in delicatessens or in the deli section of the supermarket.

———○———

SERVES 5

EQUIPMENT:
One heavy-duty 6-litre (10-pint) pot
with a lid

1. In a heavy-duty pot, combine the fat, onions and a pinch of salt. Sweat – cook, covered, over low heat without colouring until soft and translucent – about 5 minutes. Arrange the salted pork and smoked pork butt on top of the onions. Spoon the

2 tablespoons pork fat or goose fat
2 onions, peeled, halved lengthways
and finely sliced
Fine sea salt to taste
500g (1lb) salted pork
300g (10oz) smoked pork butt,
bone in
1.5kg (3lb) fresh sauerkraut
For the seasoning mix, wrapped in
cloth spice bag or wrapped securely
in cheesecloth:
2 teaspoons whole grains coriander
5 whole cloves
2 teaspoons juniper berries
1 tablespoon whole black peppercorns
1 tablespoon whole cumin seeds
½ head garlic, unpeeled and crushed
1 bottle (75 cl) Alsatian Sylvaner
or Riesling wine
1 litre (1¾ pints) water

....

6 coarse-textured smoked
pork sausages
6 pre-cooked sausages with a fine
texture, such as frankfurters
6 pre-cooked grilling sausages with a
fine texture, such as knockwurst
1 plump coarse-textured smoked pork
sausage, such as kielbasa, cut
lengthways in half

....

Various mustards, for the table

sauerkraut on top. Add the seasoning mix, salt and the wine. Add just enough water to cover (about 1 litre/1¾ pints).Cover and cook at the gentlest simmer over a low heat for 1½ hours. Stir the sauerkraut from time to time to distribute the seasoning.

2. About 10 minutes before the cooking time is over, add the smoked pork sausages and cover. Fill a large saucepan with water and bring just to a boil. Add the frankfurters. Immediately turn off the heat and cover. Let the sausages stand until firm to the touch and heated through, 10 to 15 minutes. In a large, dry, non-stick frying-pan over medium heat, lightly pan-fry the grilling sausage and the pork sausage until brown, shaking the pan from time to time so they cook evenly, 7 to 10 minutes total.

4. With a large, slotted spoon transfer the sauerkraut to several large, warmed serving platters. Cut the meats into serving pieces. Halve or quarter the sausages. Arrange the meats and sausages all around. Serve with a selection of mustards.

> Do not dare drink anything other than an Alsatian Grand Cru Riesling from Alsace. With a truly brilliant balance of sweet and acid, and a touch of dryness, the wine totally rounds out the complex salty, smoky, acid flavours of the sauerkraut, sausages and meats. I enjoy this with a Riesling from Ostertag, Vignoble d'Epfig.

CHEF STEGER SAYS:
❝ *Sauerkraut must always remain just lightly crunchy. Too cooked, and it is indigestible.* ❞

Alsaco

10, rue Condorcet

Paris 9

Telephone: 01 45 26 44 31

Métro: Poissonière

Frédéric Anton's Four-Hour Pork Roast
Rôti de Porc de Quatre Heures Frédéric Anton

———○———

For the past several years, braised meats have become increasingly popular among Parisian chefs. Rare lamb, rosy pork and duck with a touch of pink all have their place, but the homey, wholesome flavours of meat and poultry cooked until meltingly tender and falling off the bone are once again in vogue. Here Frédéric Anton, chef at the romantic restaurant Pré Catelan in the Bois de Boulogne, offers a universally appealing whole roasted pork loin, flavoured simply with mountain thyme.

SERVES 8 TO 10

EQUIPMENT:
One 6-litre (10-pint) heavy-duty covered casserole

4 tablespoons extra-virgin olive oil
A 2kg (4lb) loin pork roast, bone-in (do not trim off fat)
Sea salt
Freshly ground white pepper to taste
2 teaspoons fresh or dried thyme leaves
45g (1½oz) unsalted butter
2 carrots, peeled and finely chopped
2 onions, peeled and finely chopped
6 plump, fresh cloves garlic, peeled and chopped
2 stalks celery, finely chopped
500ml (18fl oz) Homemade Chicken Stock (page 274)
2 large bouquets of fresh thyme

PREHEAT THE OVEN TO
140°C/275°F/GAS MARK 1

1. Season the pork all over with salt, pepper and thyme. In a large, heavy-duty casserole that will hold the pork snugly, heat the oil over moderate heat until hot but not smoking. Add the pork and sear well on all sides, about 10 minutes total. Transfer the pork to a platter and discard the fat in the casserole. Wipe the casserole clean with kitchen towel. Return the pork to the casserole, bone side down. Set aside.

2. In a large, heavy-duty frying-pan, combine the butter, carrots, onions, garlic, celery and season with salt. Sweat – cook, covered, over low heat without colouring until the vegetables are soft and cooked through – about 10 minutes. Spoon the vegetables around and on top of the pork. Add the chicken stock to the casserole. Add the large bouquets of thyme. Cover.

3. Place the casserole in the centre of the oven and braise, basting about every 30 minutes, for about 4 hours, or until the pork is just about falling off the bone. Remove the casserole from the oven. Carefully transfer the meat to a carving board and season it generously with salt and pepper. Cover loosely with foil and set aside to rest for about 15 minutes.

4. While the pork is resting, strain the cooking juices through a fine-mesh sieve into a gravy boat, pouring off the fat that rises to the top. Discard the vegetables and herbs. The pork will be very soft and falling off the bone, so you may not actually be able to slice it. Rather, with a fork and spoon tear the meat into serving pieces and place on warmed dinner plates or a warmed platter. Spoon the juices over the meat.

5. Serve, accompanied by Brussels sprouts, sautéed mushrooms or a potato gratin.

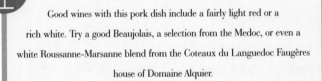

Good wines with this pork dish include a fairly light red or a rich white. Try a good Beaujolais, a selection from the Medoc, or even a white Roussanne-Marsanne blend from the Coteaux du Languedoc Faugères house of Domaine Alquier.

Le Pré Catelan

Route de Suresnes

Bois de Boulogne

Paris 16

Telephone: 01 44 14 41 14 Fax: 01 45 24 43 25

Métro: Porte-Dauphine

Le Mauzac's Hanger Steak
Onglet de Boeuf Le Mauzac

Le Mauzac is a lively lunchtime café/wine bar tucked along a romantic, tree-lined street in the busy Left Bank Latin Quarter. Their onglet – flank or hanger steak – is one of the best I've ever sampled. Following tradition, the quickly pan-seared meat is served with a mound of golden, delicious French-fried potatoes. Although restaurants do not usually offer lemon with steak, I prefer it this way and always ask for a few wedges of fresh lemon to squeeze over the beef. Note that in cooking the meat, I do not salt in the beginning, only at the end. I feel that salting in the beginning draws out too many of the delicious juices we want to save. But salted at the end helps give the meat a fine, seasoned flavour.

SERVES 4

1 tablespoon extra-virgin olive oil
750g (1½lb) beef hanger or flank steak, butterflied, about 1.25cm (½in) thick
Fine sea salt
Freshly ground black pepper to taste
Wedges of sliced, fresh lemon to garnish (optional)

1. Massage a little bit of the oil into the steak, and lightly season both sides with pepper. If you do not have a frying-pan large enough to hold the steak, cut it crosswise into two to fit.

2. Heat a large, dry, non-stick frying-pan over a high heat for about 1 minute. When the pan is very hot, sear the steak quickly on both sides, 1 to 2 minutes a side for medium-rare, longer for medium.

3. Remove the steak to a platter. Pour any juices from the pan over the meat. Season generously with fine sea salt. Let the meat rest for 5 minutes (to allow the juices to retreat back into the beef) before carving across the grain. Serve immediately, with a few drops of freshly squeezed lemon juice, if desired.

An unusual wine worth sampling at Le Mauzac is a little known Gaillac from France's southwest: Domaine Robert Plageoles syrah, a young delight that goes so well with the wine bar's meaty fare.

ONGLET: A BISTROT STAR

Onglet – flank or hanger steak – is one of the stars of bistro cooking. It is tender and beefy, and needs nothing more than salt, pepper and a touch of lemon juice to bring out its succulent brilliance. Always cooked to medium rare (rare is too chewy), this thin, narrow and boneless cut of meat comes from what butchers call 'the hanging tender' because it literally hangs down below the ribs, an extension of the tenderloin. In France, it is known as la piece de boucher, or 'the butcher's piece', because there is only one hanging tender, weighing about 1.5kg (3lb) for each steer. Since there wasn't a lot to go around, the butcher traditionally took it home to serve to his family. The meat is prized for its chewy tenderness, silken texture, and rich meaty flavour. Butchers generally butterfly the meat, cutting it horizontally through the middle to create a large piece, ideal for quickly pan-searing or outdoor grilling.

Le Mauzac

7, rue de l'Abeé de l'Epée

Paris 5

Telephone: 01 46 33 75 22

Métro: RER Luxembourg

Allobroges Braised Lamb Shanks with Garlic
Souris d'Agneau Braisée et Ail Confit

———○———

Olivier Pateyron and his wife Annette are an energetic pair, running a lovely small restaurant – Les Allobroges – hidden at the edge of town. Such sublime and simple fare as roasted Bresse chicken with a potato gratin and these meaty lamb shanks, flanked by whole cloves of garlic, can usually be found on the brief menu. I sampled these tender shanks on my first visit years ago, and keep coming back for more. Chef Pateyron first roasts the shanks, then braises them in a mixture of sweet Banyuls wine from France's southwest, and a touch of veal stock. The result is meat with a glistening mahogany colour and a thick, voluptuously shiny dark sauce. Serve with the chef's brilliant version of Garlic Confit (page 270).

———○———

SERVES 4

EQUIPMENT:
One 6-litre (10-pint) roasting pan with a lid

4 meaty lamb shanks (each about 500g/1lb), do not trim the external fat
4 teaspoons Quatre Épices (page 271)
Sea salt
Freshly ground white pepper to taste
250ml (9fl oz) Banyuls wine, vin doux naturel from Provence, or Port
1 litre (1¾ pints) Homemade Chicken Stock (page 274)
Garlic Confit (page 270)

PREHEAT THE OVEN TO 230°C/450°F/GAS MARK 8.

1. Rub the Quatre Épices all over the surface of the lamb shanks. Season with salt and pepper.

2. Stand the shanks, wider side down, narrow end up, in the roasting pan. Place in the centre of the oven and roast, uncovered, for 1 hour.

3. Transfer the lamb to a platter and set aside. Off the heat, deglaze the pan with the wine, scraping up any cooked bits that may have stuck to the bottom. Return the lamb to the pan. Add the stock. Cover. Return to the oven and braise – without intervening – until the meat is very tender and just beginning to fall off the bone, about 90 minutes.

4. Remove the pan from the oven and transfer the lamb shanks to a warmed platter. Cover them with foil and let rest for 10 minutes. Strain the sauce from the pan through a fine-mesh sieve. Serve, passing the sauce and Garlic Confit.

This simple, meaty dish calls out for one of your best reds. My first choice would be a Cairanne from wine-maker Marcel Richaud or a Gigondas from wine-maker Jean-Pierre Cartier at Domaine les Gouberts. Alternatively, try one of the new and upcoming wines from the Languedoc-Roussillon, such as a Corbières or Minervois.

OLIVER SAYS:

66 Do not trim the fat the lamb shanks! The fat forms a sort of girdle, holding the lamb shanks together, and also adding flavour, colour and body to the final sauce 99

NOTE

Lamb shanks – which the French call a souris – are the shin portion of the legs. The fore shanks are the meatiest and the easiest to find since the rear shanks are usually sold attached to the whole leg of lamb. The shank contains a good deal of connective tissue that produces a smooth, luxurious sauce when cooked by the very slow and moist heat of a braise.

Les Allobroges

71, rue des Grandes-Champs

Paris 20

Telephone: 01 43 73 40 00

Métro: Maraîchers

THE ULTIMATE COOKING WINE

Banuyls, a sweet fortified wine from the Pyrénées in France's southwest, is a powerful wine usually made from at least 75 percent Grenache grapes and aged for two years. It is a distant relation of port. The best ones bear the name Rancio, and come from the Domaine la Rectoire and du Mas Blanc. In Provence, one also finds some excellent vins doux naturels that are great for cooking. My favourites include the 16-degree alcohol red vin doux naturel from the cave co-operative in Rasteau, or the pure-Grenache Rasteau Rancio from Domaine Bressy Masson.

Eric Lecerf's Braised Leg of Lamb
Gigot d'Agneau Braisé Eric Lecerf

Sometimes I think that lamb is there just to be teamed up with the vibrant spices of coriander, cumin and curry. Here Eric Lecerf – a Joël Robuchon protégé and chef at the always satisfying restaurant Astor on the Right Bank – presents one of his most popular dishes, a leg of lamb that is braised ever so slowly in the oven until it is cooked to a welcome, melting tenderness. Typical of many modern Parisian dishes, this one reveals a contemporary French love-affair with a myriad of spices, as well as a return to old-fashioned dishes cooked slowly for a good, long time. I like to serve this with seasonal winter or early spring vegetables, such as a mixture of carrots, leeks, shallots and potatoes.

SERVES 6

EQUIPMENT:
One heavy-duty casserole, with cover,
large enough to hold the lamb

1 leg of lamb (about 2.2kg/5lb)

HERBS AND SPICES:
1 teaspoon coriander grains, ground
1 teaspoon whole ground coriander
3 teaspoons whole cumin seeds
1½ teaspoons cumin seeds, ground
2 teaspoons Curry Powder (page 268)
2 teaspoons fine sea salt
1 teaspoons coarsely ground
white pepper
4 teaspoons fresh thyme leaves
2 teaspoons chopped fresh
rosemary leaves
4 cloves garlic, peeled and
finely chopped
375ml (13½fl oz) Homemade Chicken
Stock (page 274)
4 tablespoons extra-virgin olive oil

1. In a small bowl, combine all the herbs and spices. Rub them all over the surface of the lamb. In a cast iron casserole just large enough to hold the lamb, heat the oil over moderate heat until hot but not smoking. Add the lamb and brown lightly on all sides, about 5 minutes total. Do not let the spices burn. Pour the stock around the lamb. Cover all with a piece of parchment paper. The paper will serve as a moisture tent, to keep the meat from drying out as it cooks.

2. Cover the casserole and place in the centre of the oven, braising until the meat is very tender, about 2 hours. Check the meat from time to time, basting every 30 minutes to prevent the meat from drying out.

3. Remove the casserole from the oven. Carefully remove the lamb from the casserole, carve into serving pieces, and keep warm on a serving platter.

Fine sea salt
Freshly ground black pepper to taste

PREHEAT THE OVEN TO
130ºC/250ºF/GAS MARK 1.

4. Strain the sauce through a fine-mesh sieve and into a bowl. Place the sauce in the refrigerator for about 30 minutes to allow the fat to rise to the top and firm up. Remove and discard the fat. Warm the sauce and transfer to a sauce boat. Serve with seasonal winter or early spring vegetables.

With all these spices, you need a bold red, such as Michele Laurent's velvety red Côtes-du-Rhône Domaine Gramenon, Cuvée Pascal.

The Restaurant de L'Astor

11, rue Astor

Paris 8

Telephone: 01 53 05 05 20 Fax: 01 53 05 05 30

Métro: Saint-Augustin

Jean-Guy's Basque-Spiced Leg of Lamb
Gigot d'Agneau Basquaise Jean-Guy

Jean-Guy Lousteau's heart-warming Right Bank bistro Au Bascou offers some of Paris' most unusual, hearty and delicious regional fare. Lousteau, a Basque native, receives weekly shipments of the area's finest produce, and serves it all with flair in this tiny café-bistro. This is one of my favourite dishes, prepared with the tiniest of baby lamb – weighing less than 1kg (2lb) – so tender, so flavourful. The same dish can, of course, be prepared with a larger leg of lamb.

SERVES 12

EQUIPMENT:
A roasting pan with a rack;
an instant-read thermometer

FOR THE PASTE:
40g (1½oz) coarse-grain Dijon mustard
65g (2oz) sheep's milk full-fat yoghurt
1 teaspoon finely ground dried red chilli peppers
2 teaspoons fresh or dried thyme leaves

1 whole bone-in leg of lamb (3.5 to 4kg/7 to 8lb), preferably with hip bone removed and excess fat and membrane trimmed
Several heads of plump, fresh garlic heads, halved crosswise but not peeled
Several fresh or dried bay leaves
Several springs of fresh thyme
Sea salt
Freshly ground white pepper to taste

PREHEAT THE OVEN TO 230°C/450°F/GAS MARK 8.

1. In a small bowl, combine the mustard, yoghurt, a half teaspoon hot red pepper and 1 teaspoon thyme. Stir to blend. Set aside.

2. Place the lamb on a rack in the roasting pan. Brush all over with the mustard and pepper paste. Sprinkle with the remaining pepper and thyme. Surround the lamb with reserved bones and trimmings, garlic and herbs. Add about 125ml (4½ fl oz) cold water to keep the trimmings from burning as the lamb roasts.

3. Place in the centre of the oven and roast, turning the lamb once, until an instant-read thermometer inserted into the thickest part of the meat reads 50°C/125°F for medium-rare or 60°C/140°F for medium. Allow 9 minutes per 500g (1lb) for lamb weighing under 2.5kg (5lb) and 10 to 12 minutes per 500g (1lb) for larger legs of lamb.

4. Remove from the oven and season generously with salt and pepper. Transfer the lamb to a platter, and place on an angle against the edge of an overturned plate. Cover loosely with foil.

Turn off the oven and place the platter in the oven, with the door open. Let rest a minimum of 10 minutes and up to 30 minutes. The lamb will continue to cook during this resting time.

5. Meanwhile, prepare the sauce: Place the pan over moderate heat and, with a spatula, scrape up any bits that cling to the bottom. Cook for 2 to 3 minutes, scraping and stirring until the liquid is almost caramelised. Do not let it burn. Spoon off and discard any excess fat. Add several tablespoons cold water to deglaze (hot water will cloud the sauce). Bring to a boil. Reduce the heat to low and simmer until thickened, about 5 minutes.

6. While the sauce is cooking, carve the lamb and place on a warmed platter. Strain the sauce through a fine-mesh sieve and pour into a sauce boat. Serve immediately, with the lamb.

> Jean-Guy would serve this with a good Basque red, such as Domaine Brana's Irouléguy, a wine made from a blend of cabernet franc, cabernet sauvignon and tannat grapes.

Au Bascou

38, rue Réamu

Paris 3

Telephone: 01 42 72 69 25

Métro: Arts et Métiers

Veal Flank Steak Boucherie Duciel
Bavette de Veau Boucherie Duciel

———○———

I walked into one of my neighbourhood butcher's one autumn evening in search of a nice tender and juicy onglet, *a quick-cooking cut of beef known as hanger steak or flank steak. The butcher had none, but suggested a* bavette de veau *instead, an equally muscular, fine-grained and very thin, flat, boneless cut of veal that the butcher splits open like a book, trims and scores. He also gave me the recipe. The meat pan-sears in a flash and, as he suggested, it's chewy but amazingly succulent, moist, fragrant and juicy. It quickly became of our favourite 'little time to cook tonight' dinners. Although the veal cooks quickly, do not try to rush it by cooking over high heat, or the meat will toughen.*

———○———

SERVES 4

4 pieces veal flank, skirt or hanger steak (bavette, each weighing about 250g/8oz), split open, trimmed and scored (ask your butcher to do this for you)
60g (2oz) unsalted butter
Sea salt
Freshly ground black pepper to taste
60ml (2fl oz) double cream

1. In two large frying-pans large enough to hold two steaks each, heat 2 tablespoons of butter over moderate heat until hot but not smoking. Very lightly season the veal with salt and pepper and sear gently for 4 to 5 minutes on each side. The meat should be cooked through but still tender.

2. Remove the veal to a warm platter. Deglaze each pan with 2 tablespoons of cream and pour over the steaks. Season with pepper and let the meat rest for 5 minutes before carving across the grain and serving.

This dish calls for a young red, such as one of my favourite cru Beaujolais, Moulin à Vent.

THE FRENCH BUTCHER

When I first moved to France I couldn't figure out why anyone would want to be a butcher. I understood one's love of working with sparkling fresh fish or first-of-season vegetables and fruits. But all that blood and huge animals to deal with? Well, I slowly learned the role that the butcher plays in a French woman's life. There's the way a butcher hands over a simple chicken wrapped in waxed paper, slips it into a bag and says with a wink and a certain sense of masculine assurance: 'One hour in a very hot oven. No more no less.' Women melt! I can't tell you how many times I have gone into a French butcher shop for a chicken or a rabbit and come home with two, planning to execute the recipe I had in mind, as well as the one delivered to me verbally as I scribbled on the back of an old envelope. French butchers are more than tradesmen, they are cookbook authors, seducers and philosophers, great men to have in a lady's life!

Boucherie Pascal Duciel

96, rue de Courcelles

Paris 17

Telephone: 01 47 63 40 97

Métro: Courcelles

Menu·Carte

Summer on the Seine

———o———

The Market Gardener's Courgette and
Curry Soup

———o———

The Bistrot du Dôme's Clams with Fresh Thyme

———o———

Rye Crackers and Camembert

———o———

Raspberry Pride

Desserts

Desserts
Les Desserts

The Apple Lady's Apple Cake
Gâteau aux Pommes

Benoît's Upside-Down Caramelised
Apple Tart
Tarte Tatin

Carton's Ultra-Thin Apple Tart
Tarte Fine aux Pommes

Bonbonnerie de Buci's Fresh Lemon
Juice Tart
Tarte au Jus Frais de Citron Pressé

Flaky Pastry
Pâte Brisée

Strawberry-Orange Soup with
Candied Lemon Peel
Soupe de Fraises à l'Orange, Zestes de
Citron

Rue Poncelet's Cherries in Sweet
Red Wine
Cerises au Vin Rouge Rue Poncelet

Cherry-Almond Gratin
Gratin aux Cerises et aux Amandes

Raspberry Pride
Tarte aux Framboises et Vanille

Fresh Fig and Almond Gratin
Gratin des Figues et Amandes

Fig Compote with Lavender Honey
Figues Chaudes au Miel de Lavandre

Fresh Raspberry Sauce
Coulis de Framboise

Honey-Poached Pears in Beaumes
de Venise
Poire Vigneronne aux Muscat de
Beaumes de Venise

La Maison du Chocolat's
Bittersweet Chocolate Mousse
Mousse au Chocolat La Maison du Chocolat

Joël Robuchon's Burnt Cream
Joël Robuchon's Crème Brûlée

'The Heart of Paris'
Coeur à la Crème

The Astor's Vanilla Custard Tarts
Petit Pots de Crème à la Vanille L'Astor

Blood Orange Ice Cream
Glace aux Oranges Sanguine

Almond Ice Cream
Glace aux Amandes

Alléosse Fromage Blanc Ice Cream
Glace au Fromage Blanc Fromagerie Alléosse

Maison du Miel Heather Honey Ice Cream
Glace au Miel de Bruyère Maison du Miel

Fresh Honey-Rosemary-Ginger Ice Cream
Crème Glace aux Gingembre et Romarin

Fresh Truffle Ice Cream
Glaces aux Truffes Fraîches

Truffle Panna Cotta
Crème de Truffes

Miniature Lemon Tea Cakes
Mini Madeleines

Chocolate Financiers
Financiers au Chocolat

Jean-Luc Poujauran's Shortbread Cookies
Les Sablées aux Amandes de Jean-Luc

The Apple Lady's Apple Cake
Gâteau aux Pommes

———○———

Come autumn, I begin making weekly pilgrimages to the farmer's market that rolls out along the Avenue de Breteuil, in the shadow of the Eiffel Tower. There, I seek out Evelyne Nochet and her stand from her family orchard, Le Nouveau Verger, and we talk apples. What's best for the Tarte Tatin? What's the best eating apple? When will the famed Saint Germain be ready for the apple cake? For months I begged her for her favourite apple recipe, and finally, one chilly day in November, her neat, handwritten apple cake recipe appeared on my doorstep. This is the sort of homey recipe that makes French home cooking incomparable. When you make this cake, you will be surprised by the small amount of batter and the quantity of apples. In effect, this is more of a crustless pie, in that the batter is just there to hold the apples together. What I love most about this recipe is that it allows the full flavour of the apple to shine through. I prefer a more acidic cooking apple, such as Cox's Orange Pippin or the French variety of Boskoop or Reine de Reinettes. Other good varieties include McIntosh, Cortland, Gala or Gravenstein. And if you tend towards sweeter cooking apples – Golden Delicious or Jonagold – use those. I find that this is one cake that tastes just as good the second day, should there be any left over.

———○———

SERVES 8

EQUIPMENT:
One 23cm- (9in-) springform pan

Unsalted butter and flour for preparing baking pan
70g (2½oz) plain flour
65g (2oz) sugar
1 tablespoon baking powder
⅛ teaspoon fine sea salt
½ teaspoon pure vanilla extract
2 large eggs, lightly beaten
2 tablespoons vegetable oil
80ml (3fl oz) whole milk

1. Butter the pan and set aside.

2. In a large bowl, combine the flour, sugar, baking powder and salt, and stir to blend. Add the vanilla extract, eggs, oil and milk, and stir until well-blended. Add the apples and stir to thoroughly coat the apples with the batter.

3. Spoon the mixture into the prepared cake pan. Place the pan in the centre of the oven and bake until fairly firm and golden, about 25 minutes.

4. Meanwhile, in a small bowl, combine the sugar, egg and

4 baking apples (about 1kg/2lb), cored, peeled and cut into 16ths

FOR THE TOPPING:
65g (2oz) sugar
1 large egg, lightly beaten
45g (1½oz) unsalted butter, melted

PREHEAT THE OVEN TO
200°C/400°F/GAS MARK 6.

butter for the topping and stir to blend. Set aside.

5. Once the cake has baked for 25 minutes, remove it from the oven, and pour the sugar mixture on top of the cake. Return the cake to the oven and bake until the top is a deep golden brown and the cake feels quite firm when pressed with a fingertip, about 10 minutes more, for a total baking time of 35 minutes.

6. Remove to a rack to cool. After 10 minutes, run a knife along the sides of the pan. Release and remove the side of the springform pan, leaving the cake on the pan base. Serve at room temperature, cutting into thin wedges. This is delicious with Heather Honey Ice Cream (page 246).

I adore wine with dessert, and love to serve a good German, Austrian, or Hungarian white or a lovely wine from the Loire, such as a sweet Bonnezeau, Château de Fesles.

Le Nouveau Verger Pommes et Poires de Touraine

Marché Breteuil, Avenue de Saxe

From avenue de Ségur to place de Breteuil

Paris 7

Thursday and Saturday mornings

Métro: Ségur

Benoît's Upside-Down Caramelised Apple Tart
Tarte Tatin

---○---

Each year in France high achievers in all of the nation's trades – from hairdressers to chefs to florists – compete for the top honour of 'Meilleur Ouvrier de France'. When chef Benoît Guichard of Jamin competed, he was placed first in the pastry category, outdistancing even famous pastry chefs vying for the MOF title. Come autumn, I make this tart every single chance I get. I love it so much that I make it for my birthday in November, in lieu of a cake!

---○---

SERVES 8

EQUIPMENT:
One 23cm- (9in-) Tarte Tatin pan or cast iron frying-pan

150g (5oz) sugar
150g (5oz) unsalted butter, cut into thin slices
1 teaspoon pure vanilla extract
1.5kg (3lb) large apples (about 8, peeled, cored and halved lengthways; see note)
One recipe Flaky Pastry (page 225), rolled into an 25cm- (10in-) round, placed on parchment paper and refrigerated
Crème fraîche or whipped double cream, to garnish

1. Spread the sugar evenly over the bottom of a Tarte Tatin pan (or use a heavy cast-iron or other ovenproof frying-pan). Place the butter slices evenly over the sugar. Drizzle with vanilla extract. Beginning at the outside edge of the pan, stand the apple halves on end on top of the butter: They should all face in one direction with the rounded edge of the apple against the edge of the pan and the cut halves towards the centre. Pack the apples as closely together as possible. Make a second identical circle of apple halves inside the first. Place one apple half in the centre of the circle to fill any remaining space. Note that the apples will shrink as they cook and give up their juices. Try to remember that when you turn out the tart, you want to see the nice rounded halves of apple.

2. Place the frying-pan over a low heat and cook the apples in the butter and sugar, uncovered, until the butter/sugar mixture turns a thick, golden brown and just begins to caramelise, about 1 hour. The liquid should remain at a gentle bubble. Baste the apples from time to time to speed up cooking time and to make for evenly cooked fruit. (If the apples seem to lose their place, you can carefully nudge them back into formation.)

3. Preheat the oven to 220ºC/425ºF/gas mark 7.

4. Place the Tatin pan or frying-pan on a baking sheet. Remove the pastry from the refrigerator and place it on top of the apples, gently pushing the edges of the pastry down around the edge of the pan. Place in the oven and bake until the pastry is golden, 25 to 30 minutes. Do not be concerned if the juices bubble over. This is normal.

5. Remove the tart from the oven. Immediately invert a serving platter with a lip over the frying-pan. Quickly but carefully invert the tart on top of the serving platter so that the apples are on top and the pastry is on the bottom. Should any apples stick to the bottom of the pan, remove them and place them back into the tart. Serve warm or at room temperature, with dollops of crème fraîche or whipped double cream.

An apple tart calls out for a sweet white, such as a honey-like and unctuous German Auslese or an intense Beerenauslese; a sweet Austrian Ausbruch; or a liquorous sweet Hungarian Tokay.

NOTE

Recommended varieties of apples for a Tarte Tatin include: Fuji, Criterion, Winesap, Northern Spies, Jonagold; France: Cox's Orange Pippin, Reine de Reinette, Boskoop.

WHAT I LEARNED

I have made this tart dozens of times and it took me a while to learn one thing: find one or two apple varieties you love and stick with them; there will be fewer surprises. And only make this in season, meaning when apples are at their peak in the early autumn to late winter. If you use older, softer apples, they are like to fall apart and turn into apple sauce.

Jamin

32, rue de Longchamp Paris 16

Telephone: 01 45 53 00 07 Fax: 01 45 53 00 15

Metro: Trocadéro

Carton's Ultra-Thin Apple Tart

Tarte Fine aux Pommes

———○———

Right around the corner from my office is the excellent pastry shop, Carton, on the bustling Rue de Buci on the Left Bank. There are days when this very thin tart calls out to me, satisfying my need for just a gentle touch of sugar punctuated by a nice note of fruit. This is a quick, easy tart that can be prepared in minutes. Keep prepared pastry shells on hand in the freezer.

———○———

SERVES 6

EQUIPMENT:
An apple corer; a mandolin, electric slicer, or very sharp knife

One 23cm- (9in-) flat, rimless pastry shell (page 226)
2 cooking apples
60g (2oz) unsalted butter, melted
2 tablespoons granulated sugar
Icing sugar, to garnish

PREHEAT THE OVEN TO
220°C/425°F/GAS MARK 7.

1. Trim and discard a very thin slice of apple at both the stem and bottom end. This makes the apple easier to peel, and creates more uniform slices. Peel and core the apple. Using a mandolin, electric slicer, or very sharp knife, slice the apples crosswise into paper-thin rings. With a cookie cutter, cut out one 3cm (1½ in) circle that will be used to decorate the centre of the tart.

2. Arrange the apple slices on the tart shell: Beginning on the outside edge of the shell, arrange a single apple slice. Overlap with a second slice, just covering the hole in the centre of the first slice with the second slice. Continue in this manner until the apple slices have formed a ring along the outside edge of the shell. Brush the ring of apples with melted butter. Continue with the second, inside ring, slightly overlapping the apples on the outside edge, as well as the hole in the centre of the apples in this ring. Brush this ring with butter. Place 2 or 3 overlapping slices in the centre, again covering the hole in the centre of the slices; brush with melted butter. Place the decorative circle of apple in the centre; brush with butter. Sprinkle evenly with granulated sugar.

3. Place the prepared tart on a baking sheet. Place the baking sheet in the centre of the oven and bake for 5 minutes. Remove from the oven and brush with butter and dust with sugar. Return to the oven for 10 minutes more. Remove from the oven and brush with butter and dust with icing sugar. Return to the oven for 10 minutes more. This delicate tart is best served ever so slightly warm or at room temperature. Any leftover tart may be covered with plastic wrap and refrigerated but it will not have that just-baked flavour or freshness.

This is particularly delicious with a sweet wine or semi-sweet white wine such as an Anjou-Coteaux de la Loire, a young Sauternes, or a sweet German, Austrian or Hungarian wine.

Jean-Pierre Carton

6, rue de Buci

Paris 6

Telephone: 01 43 26 04 13

Métro: Mabillon

Bonbonnerie de Buci's Fresh Lemon Juice Tart
Tarte au Jus Frais de Citron Pressé

———○———

The French love specifics, especially when it comes to food. When a pastry shop window – La Bonbonnerie de Buci on the famed market street – advertised that their tart was made with freshly squeezed lemon juice (as opposed the sort that comes in a bottle) I had to giggle over the precision. And I had to have one. This is the puckery sort of tart made for those of us who love the acidic punch of a very pungent lemon tart.

———○———

SERVES 8

One 23cm- (9in-) sweet pastry shell,
pre-baked (page 226)
4 large eggs
200g (7oz) sugar
160ml (6fl oz) freshly squeezed
lemon juice (from 2 or 3 lemons)
125ml (4½fl oz) crème fraîche
or double cream

PREHEAT THE OVEN TO
175ºC/350ºF/GAS MARK 4.

1. In a large mixing bowl, whisk the eggs to blend. Add the sugar and whisk until just combined. Add the lemon juice and cream and whisk until just combined. Strain the mixture through a fine-mesh sieve. Pour it into the prepared pastry shell.

2. Place in the centre of the oven and bake until the filling is set, 25 to 30 minutes. Remove from the oven and transfer to a rack to cool. Serve at room temperature.

WHAT I LEARNED

For more refined flavour, it is often a good idea to strain a raw egg mixture. Eggs often contain little particles that could affect the texture and appearance of the final product.

La Bonbonnerie de Buci

12, rue de Buci

Paris 6

Telephone: 01 43 26 97 13

Métro: Mabillon

Flaky Pastry
Pâte Brisée

———○———

This is my tried and true classic pastry recipe, the one I've been using in my Paris kitchens for more than twenty years. It is easy as – can one say it – 'pie'. I find that once a cook is confident with pastry making, he or she is ready to tackle just about anything. For great pastry, you need chilled ingredients and must work swiftly, without hesitation. Here I offer three ways to deal with the pastry: as two pre-baked tart shells; as flat pastry for two rimless tarts; and as pastry for a single Upside-Down Caramelised Apple Tart (page 220).

———○———

140g (5oz) unbleached, plain flour
⅛ teaspoon fine sea salt
120g (4oz) unsalted butter, chilled and cut into cubes
3 tablespoons iced water

1. Place the flour and salt in the bowl of a food processor and process to blend. Add the butter and process until well-blended, about 10 seconds. With the machine running, add the water and process just until the mixture begins to form a ball, about 10 seconds more. Transfer to a clean work surface and, with a dough scraper, smear it bit by bit across the work surface until the dough is smooth and the flour and butter well blended. Form into a flattened round, cover with plastic wrap, and refrigerate for at least 1 hour and up to 24 hours.

FOR 2 PRE-BAKED 23CM-
(9IN-) SHELLS

EQUIPMENT:
Two 23cm- (9in-) fluted tart pans with removable bottoms; a baking sheet for each tart shell

2. Divide the dough in half. Roll one half into a 25cm- (11in-) round. Fold the dough in half and, without stretching it, lift it up at the edges so that it naturally falls into the rim of the pan. Unfold the dough. With your fingertips, very delicately coax the dough into the rim. There should be a generous 2.5cm (1in) overhang: Allow it to drape naturally over the edge of the pan. Generously prick the dough lining the bottom of the tart pan. Cover loosely with aluminium foil. Freeze for at least 1 hour or up to 24 hours. Repeat with the remaining half.

3. Preheat the oven to 200°C/400°F/gas mark 6.

4. Remove the tart shells from the freezer. Unwrap and place each on a baking sheet. (Do not ignore this step or there will be bits of pastry on your oven floor.)

5. Bake until lightly and evenly browned, about 25 minutes. Remove from the oven and with a rolling pin, carefully roll over the tart to trim off the overhanging pastry and create a smooth, well-trimmed shell. Discard the overhanging pastry. Watch carefully: ovens vary tremendously and the pastry may brown both unevenly and quickly. Cool for at least 10 minutes (or up to several hours) before filling.

FOR TWO 23CM-(9IN-)
RIMLESS TARTS

EQUIPMENT:
A baking sheet for each tart

Divide the dough in half. Roll one half into a 23cm- (9in-) round. Place the rolled dough on a baking sheet and freeze for at least 1 hour or up to 24 hours. Repeat with the remaining half.

FOR ONE 23CM-(9IN-)
TARTE TATIN

EQUIPMENT:
Wax paper or baking parchment;
a baking sheet

Roll the dough into a 25cm- (10in-) round. Place it on a piece of parchment or wax paper. Refrigerate for at least 1 hour and up to 24 hours.

Strawberry-Orange Soup with Candied Lemon Peel
Soupe de Fraises à l'Orange, Zestes de Citron

———◇———

All it takes is an intelligent combination of fresh ingredients to create a dish with a pleasingly sophisticated dimension. The sweet, fruity flavour of strawberries reach another realm, enlivened by a touch of vinegar, sweetened with the intensity of freshly squeezed orange juice, and brought to a crescendo with a touch of zesty, candied lemon peel. There are just a few days in March when there are still blood oranges in the market and the first of season strawberries make their debut. That's when this dessert is at its peak. The rest of the year, make this dish with the best juice oranges you can find.

———◇———

SERVES 6

500g (1lb) strawberries, rinsed, stemmed, quartered lengthways
1 tablespoon best-quality vinegar (red wine, sherry wine or balsamic)
50g (2oz) sugar

FOR THE CANDIED LEMON ZEST:
Zest of 1 scrubbed lemon, cut into fine julienne
50g (2oz) sugar
400ml (14fl oz) freshly squeezed blood orange juice (about 5 oranges), or the juice of top-quality juice oranges

CHEF'S SECRET

Chef Emmanuel Leblay says:
To blanch lemon zest, combine the zest and cold water, bringing it just to a boil, then draining.

1. In a large bowl, combine the strawberries, vinegar and sugar. Stir gently. Cover securely with plastic wrap and refrigerate for 1 hour.

2. Blanch the lemon zest: Place the zest in a medium-sized saucepan, add 250ml (9fl oz) cold water and bring to a rolling boil over high heat. Remove from the heat. Drain the zest into a small, fine-mesh sieve. Rinse with cold water. Drain. Set aside.

3. In a small saucepan, combine the blanched and refreshed lemon zest, sugar and 60ml (2fl oz) of water and stir to dissolve the sugar. Bring to a simmer over a very low heat and cook until the zest is transparent and a thin veil of syrup remains, 8 to 10 minutes. Remove from the heat and let the zest cool in the liquid.

At serving time, add the orange juice to the strawberry mixture. Mix gently. To serve, pour the strawberry soup into shallow, individual serving bowls or champagne coupes. Garnish with the candied lemon zest and serve, accompanied by small cookies or cakes, such as financiers or madeleines.

Rue Poncelet's Cherries in Sweet Red Wine
Cerises au Vin Rouge Rue Poncelet

———◦———

The French have a saying: 'Eat peas with the rich and cherries with the poor.' In other words, the best peas are the season's first (and most expensive), the sweetest cherries the season's last (and least expensive). Come May, the Paris markets are a flood of red, with mounds and mounds of sweet red fruits. This is a favourite way to prepare the season's fruit. I prepare this with a French vin doux naturel, usually one from the co-operative in the Provençal village of Rasteau.

———◦———

SERVES 6 TO 8

EQUIPMENT
One flat-bottomed, 6-litre (10-pint) saucepan

1 bottle (75 cl) fortified red wine (vin doux naturel, port, Madeira or Banuyls)
200g (7oz) icing sugar
500g (1lb) fresh sweet cherries, pitted but left whole (see note)
Small handful fresh mint leaves, cut into fine ribbons (chiffonnade), to garnish

1. In the flat-bottomed saucepan, combine the wine and sugar, and stir to dissolve. Bring to a boil over a high heat. Boil until reduced to 250ml (9fl oz), about 10 minutes. Add the cherries and return just to a boil.

2. Remove from the heat. Cover and set aside to infuse for about 30 minutes. Serve warm or at room temperature, ladling the fruit and sauce over ice cream. Garnish with the mint chiffonnade and serve.

Marché Poncelet

Beginning at avenue des Ternes

Paris 17

9am to 1pm, and 4pm to 7pm Tuesday through Saturday

9am to 1pm Sunday

Métro: Ternes

NOTE
Cherries can most easily be pitted with a small gadget, either a cherry or an olive pitter. I find that the brands from Germany work the best. Short of that, simply squeeze the cherry between your fingers to extract the pit.

228

Cherry-Almond Gratin
Gratin aux Cerises et aux Amandes

I know of few greater food combinations that almonds and cherries. They love to grow side by side, and what's amazing is that in France they ripen at the very same moment in late May to early June. Of course the almonds are still raw then and need more time on the tree, but since I go by the rule that 'what grows together goes together', I always add a touch of almond and almond extract to any cherry dish. This gratin is simple, not too rich, and a true crowd pleaser.

SERVES 8

EQUIPMENT:
One 25cm- (10in-) round porcelain baking dish; a heavy-duty mixer with bowl and whisk

1kg (2lb) fresh cherries, rinsed, stemmed and pitted
1 tablespoon kirsch, or cherry eau-de-vie
2 tablespoons sugar

FOR THE ALMOND CREAM:
120g (4oz) finely ground almonds
120g (4oz) unsalted butter, softened
2 large eggs
2 tablespoons double cream
120g (4oz) icing sugar
Several drops of kirsch, or cherry eau-de-vie (optional)
Several drops of almond extract

Icing sugar, for dusting the gratin

PREHEAT THE OVEN TO 190°C/375°F/GAS MARK 5.

1. Butter the baking dish. Set aside.

2. In a large, heavy frying-pan, combine the cherries, kirsch and sugar, and cook over low heat, stirring regularly for 5 minutes. Transfer the cherries to the prepared baking dish. Set aside.

3. Prepare the almond cream: In the bowl of a heavy-duty mixer fitted with a whisk, combine the almonds and butter, and whisk, blending until smooth. Add the eggs, cream and icing sugar, and whisk until thick, smooth and well-blended. Add the kirsch and almond extract, mixing to blend. Pour the cream over the cherries in the baking dish.

4. Place the baking dish in the centre of the oven. Bake until the gratin is firm and a deep golden brown, 20 to 25 minutes. Remove to a rack to cool. Dust lightly with icing sugar and serve in wedges, warm or at room temperature. This dessert is best served just a few hours after it is prepared.

Raspberry Pride
Tarte aux Framboises et Vanille

———o———

When fresh raspberries first appear in the Paris markets in June, I find every excuse imaginable to make this dessert. Raspberries, vanilla, almonds and thyme, what could be better? Thyme, you ask? Yes, modern cooks are realising that herbs need not be reserved for savoury dishes alone. The wild herbal flavour of thyme is readily absorbed by the butter and cream, and marries so beautifully with the acid/sweet flavour of the raspberry. While this very elegant dessert is a showstopper, preparing it is child's play. A simple almond cream is spread between layers of thin pastry, then baked and topped with a vanilla and thyme-flavoured crème Chantilly. A crown of fresh raspberries adds the final touch of drama. Your guest will ask: You made this? A friend suggested I call this Raspberry Pride, and so I did.

———o———

SERVES 12

EQUIPMENT:
A heavy-duty mixer with bowl and whisk; a pastry brush; baking parchment

FOR THE ALMOND CREAM:
120g (4oz) finely ground almonds
120g (4oz) unsalted butter, softened
2 large eggs
2 tablespoons double cream
100g (3½oz) icing sugar
Several drops framboise, or raspberry eau-de-vie (optional)

FOR THE CHANTILLY CREAM:
375ml (13fl oz) double cream, well chilled
50g (2oz) icing sugar
1 teaspoon pure vanilla extract
2 teaspoons fresh thyme leaves

1. Place the bowl and the whisk of a heavy-duty mixer in the freezer.

2. Place an oven rack in the centre of the oven. Preheat the oven to 220°C/425°F/gas mark 7.

3. Prepare the almond cream: in the bowl of a food processor, combine the almonds and butter and process until smooth. Add the egg, cream and icing sugar, and process again until thick, smooth and well-blended. If desired, add the fruit eau-de-vie, processing to blend. Transfer to a small bowl and set aside.

4. Prepare the Chantilly cream: In the bowl of a heavy-duty mixer fitted with a whisk, whisk the cream at moderate speed until soft peaks form. Gradually increase to high speed – gradually adding the icing sugar, vanilla extract and the thyme – until stiff peaks form. Scrape down the sides of the bowl. Cover the bowl with plastic wrap and refrigerate.

FOR THE PASTRY:
Four sheets filo dough
(32 x 43cm/12½ x 17in)
60g (2oz) unsalted butter, melted
About 30g (1oz) icing sugar

500g (1lb) fresh raspberries
(or substitute fresh strawberries,
blueberries or blackberries)
Icing sugar, to garnish

5. Prepare the pastry: Butter a baking sheet. Place one sheet of filo on the baking sheet. With a pastry brush, lightly butter the dough and dust with icing sugar. Cover with a second sheet of dough. Lightly butter it and sprinkle with sugar.

6. Delicately spread all of the almond cream over the centre of the second sheet of dough. Do not spread the almond cream all the way to the edges, or it will ooze out in baking. Cover with a third sheet of dough, lightly buttering and dusting with sugar.

7. Cover with a fourth sheet of dough, lightly buttering and dusting with sugar. Cover with a sheet of baking parchment. Cover with another baking sheet, to keep the pastry even and compact. Place in the centre of the oven and bake for 5 minutes.

8. Remove from the oven and remove the baking sheet and the parchment. Return to the oven and bake until the pastry is a deep, even, golden brown, about 5 minutes more. The dough should be a deep, crispy brown. If it is undercooked, it will become soggy and tough. Remove from the oven and set aside to cool.

9. To serve: Neatly trim off any ragged edges from the pastry. With a very large, sharp chef's knife, cut the pastry lengthways into 3 even strips. Cut each strip into 4 even rectangles. With a spatula, delicately spread a thin layer of the Chantilly cream over the pastry. Arrange the raspberries over the top. Sprinkle with icing sugar and serve

A small glass of framboise, or raspberry eau-de-vie

Fresh Fig and Almond Gratin
Gratin des Figues et Amandes

I remember the first time I bought figs in Paris. I asked the vendor to select figs that were not overly ripe, because they were so delicate. He looked at me as though I was nuts. Why would anyone want an under-ripe fig? I learned my lesson, for under-ripe figs lack flavour and aroma. Ripe figs, purple figs, dripping with their honey-like nectar, are as fragile as can be, so I always carry them gingerly, and either eat or cook them the second I get home. This is a lovely gratin that is perfect for figs or ripe summer apricots. One of the best greengrocers in Paris is Les Jardins de Courcelles.

SERVES 8

EQUIPMENT:
One 27cm- (10½in-) round porcelain baking dish.

Butter for buttering the baking dish
150ml (6fl oz) crème fraîche or double cream
Several branches fresh thyme
1kg (2lb) fresh figs
4 large eggs
100g (3½oz) sugar
⅛ teaspoon fine sea salt
60g (2oz) finely ground almonds
¼ teaspoon almond extract

FOR THE THYME SUGAR:
2 teaspoons fresh or dried thyme leaves
2 teaspoons sugar

PREHEAT THE OVEN TO 190°C/375°F/GAS MARK 5.

1. Butter the baking dish and set aside.

2. In a small saucepan, combine the cream and thyme. Heat over moderate heat, stirring from time to time, just until tiny bubbles form around the edges of the pan, 2 to 3 minutes. Remove from the heat. Cover, and let steep for 1 hour. Strain through a fine-mesh sieve, discarding the thyme. Set aside.

3. In the bowl of a heavy-duty mixer fitted with a whisk, beat the eggs, sugar and salt at high speed until thick and lemon coloured, 2 to 3 minutes. Stir in the almonds, almond extract and the thyme-flavoured cream.

4. Pour half of the batter into the prepared baking dish. Place the dish in the centre of the oven and bake just until the batter begins to set, about 10 minutes. Remove the dish from the oven.

5. Arrange the fruit over the batter. Pour the remaining batter over the fruit. Return to the oven and bake until the gratin is golden brown, about 30 minutes more.

6. Meanwhile, prepare the thyme sugar. In a spice mill, combine the thyme leaves and sugar and grind to a fine powder. Once the gratin has baked for a total of 40 minutes, scatter the thyme sugar over the gratin and bake for 10 minutes more, for a total baking time of 50 minutes.

7. Remove from the oven. Serve warm, cut into wedges. This dessert is best served within an hour after it is prepared.

VARIATIONS

The gratin can be prepared with small figs that have been stemmed and cut into a cross, cutting halfway down the fruit; apricots that have been halved and pitted, and placed cut-side up in the dish; or pears that have been peeled, cored and quartered, and placed on their sides in the dish.

Le Jardin de Courcelles

96, rue de Courcelles

Paris 17

Telephone 01 47 63 70 55

Métro: Courcelles

Warm Fig Compote with Lavender Honey
Figues Chaudes au Miel de Lavande

———○———

For me, this is what dessert is all about. The freshest seasonal fruit, just a touch of sugar, a tangle of memorable tastes. Really ripe figs tend almost to drip of honey, so why not combine them with a flavour – lavender – that grows side by side with the proud fig tree? Embellish, if you will, with a scoop of fresh Heather Honey Ice Cream (page 246).

———○———

SERVES 4

FOR THE FIG COMPOTE:
500g (1lb) fresh black figs, rinsed (about 12)
100g (3½oz) sugar
1 tablespoon lavender honey
½ teaspoon ground cinnamon

500g (1lb) fresh black figs, rinsed (about 12)
45g (1½oz) unsalted butter
3 tablespoons lavender honey
3 tablespoons lemon juice

1. Prepare the fig compote: Quarter 500g (1lb) figs lengthways. In a large, heavy-duty saucepan, combine them with the sugar, honey and cinnamon. Cook over a high heat, stirring regularly, until the compote is compact, about 10 minutes. Remove from the heat and set aside.

2. Prepare the remaining figs: cut the figs to open like a flower, cutting three-quarters of the way down into quarters, leaving the stem end intact.

3. In a large frying-pan, melt the butter over a low heat, add the honey and bring the mixture just to a boil. Stand the figs in the frying-pan and cook for 4 to 5 minutes, rolling them in the butter and honey mixture. Remove the frying-pan from the heat and set aside. Do not discard the liquid in the pan.

4. Place the fig compote on 4 warmed dessert plates. Place 3 figs upright on top of the compote. Add the lemon juice to the frying-pan, and place over high heat for 1 to 2 minutes. Taste, adding additional honey or lemon juice as desired. Pour the sauce over the fig dessert. Serve immediately.

Fresh Raspberry Sauce
Coulis de Framboise

———◦———

When raspberries are plentiful in the outdoor markets of Paris during the summer months I often make up a batch of this delightful sauce and freeze it for cooler days. It can be served as a brilliant red sauce for vanilla ice cream and is lovely with Raspberry Pride (page 230), offering diners a double hit of one of my favourite fruits.

———◦———

MAKES ABOUT 250ML (9FL OZ)

250g (8oz) fresh raspberries
1 tablespoon icing sugar
2 tablespoons freshly squeezed lemon juice

In a food processor, combine the raspberries, sugar and lemon juice. Process to blend. Strain through a fine-mesh sieve to remove the seeds. Transfer to a sealed container. The sauce may be refrigerated for 2 to 3 days, or frozen for up to 1 month.

Honey-Poached Pears In Beaumes de Venise
Poire Vigneronne aux Muscat de Beaumes de Venise

———◦———

Honey, pears and sweet muscat wine make a happy triumvirate. I sampled a version of this dessert one cold wintry Paris night at Alain Dutournier's Carré des Feuillants. With just a touch of spice and a hint of rosemary you have a winter dessert that brings promise of summer and the sun. Serve with Honey-Rosemary-Ginger Ice Cream (page 247).

———◦———

SERVES 4 TO 6

4 large pears, peeled with stems intact
250ml (9fl oz) mild honey

1. In a large saucepan that will hold the pears snugly, combine all the ingredients. Bring just to a simmer over moderate heat, simmering just until the pears are cooked though, 15 to 20 minutes. Do not cover. Using a slotted spoon, very gently turn

1½ bottles Beaumes
de Venise or other sweet
muscat-based wine
2 tablespoons freshly squeezed
lemon juice
4 sprigs of fresh rosemary
1 vanilla bean, split lengthways and
seeds gently scraped out
4 whole cloves
8 black peppercorns
8 whole allspice berries
2 sticks cinnamon

the pears from time to time so they are evenly coated.

2. Remove from the heat and using a slotted spoon, transfer the pears to a large, shallow bowl. Strain the liquid, discarding the rosemary, spices and vanilla bean. Return the liquid to a saucepan and reduce by half over high heat, about 10 minutes. The liquid should be light and syrupy. Allow the liquid to cool slightly, then pour over the cooled pears. Cover and refrigerate up to 24 hours before serving.

3. To serve, cut each pear in half lengthways and place cut-side down on a small chilled dessert plate. Serve with Fresh Rosemary-Ginger Ice Cream, spooning the liquid over the ice cream and the pears.

Serve with a small glass of honey-like muscat wine, such as that from Beaumes de Venise.

WHAT I LEARNED

When cooking with wine, always leave the cooking vessel uncovered as you cook, to allow the alcohol to burn off, resulting in a liquid with a rounder, firmer, fruitier flavour.

Carré des Feuillants (Alain Dutournier)

14, rue de Castiglione

Paris 1

Telephone: 01 42 86 82 82 Fax: 01 42 86 07 71

Métro: Concorde or Tuileries

La Maison du Chocolat's Bittersweet Chocolate Mousse
Mousse au Chocolat La Maison du Chocolat

———————◦———————

When I first moved to Paris in 1980, one of my biggest treats was to walk to the end of my street and wander into La Maison du Chocolat for a mid-afternoon chocolate fix. Owner Robert Linxe remains one of the city's paramount chocolatiers, always offering quality, creativity and excellence. He kindly shared this exquisite chocolate mousse. It is light, rich with chocolate flavour, and as voluptuous as one could ever imagine.

———————◦———————

SERVES 8

EQUIPMENT:
A double boiler (bain marie); a heavy-duty mixer; a large spatula

60ml (2fl oz) double cream
200g (7oz) bittersweet or semisweet chocolate, broken into pieces (preferably Lindt Excellence 70% or Valhrona guanaja 70%)
45g (1½oz) unsalted butter
2 large egg yolks
5 large egg whites
1 tablespoon sugar
1 tablespoon Dutch process cocoa
¼ teaspoon fine sea salt
½ teaspoon pure vanilla extract

1. In the top of a double boiler set over, but not touching, boiling water, heat the cream just until warm, about 1 minute. Add the chocolate pieces, and stir until the chocolate is melted. Add the butter and stir to melt and combine. Remove from the heat. One by one, whisk in the egg yolks. Transfer to a large bowl. Set aside to cool.

2. Place the egg whites in the bowl of a heavy-duty mixer fitted with a whisk. Whisk at low speed until the whites are frothy. Gradually increase speed to high. Slowly add the sugar, cocoa, salt and vanilla extract, whisking at high speed until stiff but not dry.

3. Whisk one-third of the egg whites into the chocolate, butter and egg yolk mixture in the large bowl, and whisk until the two are thoroughly blended. This will lighten the batter and make it easier to fold in the remaining whites. With a large rubber spatula, gently fold in the remaining whites. Do this slowly and patiently. Do not overmix, but be sure that the mixture is well blended and that no streaks of white remain.

4. Pour the mousse into a large salad bowl, 8 individual ramekins, or 8 pot de crème pots. Cover with plastic wrap and store at room temperature. Preferably, serve within a few hours of preparing the mousse.

VARIATIONS

• Add about half a finely ground vanilla bean to the chocolate. Do not add too much, or the vanilla will make the chocolate taste too sweet.

• Along with the cream, heat 1 small cup of very strong coffee along with the grated zest of 1 orange or 1 lemon.

• Add 1 teaspoon of finely ground ginger to the warm cream. Let the mixture cool, then strain through a fine-mesh sieve and continue with the recipe.

Chocolate is delicious with one of France's newly popular vins doux naturels, such as Boissy-Masson's Rancio, full of body with a nuttiness that pairs so well with the richness of chocolate.

NOTE

Semisweet and bittersweet chocolate are used interchangeably, and are made of chocolate, cocoa butter and a bit of sugar to make the chocolate more palatable. Unsweetened chocolate contains no sugar at all, and is considered less palatable.

La Maison du Chocolat

225, rue du Faubourg Saint-Honoré

Paris 8

Telephone: 01 42 27 39 44

Métro: Ternes

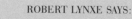

ROBERT LYNXE SAYS:

The amount of egg whites makes this a very light mousse.
Don't put the mousse in the refrigerator, but in a cool spot.
The cold will block the flavour of the chocolate and it will lose its smooth, creamy quality.
For a truly rich mousse, use an extra-bitter chocolate, Van Couva from Trinidad, the best chocolate in the world.

Joël Robuchon's Burnt Cream
Joël Robuchon's Crème Brûlée

———○———

For nearly four years during the 1980s – as I worked on a cookbook with chef Joël Robuchon – I spent many a day ensconced in the tiny kitchen on the Rue du Longchamp, the home of the famous restaurant Jamin where Robuchon held court. This was one of his most famous desserts, and I cannot count the number of times I sampled it as part of a multiple dessert medley. It is a dessert that holds up over time, and I have never known a guest to turn it down. The secret is in the huge amount of vanilla seeds used, giving it an elegant, rich flavour and texture.

———○———

SERVES 6

EQUIPMENT:
Six 15cm- (6in-) round porcelain baking dishes

4 plump, moist vanilla beans, split lengthways
9 large egg yolks
150g (5oz) granulated sugar
250ml (9fl oz) chilled whole milk
750ml (1.25 pints) crème fraîche or double cream
75g (2½oz) firmly packed dark brown sugar

PREHEAT THE OVEN TO
100°C/200°F/GAS MARK ½

1. Flatten the vanilla beans and cut them in half lengthways. With a small spoon, scrape out the seeds and place in the bowl of a heavy duty mixer fitted with a whisk.

2. Add the egg yolks and sugar to the bowl and whisk at high speed for 2 minutes. Stir in the milk and the crème fraîche. Cover with plastic wrap and refrigerate for 12 hours to allow flavours to ripen.

3. Arrange the porcelain dishes on two baking sheets. Pour the mixture into the porcelain dishes. Place the baking sheets in the oven and bake until the custard sets, 40 to 45 minutes.

4. Remove from the oven and let cool to room temperature. Cover the cooled custard with plastic wrap. Refrigerate at least 4 hours or overnight.

5. At serving time, preheat the grill. Sprinkle the brown sugar through a fine mesh sieve over the cream. Place the baking dishes under grill until the sugar forms a crust, watching carefully to see that it does not burn. Serve immediately.

'The Heart of Paris'
Coeur à la Crème

———————○———————

Around Valentine's Day, Paris cookshops love to decorate their windows with charming, heart-shaped white porcelain coeur à la crème moulds. Coeur à la crème is a very light moulded cheese dessert, usually prepared in moulds shaped like a heart. I have a treasured collection, with moulds in every size. Since I am a cheese lover at heart, this style of dessert – with its farm-fresh lactic tang and just a touch of sweetness – speaks to me. This is an ideal dessert any time of year, delicious when served with fresh berries or homemade fruit preserves. The best fromage blanc I know comes from my favourite cheese shop, Alléosse.

———————○———————

SERVES 6

EQUIPMENT:
One 500ml (18fl oz) heart-shaped perforated mould or four 125ml (9fl oz) individual heart-shaped perforated moulds

3 large egg whites
50g (2oz) sugar
500ml (18fl oz) fresh cheese (fromage blanc or yoghurt)
80ml (3½fl oz) double cream

Fresh seasonal berries or fruit preserves, to garnish

1. At least 8 hours and up to 36 hours before serving, prepare the fresh cheese dessert: Place the egg whites in the bowl of a heavy-duty mixer fitted with a whisk. Whisk at low speed until the whites are frothy. Gradually increase speed to high. Slowly add the sugar, whisking at high speed until stiff but not dry.

2. In another large bowl, using a hand whisk, blend the cheese and cream until smooth. Gradually fold in the beaten whites.

3. Set each mould on a tray or container deep enough to catch the liquid that will drip from the moulds. Spoon the mixture into the mould or moulds and even out with a spatula. Cover with plastic wrap. Place in the refrigerator to drain for at least 8 hours and up to 36 hours. To serve, turn each mould onto a serving plate and pass fruits, preserves and sugar to taste.

Alléosse

13, rue Poncelet, Paris 17

Telephone: 01 46 22 50 45

Métro: Ternes

The Astor's Vanilla Custard Tarts
Petit Pots de Crème à la Vanille L'Astor

———◦———

These simple, sublime traditional desserts have long been part of the repertoire of chef Joël Robuchon and his acolyte, Eric Lecerf. These delicate creams – often served in lovely antique pots de crème moulds of all colours – can be prepared up to one day in advance, allowing flavours to mellow with age.

———◦———

SERVES 8

EQUIPMENT:
Eight 125ml (9fl oz) ovenproof ramekins, custard cups or petits pots

400ml (14fl oz) whole milk
2 plump moist vanilla beans, split lengthways
4 large egg yolks
65g (2½oz) sugar

PREHEAT THE OVEN TO
160°C/325°F/GAS MARK 3

1. Cut 3 slits in a piece of wax paper, and use it to line a baking pan large enough to hold the ramekins. Place the ramekins in the pan, on top of the paper, and set aside. The paper will prevent the water from boiling and splashing up on the custards.

2. In a medium-size saucepan, combine the milk and vanilla beans over a high heat. Bring to a boil and remove from the heat. Cover and set aside to infuse for 15 minutes.

3. In the bowl of an electric mixer, whisk the egg yolks and sugar until thick and lemon-coloured. Set aside.

4. Bring the vanilla-infused milk back to a boil, and very gradually add to the yolk mixture in a thin stream, whisking constantly. Strain into a bowl through a fine-mesh sieve or several layers of cheesecloth. Let stand for 2 to 3 minutes, then remove any foam that has risen to the top.

5. Divide the cream evenly among the individual ramekins. Pour enough boiling water into the pan to reach about halfway up the side of the ramekins. Cover the pan loosely with aluminium foil, to prevent a skin from forming on the custards.

Place in the centre of the oven, and bake until the custard is just set at the edges but still trembling in the centre, 30 to 35 minutes.

6. Remove the pan from the oven and carefully remove the ramekins from the water. Refrigerate, loosely covered, for at least 2 hours or up to 24 hours. Serve the pots de crème chilled, without unmoulding.

> ### TRUC
> To prevent those moist and precious vanilla beans from drying out, place the beans in a small jar, add rum just to keep the tip of the beans wet, and cover securely. The beans will absorb a bit of the liquid and will not dry out with time.

Any good sweet, regional French wine would be ideal here. Try a Loupiac, Ste-Croix-de-Mont, or Monbazillac and, of course, one will never go wrong with a Sauternes.

Astor

11, rue Astor

Paris 8

Telephone: 01 53 05 05 20 Fax: 01 53 05 05 30

Métro: Saint-Augustin

Blood Orange Ice Cream, Le Jardin de Courcelles
Le Jardin de Courcelles Glace aux Oranges Sanguines

———○———

I consider blood oranges – those ruby-dappled oranges with their rich red juice – a ray of sunshine in the often grey winters of Paris. I keep my refrigerator stocked with citrus in the winter, and when I am in the mood for an ice cream splurge, I head over to one of the city's best fruit and vegetable shops – Le Jardin de Courcelles – for a fresh stock. If you cannot get blood oranges, best-quality juice oranges can be substituted.

———○———

*MAKES ABOUT 1 LITRE
(1¾ PINTS)*

*EQUIPMENT:
An ice cream maker*

*375ml (13fl oz) water
Grated zest of 4 blood oranges (or
substitute juice oranges)
200g (7oz) sugar
250ml (9fl oz) freshly squeezed blood
orange juice (or substitute juice of
juice oranges)
375ml (13fl oz) double cream*

1. In a small saucepan, combine the water, orange zest, sugar and orange juice. Bring to a boil over a moderate heat. Boil vigorously for 2 minutes. Place a sieve over a bowl and strain the syrup through the sieve. Discard the solids. Let the syrup cool to room temperature. To speed cooling, place the bowl inside a larger bowl filled with ice cubes and water. Stir occasionally. The mixture should be cold to the touch. The process should take about 30 minutes.

2. When the syrup is thoroughly cooled, stir in the double cream. Transfer to an ice cream maker and freeze according to manufacturer's instructions.

Le Jardin de Courcelles

96. rue de Courcelles

Paris 17

Telephone: 01 47 63 70 55

Métro: Courcelles

Almond Ice Cream
Glace aux Amandes

———◇———

I never get enough almonds in my life. This is delicious all on its own, or served with
Miniature Lemon Tea Cakes (Mini Madeleines; page 250) or Chocolate Financiers (page 252).

———◇———

SERVES 8 TO 10

EQUIPMENT:
An ice cream maker.

125g (4oz) finely ground almonds
750ml (1.25 pints) double cream
375ml (13fl oz) whole milk
150g (7oz) sugar
Several drops almond extract

1. In a large saucepan, combine the almonds, cream, milk and sugar. Stir to dissolve the sugar. Heat over moderate heat, stirring from time to time, just until tiny bubbles form around the edges of the pan, 2 to 3 minutes. Remove from the heat and let steep, covered, for 1 hour.

2. Strain through a fine-mesh sieve, discarding the almonds. Cover and refrigerate until thoroughly chilled. Stir in the almond extract. Transfer to an ice cream maker and freeze according to manufacturer's instructions.

Alléosse Fromage Blanc Ice Cream
Glace au Fromage Blanc Fromagerie Alléosse

———◦———

Made without egg yolks, and sweetened just enough to make the ice cream only mildly tangy, this fromage blanc ice cream is always a hit. I purchase my fresh cheese – the French fromage blanc that is like yoghurt in texture, but with a much sharper flavour – at the city's best cheese shop, Alléosse. Philippe Alléosse and his family offer the city's finest selection of cheeses, ranging from their thick and creamy fromage blanc to an astonishing array of goat's, sheep's and cow's milk cheeses from all over France.

———◦———

MAKES 1 LITRE (1¾ PINTS)

EQUIPMENT:
An ice cream maker

3 large egg whites
140g (5oz) sugar
500ml (18fl oz) fresh cheese (fromage blanc or full-fat yoghurt)
250 ml (9fl oz) double cream
Fresh seasonal berries or fruit preserves, to taste

1. Place the egg whites in the bowl of a heavy-duty mixer fitted with a whisk. Whisk at low speed until the whites are frothy. Gradually increase speed to high. Slowly add the sugar, whisking at high speed until stiff but not dry.

2. In another large bowl whisk the cheese and the cream until smooth. Gradually fold the beaten egg whites into the cream mixture. Transfer to an ice-cream maker and freeze according to manufacturer's instructions.

At serving time, pass a bowl of fruit and preserves to flavour to taste.

Fromagerie Alléosse
13, rue Poncelet
Paris 17
Telephone: 01 46 22 50 45
Métro: Ternes

Maison du Miel Heather Honey Ice Cream
Glace au Miel de Bruyère Maison du Miel

————o————

La Maison du Miel – The House of Honey – is one of Paris' most traditional shops, devoted to nothing but honey and honey-related products. My favourite selection is the deep, rust-toned heather honey – bruyère – which is strong and pungent. I use it to make a rich honey ice cream, delicious with The Apple Lady's Apple Cake (page 218) or with crusty Miniature Madeleines (Miniature Lemon Tea Cakes; page 250).

————o————

SERVES 6 TO 8

EQUIPMENT:
An ice cream maker

2 plump moist vanilla beans
500ml (18fl oz) double cream
250ml (9fl oz) whole milk
125ml (4½fl oz) heather honey (or other aromatic honeys, such as chestnut or eucalyptus)

1. Flatten the vanilla beans and cut them in half lengthways. With a small spoon, scrape out the seeds and place them and the pods in a large saucepan. Add the cream, milk and honey. Stir to dissolve the honey. Heat over moderate heat, stirring from time to time, just until tiny bubbles form around the edges of the pan, 3 to 4 minutes.

2. Remove from the heat and let steep, covered, for 1 hour.

3. Cover and refrigerate until thoroughly chilled. When preparing the ice cream, stir again to blend. Remove the vanilla pods. Transfer to an ice cream maker and freeze according to manufacturer's instructions.

La Maison du Miel

24, rue Vignon

Paris 8

Telephone: 01 47 42 26 70

Métro: Madeleine

Fresh Honey-Rosemary-Ginger Ice Cream
Crème Glace aux Gingembre et Romarin

———◦———

Paired with Honey-Poached Pears in Beaumes de Venise (page 235), this is one of my favourite winter desserts, inspired by a visit to Alain Dutournier's Carré des Feuillants.

———◦———

SERVES 8

EQUIPMENT:
An ice cream maker

500ml (18fl oz) double cream
250ml (9fl oz) whole milk
125ml (4½fl oz) mild honey, such as lavender
A small thumb-sized knob of fresh ginger, peeled
20 sprigs fresh rosemary

1. In a large saucepan, combine the cream, milk, honey, ginger and rosemary. Heat over a moderate heat just until tiny bubbles form around the edges of the pan, 3 to 4 minutes. Remove from the heat, cover, and let steep for 1 hour.

2. Strain through a fine-mesh sieve, discarding the rosemary and ginger. Refrigerate until thoroughly chilled. Transfer to an ice cream maker and freeze according to manufacturer's instructions.

WHAT I LEARNED

When you want to infuse a liquid with the flavour of an herb or a spice, heat the liquid and then set aside, covered. Sealed in this manner, the herb or spice will then have an opportunity to transfer its oils and flavours, permeating the liquid.

Carré des Feuillants (Alain Dutournier)

14, rue de Castiglione

Paris 1

Telephone: 01 42 86 82 82 Fax: 01 42 86 07 71

Métro: Concorde or Tuileries

Fresh Truffle Ice Cream
Glaces aux Truffes Fraîches

I know, the first time you hear the words 'Truffle Ice Cream' you make a face and say, 'It can't be true. It can't taste good.' I used to be totally against mixing sweet and savoury, sort of like polka dots and plaid together. But I've changed my tune. This dessert is always on the menu when a truffle feast is in order.

SERVES 8 TO 10

EQUIPMENT:
An ice cream maker

750ml (1.25 pints) double cream
375ml (13fl oz) whole milk
200g (7oz) sugar
About 2 tablespoons fresh black truffle, chopped

1. In a large saucepan, combine the cream, milk and sugar. Stir to dissolve the sugar. Heat over a moderate heat, stirring from time to time, just until tiny bubbles form around the edges of the pan. Remove from the heat, add 1 tablespoon and 1 teaspoon of the truffles, and let steep, covered, for 1 hour.

2. Cover and refrigerate until thoroughly chilled. Just before churning the ice cream, stir in the remaining 2 teaspoons of chopped truffles. Transfer to an ice cream maker and freeze according to manufacturer's instructions.

Truffle Panna Cotta
Crème de Truffes

———○———

I have decided that truffles are nature's way of saying February is OK! In France, the precious black truffle is in season from late November to the first of March, giving us reason to indulge when truffle season is at its peak. Chopped truffles and cream make a great combination, for the fat of the cream seems virtually to inhale the fragrance and flavour of the truffle. What's more, when using fresh truffles there are always little bits that can be set aside for mincing and, when purchasing canned truffles, the sliced or chopped version is generally less expensive. While the name – panna cotta, or 'cooked cream' in Italian – implies that the mixture is cooked, it is only brought to a boil then mixed with gelatin, which helps it set. The recipe without truffles is also delicious – it is the traditional dessert of Italy's Piedmont. I created this dish to keep smiles on our faces until the first blossoms of spring appear.

———○———

SERVES 8

EQUIPMENT:
Eight 125ml (4½fl oz) ramekins

(1 package) 2 teaspoons
unflavoured gelatin
500ml (18fl oz) whole milk
200g (7oz) icing sugar
500ml (18fl oz) Truffle Cream
(see page 263)
30g (1oz), chopped truffle shavings

1. Chill eight dessert plates.

2. Place the ramekins on a tray. Set aside.

3. In a small bowl, sprinkle the gelatin over 60ml (2fl oz) of the milk and stir to blend. Set aside until the gelatin completely absorbs the milk, 2 to 3 minutes.

4. In a large saucepan, combine the remaining milk, the icing sugar and the cream. Bring to a boil over moderate heat, whisking to dissolve the sugar. Remove from the heat.

5. Stir in the softened gelatin and milk mixture. Strain the mixture through a fine-mesh sieve set over a large measuring cup with a pouring spout. Pour the mixture into the ramekins. Cover with plastic wrap and refrigerate until set, about 4 hours.

The panna cotta can be prepared up to 1 day in advance. Refrigerate until serving time.

6. To serve, run a sharp knife along the inside of each ramekin. Dip the bottom of each ramekin into a bowl of hot water, shaking to completely loosen the cream. Invert onto chilled dessert plates. Sprinkle with the chopped truffle shavings. Serve.

Miniature Lemon Tea Cakes
Mini Madeleines

———o———

Ever since I moved to Paris in 1980, madeleines – tiny scallop-shaped sweets that look like a cookie but taste like a miniature cake – have been one of my greatest treats. When working on the The Food Lover's Guide to Paris *in the early 1980s, I was obsessed with these tiny cakes. I couldn't pass a pastry shop without examining the golden sweets. When I deemed the shop's madeleines potentially worthy, I'd purchase one and decide whether or not this pastry chef made the cut. Today, my preference is for the miniature version, which has more crust and crunch than the more traditional ones twice the size.*

———o———

MAKES 60 4CM (1¼IN) MADELEINES

EQUIPMENT: Madeleine tins for 60 mini-madeleines

Butter for preparing the madeleine tins

1. Butter the madeleine tins and place in the freezer.

2. Place the eggs and sugar in the bowl of a heavy-duty mixer fitted with a whisk. Beat the eggs and sugar at high speed until thick and lemon coloured, 2 to 3 minutes. Stir in the zest. Stir in the flour and salt. Stir in the butter. Cover and refrigerate for at least 1 hour and up to 24 hours.

2 large eggs
100g (3½oz) sugar
Grated zest of 1 lemon
120g (4oz) plain flour
⅛ teaspoon fine sea salt
90g (3oz) unsalted butter, melted
and cooled

3. Preheat the oven to 190°C/375°F/gas mark 5.

4. Remove the madeleine tins from the freezer. Spoon the batter into the prepared moulds, filling nearly to the top. Tap down the moulds to distribute the batter evenly. Place in the centre of the oven and bake until the madeleines are golden brown, 10 to 12 minutes.

5. Remove the madeleines from their tins as soon as they are cooled. Wash the tins immediately with a stiff brush and hot water but no detergent, so they retain their seasoning. The madeleines are best eaten as soon as they have cooled. They may, however, be stored for several days in an airtight container.

Miniature moulds can be found at:

Geneviève Lethu

95, rue de Rennes

Paris 6

Telephone: 01 45 44 40 35

Métro: Rennes

Chocolate Financiers

Financiers au Chocolat

———○———

Jean-Paul Hévin is one of Paris' finest chocolate-makers. His Left Bank shop offers no less than 28 different dark chocolate confections. I admit to a serious weakness for these shiny, rich financiers – pure, hedonistic and chocolatey. Financiers are small, rectangular cakes, most often made with almonds. They are so called because a financier *is a banker and the rectangles resemble a gold brick. While one finds financiers in all sorts of 'fantasy' shapes – round, square, even made in madeleine pans – I am a purist and insist on the authentic, traditional shape.*

———○———

MAKES 21 FINANCIERS

EQUIPMENT:
21 rectangular financier moulds, measuring 5 x 10cm (2 x 4in)

Butter for preparing the financier moulds
160ml (5½fl oz) double cream
150g (5oz) bittersweet chocolate, broken into pieces (preferably Lindt Excellence 70% or Valhrona guanaja 70%)
60g (2oz) icing sugar
35g (1oz) flour
60g (2oz) finely ground almonds
½ teaspoon baking powder
¼ teaspoon fine sea salt
60g (2oz) unsalted butter
3 egg whites, lightly beaten
½ teaspoon pure vanilla extract

PREHEAT THE OVEN TO 190°C/375°F/GAS MARK 5.

1. Butter the financier moulds. Place them side by side on a baking sheet. Place the baking sheet in the freezer.

2. In a small saucepan, heat the cream to a gentle simmer over a moderate heat. Add the chocolate and mix until melted. Set aside to cool.

3. In a large bowl, stir together the sugar, flour, almonds, baking powder and salt. Set aside.

4. In a small saucepan, heat the butter over moderate heat until it is golden, and gives off a nutty aroma. Immediately remove from the heat and transfer to a small bowl to prevent the butter from burning. Set aside to cool.

5. Add the egg whites to the sugar/flour mixture and stir until thoroughly blended. Add the butter and stir until thoroughly blended. Add the chocolate mixture and stir until thoroughly blended. Finally, add the vanilla extract, stirring until thoroughly blended.

6. Remove the financier moulds from the freezer. Spoon the batter into the prepared moulds, filling nearly to the top. Tap each mould gently against a flat surface to evenly distribute the batter.

7. Place the baking sheet in the centre of the oven and bake until the financiers are firm and springy, 20 to 25 minutes. Remove from the oven. Transfer the moulds to a cooling rack for 5 minutes before unmoulding.

Jean-Paul Hévin

3, rue Vavin

Paris 6

Telephone: 01 43 54 09 85

Métro: Vavin or Nôtre-Dame des Champs

Jean-Luc Poujauran's Shortbread Cookies
Les Sablées aux Amandes de Jean-Luc Poujauran

———○———

These delicate cookies come from one of my favourite bakers in Paris, the outgoing and talented Jean-Luc Poujauran. This recipe is dedicated to Susan Marcus, one of my students who begged that these be put on the menu for the Paris cooking class. So here they are!

———○———

MAKES ABOUT 50 COOKIES

2 tablespoons finely ground blanched almonds
60g (2oz) icing sugar
140g (5oz) bleached plain flour
⅛ teaspoon fine sea salt
75g (3oz) unsalted butter, cubed and chilled
1 large egg, at room temperature
Grated zest of 1 lemon

PREHEAT THE OVEN TO 180°C/350°F/GAS MARK 4.

1. Place the almonds and sugar in the bowl of a food processor and process to blend. Add the flour and salt, and process to blend. Add the butter and process until the mixture resembles coarse crumbs, about 10 seconds. Add the egg and lemon zest, and pulse until the dough begins to hold together, about 10 times. Do not overprocess – the dough should not form a ball.

2. Transfer the dough to a clean work surface, and with a dough scraper, smear it bit by bit across the work surface until the dough is thoroughly incorporated. Form into a flattened round, cover with plastic wrap, and refrigerate for at least 1 hour and up to 48 hours.

3. Divide the dough into four equal parts. Refrigerate three of the parts to keep cool while you are working with the fourth. Place the fourth on a lightly floured surface. Roll out the dough 3mm (⅛th-inch) thick. Use flour sparingly and touch the dough has little as possible while rolling. After each few strokes of the rolling pin, gently unstick the dough from the surface and spread a bit more flour underneath if necessary. Once the pastry is rolled to desired thickness, use a pastry brush to dust off any flour that sticks to both sides of the dough.

4. Using a 4cm-(1½ in-) round or fluted biscuit cutter, cut out circles of dough and place them on a paper-lined baking sheet about 2.5cm (1in) apart. Refrigerate until firm, about 20 minutes.

5. Place in the centre of the oven and bake for 20 to 25 minutes. The cookies should only colour slightly, but must be cooked through. Cool completely.

Menu·Carte

A Special Winter Feast

———○———

Arpège Eggs with Maple Syrup

———○———

Taillevent's Cream of Watercress Coup
with Caviar

———○———

Memories of Brittany Lobster with Cream

———○———

La Maison du Chocolat's Chocolate Mousse

The Pantry

The Pantry
Les Recettes de Base

Classic Vinaigrette
Vinaigrette Classique

Le Grand Vefour's Vinaigrette
Vinaigrette Le Grand Vefour

Niçoise Vinaigrette
Vinaigrette Niçoise

Mustard Vinaigrette
Vinaigrette Moutardé

Mustard Mayonnaise
Mayonnaise Moutardé

Truffle Cream
Créme de Truffes

Black Truffle Mayonnaise
Mayonnaise aux Truffes

Black Truffle Butter
Beurre aux Truffes

Thai Curry Paste
Pâte à Curry Thai

Curry Powder
Poudre de Curry

Tomato Sauce
Sauce aux Tomates

Allobroges Garlic Confit
Confit d'Ail Allobroges

Four-spice Blend
Quatre Épices

Cherry Jam
Confiture de Cerise

Sorrel Sauce
Sauce à l'Oseille

Homemade Chicken Stock
Fond de Volaille

Sun-Dried Tomato Paste
Purée de Tomates Séchées

Classic Vinaigrette
Vinaigrette Classique

———o———

This is the simple, classic vinaigrette always found on my kitchen counter, along with salt and pepper mills. I insist upon two vinegars – a top-quality red wine vinegar and a Spanish sherry wine vinegar – to give greater depth of flavour to my salad dressing. I keep the mixture corked in a small wine bottle, so I always have a vinaigrette on hand when in the mood for a salad. Since the mixture contains only vinegars, oil and salt, there is no fear of spoilage.

———o———

MAKES ABOUT 310ML

(11FL OZ)

2 tablespoons best-quality sherry
wine vinegar
2 tablespoons best-quality
red wine vinegar
Fine sea salt to taste
250ml (9fl oz) extra-virgin olive oil

1. Place the sherry and red wine vinegars and salt in a bottle. Cover and shake to dissolve the salt. Add the oil and shake to blend. Taste for seasoning. The vinaigrette can be stored at room temperature or in the refrigerator for several weeks. Shake again at serving time to create a thick emulsion.

Le Grand Vefour's Vinaigrette
Vinaigrette Le Grand Vefour

———o———

This brilliant, unusual creation of Grand Vefour chef Guy Martin quickly became a staple in my home. I love the complex blend of hazelnut, walnut and olive oil, enriched by a bit of home-made chicken stock, then given that proper bite with just a touch of sherry wine vinegar. Use it to dress any green salad or fresh, blanched vegetables. The easy-to-prepare vinaigrette is typical of Guy Martin's style: modern, classic and thoughtful – all in one.

———o———

MAKES ABOUT 185ML (6½FL OZ)

1 tablespoon best-quality
sherry wine vinegar
Sea salt
4 tablespoons extra-virgin olive oil
2 tablespoons hazelnut oil
1 tablespoon walnut oil
3 tablespoons Homemade Chicken
Stock (page 274)

1. In a small, covered jar, combine vinegar and salt. Shake to blend. Add the remaining ingredients. Shake to blend. Taste for seasoning. The vinaigrette can be stored in the refrigerator for up to two days. To keep longer, omit the chicken stock.

Le Grand Vefour

17, rue de Beaujolais

Paris 1

Telephone: 01.42.96.56.27 Fax: 01 42 86 80 71

Métro: Palais Royal-Musée du Louvre

LE GRAND VEFOUR

Le Grand Vefour is one of the most alluring restaurants in Paris. There are few greater gastronomic pleasures than sitting in the sparkling eigteenth-century dining room, a former café set at the edge of the historic Palais Royal gardens. The restaurant always makes me feel just a bit like a princess, or maybe a queen, sitting at the table once shared by Colette, Victor Hugo or even Napoleon. The restaurant's decorative painted glass panels and ceilings, the *trompe l'oeil* painted chimney in the private dining room upstairs, its red velvet banquettes and swirling red, white and black carpet are all there to be admired as one dines in pampered splendour on chef Guy Martin's inventive food that is very much of today.

Niçoise Vinaigrette
Vinaigrette Niçoise

———o———

This zesty vinaigrette can turn simple grilled vegetables into a satisfying meal all on its own:
My favourite version is with baby grilled asparagus or leeks.

SERVES 4 TO 6

Grated zest of 1 lemon
1 tablespoon freshly squeezed
lemon juice
3 tablespoons extra-virgin olive oil
2 teaspoons capers, rinsed
12 top-quality black olives
(such as Nyons)
4 tablespoons finely chopped fresh
parsley leaves
4 anchovy fillets, preferably
salt-cured, chopped

1. Combine all the ingredients in a small bowl. Taste for seasoning. Pour over warm or room temperature vegetables.

Mustard Vinaigrette
Vinaigrette Moutardé

———○———

The addition of a touch of walnut oil adds that perfect, slightly mysterious touch to a rather classic dressing. If you want to experiment, try substituting hazelnut or grilled peanut oil.

———○———

*MAKES ABOUT 250ML
(9FL OZ)*

*3 tablespoons French Dijon mustard
1 tablespoon best-quality
red wine vinegar
Fine sea salt to taste
160ml (5½fl oz) extra-virgin olive oil
80ml (3½fl oz) French walnut oil*

1. Place the mustard and vinegar in a bottle. Cover and shake to blend. Add the oils and shake to blend. Taste for seasoning. The vinaigrette can be stored at room temperature or in the refrigerator for several weeks. Shake again at serving time to create a thick emulsion.

Truffle Cream
Crème de Truffes

———○———

During the truffle season, I always keep some truffle cream on hand, for seasoning everything from soups to desserts with the fragrant richness of truffle essence.

———○———

*MAKES ABOUT 500ML
(1 PINT)*

*30g (1½oz) finely chopped truffle
500ml (1 pint) cream*

1. Combine the chopped truffle and the cream. Refrigerate for at least two days before serving.

Mustard Mayonnaise

Mayonnaise Moutardé

———◦———

When I want a bit of tang in a dressing, this is the mayonnaise I like to have on hand. I prefer using grapeseed oil, since it does not firm up too much when refrigerated, making for a looser, lighter mayonnaise.

———◦———

*MAKES ABOUT 250ML
(9FL OZ)*

2 teaspoons freshly squeezed lemon juice, or to taste
½ teaspoon fine sea salt, or to taste
1 tablespoon French Dijon mustard
2 large egg yolks, at room temperature
250ml (9fl oz) grapeseed oil, or substitute canola, peanut or safflower oil

BY HAND:

1. In a small bowl, combine the lemon juice, salt and mustard and whisk to blend. Place the oil in a glass measuring cup with a pouring spout. In a medium-size bowl, whisk the egg yolks until light and thick. Add the lemon juice mixture and whisk until thick and smooth.

2. Continue whisking and gradually add just a few drops of the oil, whisking until thoroughly incorporated. Do not add too much oil at the beginning, or the mixture will not emulsify.

3. As soon as the mixture begins to thicken, add the remaining oil in a slow and steady stream, whisking constantly. Taste for seasoning. Transfer to a bowl.

IN A FOOD PROCESSOR:

1. In the bowl of a food processor, combine the lemon juice, salt, mustard and egg yolks and pulse until well blended. With the motor running, very slowly add several tablespoons of oil, processing until the mixture thickens.

2. With the motor running, add the remaining oil in a slow and steady stream. Taste for seasoning. Transfer to a bowl. The mayonnaise can be covered and refrigerated for up to 3 days.

Black Truffle Mayonnaise
Mayonnaise aux Truffes

———o———

This is unquestionably one of the best and most full-flavoured uses of fresh black truffles. The mayonnaise is delicious on just about everything, from warm sautéed potatoes to cold chicken, to cubed chicken brochettes. Try it also the dressing for a fresh Celeriac Rémoulade (page 28).

———o———

MAKES ABOUT 375ML
(13FL OZ)

250ml (9fl oz) grapeseed oil (or substitute canola, peanut or safflower oil)
2 large egg yolks, at room temperature (preferably eggs that have been enclosed in a glass jar with the truffles for 1 day)
1 teaspoon freshly squeezed lemon juice, or to taste
1 teaspoon imported mustard
¼ teaspoon fine sea salt, or to taste
3 tablespoons (15g/½oz) finely chopped fresh truffle

BY HAND:

1. Place the oil in a glass measuring cup with a pouring spout. In a medium-size bowl, whisk the egg yolks, lemon juice, mustard and salt until light and thick. Continue whisking and gradually add just a few drops of the oil, whisking until thoroughly incorporated. Do not add too much oil at the beginning, or the mixture will not emulsify.

2. As soon as the mixture begins to thicken, add the remaining oil in a slow and steady stream, whisking constantly. Stir in the chopped truffles. Taste for seasoning. Transfer to a bowl, cover, and refrigerate up to 3 days.

IN A FOOD PROCESSOR:

1. In the bowl of a food processor, combine the eggs, lemon juice, mustard and salt, and pulse until well blended. With the motor running, very slowly add several tablespoons of oil, processing until the mixture thickens.

2. With the motor still running, slowly add the remaining oil in a slow and steady stream. Taste for seasoning. Transfer to a small bowl. Stir in the chopped truffles. Cover and refrigerate up to 3 days.

Black Truffle Butter

Beurre aux Truffes

———o———

This incredible butter becomes an essential ingredient during the dreary winter months! It has unlimited uses. Use it wherever you would use butter in a recipe – everything from omelettes to cooked lentils to macaroni to cannelloni profits from this rich and intensely flavoured concoction. And of course there's nothing to stop you from simply spreading this on toast!

———o———

MAKES 60G (2OZ)

60g (2oz) unsalted butter, at room temperature
12g (½oz) chopped truffle peelings
½ teaspoon coarse sea salt (sel de Guérande)

1. On a small plate, mash the softened butter with a fork. Sprinkle with the truffles and salt, distributing as evenly as possible. Transfer the butter to a ramekin. Cover securely. Refrigerate for up to 3 days or freeze up to 1 month. Serve at room temperature.

Thai Curry Paste
Pâte à Curry Thai

This is a curry paste to knock your head off. The explosion of flavours is wild, so fasten your seat belt with this one! Use it to baste Olivades chef Flora Mikula's Spicy Spare Ribs (page 198), or a simple pork roast. During the past decade Asian food has taken on an increased popularity in France. So much so that ingredients that were not a part of classic French cuisine – from Japanese wasabi to Indian spices – are now looked upon as commonplace. But don't get me wrong: French chefs rarely stray far from centre and tend to use foreign ingredients with a great deal of forethought.

MAKES 250ML (9FL OZ)

EQUIPMENT:
A spice grinder or coffee mill

2 teaspoons whole coriander seeds
1 teaspoon whole cumin seeds
1 teaspoon whole fennel seeds
1 teaspoon whole black peppercorns
2 large handfuls packed coriander leaves
Two ½cm (¼in-) slices fresh ginger, peeled
1 stalk lemon grass, bottom third only, chopped
1 tablespoon finely ground dried red chilli peppers
2 shallots, chopped
4 plump fresh garlic cloves, chopped
Grated zest of 1 lime
1 teaspoon shrimp paste (optional)
1½ teaspoons fine sea salt
1 teaspoon freshly grated nutmeg
80ml (3fl oz) peanut oil

1. In a small dry frying-pan combine the coriander, cumin, fennel and peppercorns over medium heat and toast – shaking the pan often to prevent burning – 2 to 3 minutes. Remove from the heat, and let cool to room temperature. In a spice grinder or coffee mill, grind to a fine powder. Transfer to a small bowl.

2. In a blender or food processor combine the coriander, lemongrass, ginger, hot peppers, shallots, garlic, lime, shrimp paste (if using), salt and nutmeg and process until very finely chopped.

3. Add the toasted spices and, with the machine running, slowly pour in the peanut oil. Cover and refrigerate until ready to use. The paste will keep, covered and refrigerated, for up to 1 week.

Les Olivades

41, avenue de Ségur

Paris 7

Telephone: 01 42 83 70 09 Fax: 01 42 73 04 75

Metro: Ségur

Curry Powder
Poudre de Curry

———o———

While excellent commercial versions of curry powder exist on the market, I prefer to make my own. Here is a recipe that I have been using for years. In truth, my husband Walter teased me back into making my own after he found a commercial jar in my spice drawer. His response was, 'I remember when you used to make your own curry powder', as though my standards had slipped drastically. Well, he teased me enough. From now on, it's homemade curry powder or none at all. Although one may not instantly associate curry powder with French cuisine, the French actually use quite a bit of it, more as a delicate seasoning to nudge flavours a bit rather than as a huge hit of spice. When I worked with chef Joël Robuchon in the 1980s, curry powder became a joke between us. For as he would dictate recipes, he often ended with 'and at the end, add just a little speck of curry powder'.

———o———

MAKES 5 TABLESPOONS

EQUIPMENT:
A spice grinder or coffee mill

2 whole, small dried red
chilli peppers
2 tablespoons whole coriander seeds
1 tablespoon whole cumin seeds
½ teaspoon black mustard seeds
1 teaspoon whole black peppercorns
1 teaspoon whole fenugreek seeds
½ teaspoon ground ginger
½ teaspoon ground turmeric

1. In a small dry frying-pan combine the chilli peppers, coriander, cumin, mustard seeds and peppercorns over medium heat and toast – shaking the pan often to prevent burning – 2 to 3 minutes. Remove from the heat, transfer to a bowl, and let cool to room temperature.

2. Transfer the cooled spice mixture to a spice grinder or coffee mill. Add the fenugreek seeds. Grind to a fine powder. Transfer to a small container. Stir in the ground ginger and turmeric. Store in an airtight container in a cool place for up to 3 months.

Tomato Sauce
Sauce aux Tomates

———○———

This simple, classic homemade tomato sauce can always be found next to my homemade chicken stock in my freezer. I depend on both of these staples for so many dishes. People are always surprised that most homemade tomato sauce is made from canned tomatoes. But good-quality canned tomatoes offer excellent flavour and colour, something that fresh tomatoes generally do not.

———○———

*MAKES ABOUT 750ML
(1¼ PINTS)*

*4 tablespoons extra-virgin olive oil
1 small yellow onion, sliced
2 plump fresh garlic cloves, chopped
Sea salt to taste
Two 765g (28oz) tins peeled
tomatoes in juice
Bouquet garni: several sprigs of fresh
parsley, bay leaves and celery leaves,
tied in a bundle with cotton twine*

1. In a large frying-pan heat the oil, onions, garlic and salt over moderate heat. Cook just until the onions are soft and translucent, 3 to 4 minutes. Place a food mill over the frying-pan and purée the tomatoes directly into the pan. Add the bouquet garni. Stir to blend and simmer, uncovered, until the sauce begins to thicken, about 15 minutes. Taste for seasoning.

2. Remove and discard the bouquet garni. The sauce may be used immediately, stored in the refrigerator for up to 2 days, or frozen for up to 3 months.

Allobroges Garlic Confit
Confit d'Ail Allobroges

———————◦———————

Garlic lover's delight! This is the simplest and purest way to enjoy whole cloves of garlic, popping them out of their skins and into your mouth, like candy. No more burnt garlic at the bottom of the roasting pan. These tender cloves are cooked to what the French call a confit, *an ingredient 'cooked slowly to a melting tenderness'. Serve this with roast chicken or lamb, or Allobroges chef Olivier Pateyron's Braised Lamb Shanks (page 270).*

———————◦———————

4 plump, fresh heads garlic, separated into cloves but skin intact
250ml (9 fl oz) extra-virgin olive oil

1. Place the garlic in a small saucepan. Cover with oil. Cook, uncovered, at a tiny bubble over lowest possible heat until the garlic is soft and small knife inserted into the clove meets no resistance, 45 minutes to 1 hour. Watch carefully to avoid burning the garlic. You may need to place the saucepan on a flame tamer. The garlic can be served immediately or allowed to cool in the oil. The oil can be used in cooking or for preparing a vinaigrette.

Les Allobroges

71, rue des Grandes-Champs, Paris 20

Telephone; 01 43 73 40 00

Métro: Maraîchers

WHAT IS A *CONFIT*?

The word confit comes from the word 'confire', a process of conserving or preserving an ingredient: either enrobing it in fat (such as a confit of pork, duck or goose), preserving it in a sugar syrup (such as candied fruits), putting it in a jar with alcohol (such as cherries or plums in eau de vie) or in vinegar (capers and pickles), or in a sweet and sour preparation (such as a chutney). Today, the word is used quite liberally in French cuisine, and applies to just about any method of conserving an ingredient in liquid, such as lemon confit (preserved in lemon juice, salt and sometimes oil), as well as this garlic confit, preserved in oil.

Four-Spice Blend
Quatre Épices

———○———

Quatre épices, literally 'four spices', is a classic, evenly flavoured French seasoning used to flavour meats, terrines, beef or chicken stock, as well as dried vegetables, tomato sauces, marinades, wine sauces or gingerbread. I prepare the mixture in small amounts, grinding each spice in a spice mill or coffee grinder.

———○———

MAKES 4 TEASPOONS

EQUIPMENT:
A spice or coffee mill; nutmeg grater

1 teaspoon cinnamon
1 teaspoon allspice
1 teaspoon cloves
1 nutmeg

1. Grind the cinnamon, allspice and cloves in a spice grinder or coffe mill.

2. Grate the nutmeg with a nutmeg grater until you have 1 teaspoon of .freshly ground nutmeg

3. Combine the spices in a small bowl. Use immediately.

Cherry Jam
Confiture de Cerise

———◇———

Cherries have always held a fascination for me. As a child growing up in Wisconsin, we always had cherry trees in the back yard. Then, I considered cherry trees the best climbing trees in the world, for they were tough and sturdy and did not permit me to climb too far. Today, in Provence, we are blessed with half a dozen giant trees, which, in fact, I never climb. Rather, I stand on tip-toes to reach the best and ripest red fruit and leave the ladder for others to manipulate.

Over the past few years I have acquired the wonderful Basque habit of serving a few spoonfuls of cherry jam with the rich sheep's milk cheese – fromage de brebis – of the region. The jam, of course, can be used in more traditional ways – spread on toast at breakfast-time or spooned over vanilla ice cream. This simple, straightforward jam recipe is embellished with a touch of kirsch, or cherry liqueur, and a bit of almond extract, to bring out the almond flavour of the fruit.

The task of pitting cherries can be eased if you have a cherry pitter handy, a utensil found at most kitchen shops. I find that I prefer the German brand, Westmark

———◇———

MAKES ABOUT 1¾ LITRES

(3 PINTS)

EQUIPMENT:
A copper jam pot (optional)

2.5kg (5lb) fresh cherries, pitted
1.5kg (3lb) preserving sugar
3 tablespoons cherry liqueur (kirsch)
1 teaspoon almond extract

1. Rinse and drain the cherries. Stem and pit them. Place in a large copper jam pot with the sugar. Stir to blend. Bring to a boil over moderately high heat, stirring regularly, about 7 minutes total.

2. Place a large sieve over a large bowl. Pour the cherries into the sieve to separate the cherries and the juice. Return the juice to the jam pot, bring to a boil and boil until the juice is thick and syrupy (130°C/240°F on a jelly thermometer or when it is at the 'soft ball' stage), about 6 minutes. Carefully skim off any foam that rises to the top. There will be a lot of foam. Skim carefully or the jelly will be cloudy and the foam will rise to the top in the jar.

3. Return the cherries to the jam pot with the syrup. Bring to a

boil over high heat, skimming all the time, and boil for 2
minutes. Remove from the heat and let rest for 2 minutes.
Repeat this 2 more times for a total cooking time of 12
minutes. Examine the syrup – it should be clear and about as
thick as maple syrup. Off the heat, stir in the kirsch and
almond extract.

4. Carefully pour the jam into sterilised jars and seal according
to manufacturer's instructions.

Sorrel Sauce
Sauce à l'Oseille

*This is my favourite sauce to serve with the elegantly simple confit of salmon. It is also
delicious with roast or broiled chicken, in place of mayonnaise in a chicken salad, or as a
sandwich spread. Alongside, I often serve a chiffonnade of sorrel, sorrel leaves cut into fine strips
and tossed with a classic vinaigrette.*

MAKES 250ML (9FL OZ)

100g (3oz) fresh sorrel leaves,
trimmed and stemmed
2 large egg yolks, at room
temperature
2 teaspoon freshly squeezed lemon
juice, or to taste
½ teaspoon fine sea salt, or to taste
250ml (9fl oz) grapeseed or
canola oil

1. In the bowl of a food processor, combine the sorrel, egg yolks,
lemon juice and salt. Pulse until well blended. With the motor
running, very slowly add several tablespoons of oil, processing
until the mixture thickens.

2. With the motor still running, slowly add the remaining oil in
a slow and steady stream. Taste for seasoning. Transfer to a
small bowl. The sauce can be stored, covered and refrigerated,
up to 3 days.

Homemade Chicken Stock
Fond de Volaille

———o———

If you ask me what ingredient I could not be without in the kitchen, I would say a good, homemade chicken stock. Many a day in Paris – when I know that I will be working in my office all day long – I buy a batch of chicken wings and make this stock, inhaling the healthy aroma of the simmering stock throughout the afternoon.

———o———

MAKES 2 LITRES (3½ PINTS)

2kg (4lb) raw chicken parts or raw or
cooked carcasses
Pinch of salt
4 carrots, scrubbed and halved
2 large onions, 1 stuck with 2 cloves
4 ribs celery, with leaves
1 whole head garlic, halved
but not peeled
1 leek (white and tender green parts),
halved lengthways and rinsed
1 bouquet garni: parsley leaves, bay
leaves and celery leaves
tied with twine

1. Place the chicken pieces in a heavy stockpot and cover with cold water by at least 5cm (2in). Bring to a gentle simmer over medium heat. Skim to remove the scum that rises to the surface. Add additional cold water to replace the water removed and continue skimming until the broth is clear.

2. Add a pinch of salt, the vegetables and bouquet garni. Return the liquid to a gentle simmer and simmer gently for 2 hours. Skim and degrease as necessary.

3. Line a large colander with a double layer of dampened cheesecloth and place the colander over a large bowl. Ladle – do not pour – the broth into the colander; discard the solids.

4. Refrigerate the stock, and spoon off all traces of fat that rise to the surface. The stock may be safely refrigerated for 3 or 4 days, or can be frozen for up to 6 months.

Sun-Dried Tomato Paste
Purée de Tomates Séchées

———◦———

This delicious, herb-flecked paste is a versatile condiment. It's an integral part of Taillevent's Goat's Cheese and Dried Tomato Appetiser (page 14) and can also be used as a sauce for your favourite pasta.

———◦———

MAKES 125ML (4½FL OZ)

10 sun-dried tomatoes
1 plump fresh garlic clove, degermed and chopped
½ teaspoon crushed red peppers (hot red pepper flakes), or to taste
6 tablespoons extra-virgin olive oil
2 teaspoons chopped fresh thyme leaves
2 teaspoons chopped fresh rosemary leaves

1. In the bowl of a food processor, combine all the ingredients and process until the paste is lightly emulsified but still quite coarse and almost chunky. You do not want a smooth paste. The paste can be stored in a jar in the refrigerator for up to 1 month. If you do so, first cover the paste with a film of olive oil. When using the paste, stir to incorporate the oil.

Menu·Carte

A New Year's Celebration

———◇———

Taillevent's Goat's Cheese and Dried
Tomato Appetiser

———◇———

Le Duc's Hot Curried Oysters

———◇———

Scrambled Eggs with Truffles

———◇———

Jean-Luc Poujauran's Shortbread Cookies

———◇———

Fresh Truffle Ice Cream

Address Book

———○———

The following is a list of the shops, restaurants, bistros, cafes and markets mentioned throughout the book.

SHOPS

La Bonbonnerie de Buci
12, rue de Buci
Paris 6
Telephone: 01 43 26 97 13
Métro: Mabillon
Confectionery

Boulangerie-Patisserie Gérard
Mulot
76, rue du Seine
Paris 6
Telephone: 01 43 26 85 77
Métro: Mabillon
Bread and pastries

Boucherie Pascal Duciel
96, rue de Courcelles
Paris 17
Telephone: 01 47 63 40 97
Métro: Courcelles
Meat

Boutique Maille
6, place de la Madeleine,
Paris 8
Telephone: 01 40 15 06 00
Métro: Madeleine
Mustards

Bruno Gauvain
16, rue Dupin
Paris 6
Telephone: 01 42 22 46 65
Métro: Sèvres-Babylone
Fishmonger

Cave Viard
9, rue de Quatre Vents
Paris 6
Telephone: 01 43 54 99 30
Fax: 01 44 07 27 73
Métro: Odéon
Wine merchant

Daguerre Marée
4, rue Bayen
Paris 17
Telephone: 01 43 80 16 29
Métro: Ternes
Fishmonger

La Derniere Goutte
6, rue Bourbon-le-Château
Paris 6
Telephone: 01 43 29 11 62
Métro: Saint-Germain des Prés or
Odéon
Wine merchant

Fromagerie Alléosse
13, rue Poncelet
Paris 17
Telephone: 01 46 22 50 45
Métro: Ternes
Cheeses

Geneviève Lethu
95, rue de Rennes
Paris 6
Telephone: 01 45 44 40 35
Métro: Rennes
For madeleine moulds

La Grande Epicerie de Paris Bon
Marché
38, rue de Sèvres
Paris 7
Telephone: 01 44 39 81 00
Métro: Sèvres-Babylone
For Bresse poultry and fresh beans

Huilerie Artisanale Leblanc et Fils
6, rue Jacob
Paris 6
Telephone: 01 46 34 61 55
Métro: Mabillon
Oils

Jean-Pierre Carton
6, rue de Buci
Paris 6
Telephone: 01 43 26 04 13
Métro: Mabillon
Pastries

Jean-Paul Hévin
3, rue Vavin
Paris 6
Telephone: 01 43 54 09 85
Métro: Vavin or Nôtre-Dame des
Champs
Fine chocolate

La Maison du Chocolat
225, rue du Faubourg Saint-
Honoré
Paris 8
Telephone: 01 42 27 39 44
Métro: Ternes

La Maison du Fromage 'Molard'
48, rue de Martyrs
Paris 9
Telephone: 01 45 26 84 88
Métro: Nôtre Dame de Lorette
Cheeses

La Maison du Miel
24, rue Vignon
Paris 8
Telephone: 01 47 42 26 70
Métro: Madeleine
Honey

Oliviers & Co.
28, rue de Buci
Paris 6
Telephone: 01 44 07 15 43
Métro: Saint-Germain des Prés or
Odéon
Olives

Poissonerie de Bac
69, rue de Bac
Paris 7
Telephone: 01 45 48 06 64
Métro: Rue du Bac
Fishmonger

RESTAURANTS, BISTROs AND CAFES

Les Allobroges
71, rue des Grandes-Champs
Paris 20
Telephone: 01 43 73 40 00
Métro: Maraîchers

Alsaco
10, rue Condorcet
Paris 9
Telephone: 01 45 26 44 31
Métro: Poissonière

Ambassade d'Auvergne
22, rue du Grenier Saint-Lazare
Paris 3
Tel: 01 42 72 31 22
Fax: 01 42 78 85 47
Métro: Rambuteau

Les Ambassadeurs Hôtel Crillon
10, place de la Concorde Paris 8
Telephone: 01 44 71 15 02
Métro: Concorde

L'Ambroisie
9, place des Vosges
Paris 4
Telephone: 01 42 78 51 45
Métro: Saint-Paul

Arpège
84, rue de Varenne
Paris 7
Telephone: 01 45 51 47 33
Fax: 01 44 18 98 39
Métro: Varenne

Astor
11, rue Astor
Paris 8
Telephone: 01 53 05 05 20
Fax: 01 53 05 05 30
Métro: Saint-Augustin

Au Bascou
38, rue Réamu
Paris 3
Telephone: 01 42 72 69 25
Métro: Arts et Métiers

Benoît
20, rue Saint Martin
Paris 4
Telephone: 01 42 72 25 76
Fax: 01 42 72 45 68
Métro: Châtelet or Hôtel de Ville

Le Bistrot du Dôme
1, rue Delambre
Paris 14
Telephone: 01 43 35 32 00
Métro: Vavin

Bistrot Mazarin
42, rue Mazarine
Paris 6
Telephone: 01 43 29 99 01
Métro: Mabillon

Le Bonaparte
42, rue Bonaparte
Paris 6
Telephone: 01 43 26 41 81
Métro: Saint-Germain des Prés

Les Bookinistes
53, quai des Grands-Augustins
Paris 6
Telephone: 01 43 25 45 94
Fax: 01 4325 23 07
Métro: RER Saint-Michel

Brasserie Balzar
49, rue des Ecoles,
Paris 5
Telephone: 01 43 54 13 67
Métro: Odéon or Cluny-La-Sorbonne

La Cagouille
10-12 Place Brancusi
(across from 23, rue de l'Ouest)
Paris 14
Telephone: 01 43 22 09 01
Fax: 01 45 38 57 29
Métro: Gaîté

Cap Vernet
82, avenue du Marceau
Paris 8
Telephone: 01 47 20 20 40
Fax: 01 47 20 95 36
Métro: Charles de Gaulle-Etoile

Carré des Feuillants (Alain
Dutournier)
14, rue de Castiglione
Paris 1
Telephone: 01 42 86 82 82
Fax: 01 42 86 07 71
Métro: Concorde or Tuileries

Aux Charpentiers
10, rue Mabillon
Paris 6
Telephone: 01 43 26 30 05
Fax: 01 46 33 07 98
Métro: Mabillon

Chez Allard
1, rue de l'Epéron
Paris 6
Telephone: 01 43 26 48 23
Métro: Odéon

Chez Maître Paul
12, rue Monsieur le Prince
Paris 6
Telephone: 01 43 54 74 59
Fax: 01 46 34 58 33
Métro: Odéon or RER
Luxembourg

Chez Michel
10, rue Belzunce
Paris 10
Telephone: 01 44 53 06 20
Fax: 01 44 53 61 31
Métro: Poissonnière or Gare du
Nord

Le Dôme
108, Boulevard du Montparnasse
Paris 14
Telephone: 01 43 35 25 81
Fax: 01 42 79 01 19
Métro: Vavin

Le Duc
243, boulevard Raspail
Paris 14
Telephone: 01 43 20 96 30
Fax: 01 43 20 46 73
Métro: Raspail

Gallopin
40, rue Notre-Dames-des-Victories
Paris 2
Telephone: 01 42 36 10 32
Métro: Bourse

Le Grand Vefour
17, rue de Beaujolais
Paris 1
Telephone: 01.42.96.56.27
Fax: 01 42 86 80 71
Métro: Palais Royal-Musée du
Louvre

Jamin
32, rue de Longchamp
Paris 16
Telephone: 01 45 53 00 07
Métro: Trocadéro

Le Jardin de Courcelles
96. rue de Courcelles
Paris 17
Telephone: 01 47 63 70 55
Métro: Courcelles

Ladurée
73, avenue Champs-Elysées
Paris 8
Telephone: 01 40 75 08 75
Métro: Georges V

Laurent
41, avenue Gabriel
Paris 8
Telephone: 01 42 25 00 39
Fax: 01 45 62 45 21
Métro: Champs Elysées-
Clemenceau

Ledoyen
Carré des Champs-Elysées
Paris 8
Telephone: 01 47 42 35 98
Fax: 01 47 42 55 01
Métro: Champs Elysées-
Clemenceau

Le Maxence
9 bis, Boulevard du Montparnasse
Paris 6
Telephone: 01 45 67 24 88
Fax: 01 45 67 10 22
Métro: Falguière

Le Mauzac
7, rue de l'Abeé de l'Epée
Paris 5
Telephone: 01 46 33 75 22
Métro: RER Luxembourg

Monsieur Lapin
11, rue Raymond-Losser
Paris 14
Telephone: 01 43 20 21 39
Fax: 01 43 21 84 86
Métro: Gaîté

Au Moulin à Vent (Chez Henri)
20, rue des Fossés Saint-Bernard
Paris 5
Telephone: 01 43 54 99 37
Métro: Jussieu or Cardinal
Lemoine

Le Nemrod
51, rue du Cherche-Midi
Paris 6
Telephone: 01 45 48 17 05
Métro: Sèvres-Babylone

Les Olivades
41, avenue de Ségur
Paris 7
Telephone: 01 42 83 70 09
Métro: 01 42 73 04 75
Metro: Ségur

Le Pré Catelan
Route de Suresnes
Bois de Boulogne
Paris 16
Telephone: 01 44 14 41 14
Fax: 01 45 24 43 25
Métro: Porte Dauphine

Restaurant Alain Ducasse au Plaza
Athenée
25, avenue Montaigne
Paris 8
Telephone: 01 53 67 65 00
Fax: 01 53 67 65 00
Métro: Franklin D. Roosevelt

Restaurant La Fontaine de Mars
129, rue Saint-Dominique
Paris 7
Telephone: 01 47 05 46 44
Métro: Ecole Militaire.

Restaurant Guy Savoy
18, rue Troyon
Paris 17
Telephone: 01 43 80 40 61
Fax: 01 46 22 43 09
Métro: Charles de Gaulle-Etoile

Restaurant Hélène Darroze
4 rue d'Assas
Paris 6
Tel: 01 42 22 00 11
Fax: 01 42 22 25 40
Métro: Sèvres-Babylone

Taillevent
15, rue Lammenais
Paris 8
Telephone: 01 44 95 15 01
Fax: 01 42 25 95 18
Métro: Charles-de-Gaulle-Etoile
or George V

Le Violin d'Ingres
135, rue Saint-Dominique
Paris 7
Telephone: 01 45 55 15 05
Fax: 01 45 55 48 42
Métro: Ecole Militaire

MARKETS

Marché Richard Lenoir,
Boulevard Richard-Lenoir,
beginning at rue Amelot
Paris 11
Thursday and Saturday mornings
Métro: Bastille or Richard Lenoir.

Marché Breteuil
Avenue de Saxe,
from Avenue de Segur to Place
Breteuil
Paris 7
9am to noon, Thursday and
Sunday

Marché Poncelet
Beginning at avenue des Ternes
Paris 17
9am to 1pm, and 4pm to 7pm
Tuesday through Saturday
9am to 1pm Sunday
Métro: Ternes

Marché Carmes
Place Maubert
Paris 5
Open 7am to 1.30pm, Tuesday,
Thursday and Saturday
Métro: Maubert-Mutualité

Marché Biologique
Boulevard Raspail
Between Rue de Cherche-Midi
and Rue de Rennes
Sunday 9am to 1pm

Place Monge Market
Place Monge
Paris 5
Wednesday, Friday and Sunday
mornings
Metro: Monge

Index

---○---

Author's Acknowledgments

Over more than two decades of life in Paris, perhaps the greatest acknowledgement should go to the city itself, a place in the world that is born anew with each day, every moment a surprise and an inspiration.

But people are the ones who affect one most deeply, and I owe thanks to every baker and chef, fruit and vegetable merchant, fishmonger and butcher, pastry chef and simple cook who has enhanced my life here. Thanks to the known and the unknown.

My life would be much less enriched without having met the chefs and artisans who still serve as my teachers and mentors: Joël Robuchon, Guy Savoy, Jean-Claude Vrinat, Alain Dutournier, baker Lionel Poilâne, those no longer in Paris, such as the dear Pile ou Face trio of Alain Dumergue, Claude Udron and Philippe Marquet, and those no longer at the stove, such as the famed Antoine Magnin from L'Ami Louis and the indefatigable Adrienne Biasin from Chez la Vieille.

I want to say a special thanks to those who make my life that much easier by eagerly joining me at restaurants known and unknown, beginning with my husband Walter (who after 21 years never says 'No' to yet another meal out), friends Susan Loomis, Pat Thompson and Jim Bitterman, Rita and Yale Kramer, Devon Fredericks and Eli Zabar, Ina and Jeffrey Garten, Doire and Michael Greenspan.

In the publishing world, many people have helped this book see the light of day. A special thank you to agent Susan Lescher and publisher Kyle Cathie.